WAREHOUSING PROFITABLY

A MANAGER'S GUIDE

"How to tell what's wrong with your warehouse ... and fix it!"

KEN ACKERMAN

ACKERMAN
PUBLICATIONS
COLUMBUS, OHIO, U.S.A.

ISBN: 0-9631776-1-3

Library of Congress Catalog Number: 94-78956

Printed in the United States of America

Designed and edited by William F. Blinn, Worthington, Ohio

Ackerman Publications
1328 Dublin Road
Columbus, Ohio 43215-1059
614-488-3165

Table of Contents

Part 2: Warehouse Control

Part 3: Warehouse Management

Part 4: Security

Part 5: Handling of Cargo

Part 7: Starting a New Warehouse Operation

Part 8: The Future

Why you should read this book, and why I wrote it

Another book about warehousing! Why should you read it? Why did I write it?

My three earlier books about warehousing were all designed to be handbooks for warehouse managers. They were designed to collect everything about the field and to organize it in a fashion that would help people manage warehouses. In my zeal to collect information, I was tempted to throw in "everything but the kitchen sink."

This book is different. *Warehousing Profitably* is designed for the warehouse manager's **boss**, although we hope it will be used by warehouse managers as well. At the end of each chapter, you will find a page with *"Questions that solve problems"*. Each question is followed by a comment rather than an answer. The purpose of this is not to test your ability to read and remember, but rather to help management review warehousing problems. When your warehouse is not working well, discussion of these questions will lead to the ways to make the warehouse run better.

Warehousing is a deceptively simple business. Many think that the function is so basic that any decent manager could run a good warehouse. When it doesn't run smoothly, nobody can understand why.

Our prime goal is to illustrate what it takes to manage warehouses profitably. While other writings in warehousing may seem to tell you how to build a watch, this book is designed to tell you what time it is. Furthermore, I hope you will find it capable of telling you how to adjust the watch if it isn't keeping accurate time. ❖

About the author

Ken Ackerman has been active in logistics and warehousing management for his entire career.

Before entering the consulting field, he was chief executive of Distribution Centers, Inc., a public warehousing company that is now part of Exel Logistics USA. In 1980, Ackerman sold the company and joined the management consulting division of Coopers & Lybrand. In 1981, he formed the Ackerman Company, a management advisory service.

He is editor and publisher of *Warehousing Forum*, a monthly subscription newsletter. His three earlier warehousing books became recognized reference works on this subject. *Harvard Business Review* published "Making Warehousing More Efficient" that Ackerman co-authored with Bernard J. La Londe. He is the author of numerous other articles dealing with warehousing and management as well as a glossary called *Words of Warehousing*.

Ackerman holds a Bachelor of Arts degree from Princeton and a Master of Business Administration from Harvard. He is a past president of Council of Logistics Management and the 1977 winner of its Distinguished Service Award.

Ken Ackerman has provided management advisory services to companies throughout the United States, Canada, and Latin America. These clients include manufacturers, wholesale distributors, retailers, warehousing firms, and carriers. He has provided consulting support to several large consulting firms. In addition to advisory services, he conducts training seminars on warehousing. He has served as a speaker at conferences and conventions in North and South America as well as in Europe, Asia, and Australia. His fluency in Spanish enables him to lecture and consult in that language.

Ken Ackerman served as Columbus chapter chairman for Young President's Organization, and as a director of American Warehouse Association. He has been active in civic activities, serving as trustee and founding president of the Wellington School. He was a trustee of Columbus Association for the Performing Arts and a past president of Opera Columbus. ❖

Acknowledgements

We fear that we can never thank all of the people who contributed to this book. Dozens of footnotes throughout this work are some effort to recognize the contributions of friends who were willing to share their ideas and writing with me.

Larry Gadd of North River Press originally suggested the concept of this work. William J. Ransom gets all the credit for the name on this book, as well as his many significant contributions to our writings about warehousing.

For the past several years, Dewey Abram has been our advisor and coach in the preparation of *Warehousing Forum*, and his suggestions have certainly improved our writing.

This book is a successor to three earlier books. A 1972 work titled *Understanding Today's Distribution Center* was co-authored by R. W. Gardner and Lee P. Thomas.

This book was capably edited by William F. Blinn, who provided valuable suggestions on production as well as composition of the material. Cathy Avenido handled the word processing and the organization of the material. Doug Bosse and Jeannette Faelchle checked the proofs.

We are most grateful to all who helped us produce this book. ❖

PART

1

Understanding
Today's Warehouse

Chapter 1

Warehousing: an overview

Why start a book about warehousing with a chapter on business logistics? Because most people consider warehousing to be one of several cogs in a gear wheel we call *business logistics* today. The other cogs include transportation, inventory management, and customer service. Since it is not possible to understand warehousing except as part of a larger field, we need to describe the development of business logistics as a management tool.

Many of today's accepted logistics management methods were either unknown or experimental in 1980. Some say the field of business logistics went through a revolution during the '80s. If that word is too strong, it is at least fair to say that this field changed as much in the last decade as in the previous century.

These changes have been caused by the deregulation of nearly all transportation functions, the general acceptance of a concept referred to as 'Just-in-time,' the internationalization of the logistics function, and the rise of a whole new industry — the overnight express business.

The revolution has displaced many executives and caused whole businesses to disappear when they were unable to cope with the revolutionary tide. Of the top 40 motor freight companies in existence in 1979, just 15 survived the decade of the 1980s. Before exploring the revolution, let's look first at definitions and then at history.

Business logistics is a process

Business logistics can be described in many ways. It is certainly a process of integration, and the most ambitious definitions suggest that it is an integration of everything but the kitchen sink. Logistics managers frequently control many business functions that were formerly separate. These include both transportation and warehousing, and sometimes purchasing, inventory control, packaging, site selection, customer service, and order processing.

In its simplest form, business logistics is nothing more than the art of delivering the right goods to the right place at the right time. That was the military definition in World War II, and it is still valid.

An even simpler definition states that business logistics is the use of inventory to create customer satisfaction. If that seems too simple, consider the fact that relatively few places in the world enjoy a wide selection of food products nearly as fresh as could be found at a roadside fruit stand in July delivered to the shelves of their markets. In the United States, we take this for granted, but in many places a high percentage of food is lost to spoilage, rodents, insects, damage, or thievery.

Tragically, this condition is prevalent in those very countries that need food most desperately. The next time you go to your favorite market and see blueberries from New Zealand, consider the fact that there was a time when you seldom saw fresh produce from halfway around the world in the grocery store. Take a look at the price, and consider the miracle of transporting this fruit so far while still delivering it fresh and at an affordable price. In essence, this is the fruit of the business logistics revolution of the 1980s.

Early history of logistics

There is nothing new about business logistics — it is one of the oldest recorded commercial functions. Consider Chapter 41 of the *Book of Genesis*. In ancient Egypt, a monarch was troubled by nightmares. He brought in a management consultant from a neighboring country and described his dreams of fat cows and thin cows, of plump ears of corn and withered cornstalks. The consultant suggested these dreams were a prophecy and Egypt was destined to enjoy seven years of agricultural surpluses, followed by seven years of famine.

The solution was to build granaries, store the surpluses, and then distribute the surpluses when crops failed. This may have been the first and last time in history when the client followed a management consultant's advice to the letter. The results caused the consultant, Joseph, to become a hero in the land of Egypt, and the event was recorded as one of the great events of history.

Since the beginning of civilization, the most critical function of business logistics has been to keep us alive by effectively handling, storing, and distributing food. It is simply a function of our enormous prosperity that today we enjoy a logistics system that allows us to buy fresh fruit from New Zealand in February.

Logistics developments changed business history in other ways. Marco Polo and others from the northern Italian provinces explored the Orient and developed sources for the spices needed to preserve food without refrigeration. Marco Polo adopted a Chinese invention that changed not only logistics but other commercial functions as well.

This simple concept amazed the Europeans, but it caught on. The Chinese had perfected the idea that a piece of paper could represent something else, and that it could be bought and sold in place of the more valuable thing it represents. Today we all carry paper currency.

Our paper dollars once had the words 'silver certificate' printed on them, promising that an appropriate amount of silver, payable to the bearer, was available to back up the value of this almost-worthless piece of paper called a bank note.

The people of the Lombard region of Italy extended the principle to merchandise, developing negotiable receipts for merchandise held in storage. If you had 1,000 bushels of wheat in a warehouse, you could sell a negotiable warehouse receipt representing that wheat without moving it from the warehouse. These negotiable receipts were originally called *Lombards*, named after the province of Lombardy.

Trading in negotiable warehouse receipts for general merchandise has almost died out in the United States today, though it still exists with some agricultural commodities. In Latin America, most third-party warehousing is done by banks and the stored inventory is collateral for loans.

As transportation developed in the industrial revolution, the logistics system developed with it. Terminal warehouses were established close to railroad freight terminals and these relics of terminal warehousing are still seen in the centers of most of our cities.

The United States is unique

Logistics systems developed in this country differently from the rest of the world, and this was a product of both our geography and our history. The extensive land mass of the United States was explored and populated when overland transportation was primitive. Then came railroads, accompanied by some gross abuses of power.

Many farmers and business managers believed they were at the mercy of a few moguls who ran the railroads. They felt these powerful people could not be trusted.

Sometimes the titans fought each other. The route of the original Pennsylvania turnpike, the part that connected New Stanton and Carlisle in the late 1930s, was originally the road-bed of a railroad Andrew Carnegie built because his steel mills had a dispute with the Pennsylvania Railroad. The railroad people obviously thought that Andy was bluffing, but after he had constructed the tunnels and cleared the right-of-way, they decided that they needed to deal with him. The road-bed remained idle for decades until somebody realized that it could be converted into America's first four-lane limited-access highway.

In the 1880s there was a growing body of opinion that **big** business was **bad** business, just as **big** government had been **bad** government a century earlier. Subconsciously, perhaps citizens then equated Gould and Vanderbilt with George III. The public wanted to put a leash on the railroad barons.

That leash was devised in 1887 as the Interstate Commerce Act, the first consumerist legislation in the United States. That act created the Interstate Commerce Commission to watch over the railroads, and it required that common carriers publish all prices for moving both passengers and freight.

The Commission had the right to judge the reasonableness of those prices, and to rule on any applications to change them. The new law would allow the small business owner and farmer to compete equitably with musclemen like Andy Carnegie who could build their own railroads if they couldn't get along with the ones already there.

De-regulation

For nearly 100 years, the United States was one of the few places in the world with a heavily regulated transportation system. Most other nations never had regulation, partially because they didn't need it, and partially because they didn't want it. The idea that corporate trusts or monopolies must be broken is not as popular in some parts of the world as it is here.

When American railroads offered either free or low-cost storage as a way to attract new business, one of America's oldest trade associations was formed. The prime mission of the American Warehouse Association in its early years was to achieve legislation to prohibit the railroads from offering free storage. As a result of this success, the third-party warehousing industry in the United States became a business dominated by small owner-operators. In other parts of the world, warehousing is provided by much larger companies — sometimes branches of banks and sometimes divisions of major transport companies.

As transport developed the new modes of motor freight and air freight, federal regulation grew to accommodate it. However, by the middle of the 20th century, a few observers began to suspect foul play. They recognized that we now had a new kind of abuse — a three-legged oligopoly composed of corporate management, unions, and regulators.

Some saw a conspiracy. The Teamsters negotiated a sizable wage raise, the truckers went to the ICC and asked for a rate increase, and the public paid the bill. Other transport modes recorded similar abuses. During 1989, we heard about $35,000-per-year baggage handlers in connection with a bitter airline strike; but nobody pointed out that these wage scales were a legacy of federal rate regulation.

Perhaps it was the Kennedys who first suggested that something was rotten in the nation's logistics system. Bobby Kennedy declared war on the Teamsters and vowed to put Jimmy Hoffa in jail. He achieved his goal, and there are some who suspect his violent death was related to that dispute.

By the early 1970s, consumerists such as Ralph Nader had joined the cry. In the Carter administration, the moves to de-regulate transportation began. It is ironic that the consumerists moved to dismantle a piece of legislation that was originally designed to protect the small-business owner and the consumer.

Airline de-regulation was followed by legislation to de-regulate motor freight and rail. The Teamsters Union supported the Republican candidate in 1980, hoping that Ronald Reagan would be more reasonable. Instead, the Republicans intensified the move to de-regulation, striking out at regulations in other industries as well.

In 1980, de-regulation was still an economic experiment. Today, few people would advocate turning back the clock despite the new problems de-regulation has caused. We see signs of abuse in air transportation, where passengers in fortress hubs such as Nashville, St. Louis, and Detroit have little choice of airlines. Yet de-regulation has saved billions for American consumers, and most people recognize any abuses can be corrected without a return to the 1880s.

Internationalization

What is now known as business logistics was first called physical distribution. The concept was similar except that physical distribution was limited to finished products. The discipline's first professional society, known as the National Council of Physical Distribution Management, changed its name to the Council of Logistics Management in 1985.

Two aspects of this name change reflected the revolution of the 1980s. The broader term of logistics allows practitioners to look at the movement of raw materials as well as finished products, and the word *national* has been deleted. In 1973, the president of NCPDM advocated a move to internationalization, but the idea was ahead of its time — most members had no responsibility for import or export, and they said that their companies would not support them in any international activity.

A decade later, the question of whether logistics was a national or international function was no longer a subject of debate. Next time you are on an interstate highway, watch the lettering on the freight trailers you pass. You won't go far before you find one that obviously came from outside the United States.

Japanese warehousing and transportation companies exist today in many U.S. cities, and you are likely to see much foreign logistics activity in America's heartland. The Japanese have come in because they felt that they could best support their major automotive manufacturing enterprises with their own people. Others have come in simply because they wanted to make an investment in American business.

One of the leading third-party warehousing companies became a subsidiary of a British company. Other European companies and the Australians have produced some notably successful logistics service companies.

A critical labor dispute

The decade of the 1980s also produced some revolutionary activities in labor relations, and many affected logistics operations. The two-tier wage contract started in the logistics field because regulation had created some uneconomic pay scales. You can now find baggage handlers who are happy with a pay scale less than $35,000 per year. Most companies and unions were willing to resolve this issue peacefully.

Early in the 1980s, the union representing air traffic controllers either forgot or did not heed the lessons of the 1919 Boston police strike, which propelled Calvin Coolidge to national prominence. As governor of Massachusetts, Coolidge declared 'there is no right to strike against the public safety by anybody, anywhere, or at any time.'

Ronald Reagan and his Secretary of Transportation, Drew Lewis, decided to draw the line with the Professional Air Traffic Controllers Organization (PATCO). When the union struck, The Reagan administration used military air traffic controllers to break the strike.

The PATCO strike may have been the most important labor dispute in American history. If PATCO had won, we might have seen a strike at the U.S. Postal Service and possibly even in the U.S. Army. The PATCO strike demonstrated that while there were many privileges available to government workers, the right to strike was not one of them. Furthermore, the air traffic controllers learned that the American public was not sympathetic, particularly when their wage scales were publicized. Like the high-priced baggage handlers, wages of air traffic controllers were a product of rate regulation abuses.

The information revolution

A key development of the 1980s was the enormous advance in our ability to process information. One of the few prices that has gone **down** rather than **up** is the cost of computing and transmitting information. Many jobs routinely performed in logistics today depend upon electronic capabilities that either did not exist, or were far more expensive, a decade or two ago.

A leading example of this change is bar coding, which has changed the way freight is handled. Watch a Federal Express courier next time you receive a delivery envelope. This company relies on bar coding to track the location of every package from receipt until delivery.

Similar things are done with other cargo, including full truckloads. Many of today's truckers have on-board computers that can locate and expedite a box that's already in transit.

Communication systems that rely on satellites for both communication and tracking exist today in the cabs of tractor/trailer units.

Third-party growth

Another aspect of the 1980s revolution was the growth of third-party services. Peter Drucker wrote 'Sell the mail room,' reflecting the idea that today's corporate managers succeed by shrinking their empires, not expanding them. If you are in the business of building automobiles, perhaps you should concentrate your energy on production of cars — not on managing warehouses, truck lines, or air freight fleets.

During the days of regulation, the largest truck fleets in the United States were privately owned by companies like Kroger and Sears. This was true partly because the relatively high prices of regulated transport made private fleets economical. With de-regulation, there was growing realization that third parties might do the job for less money, and the third-party logistics industry spread like wildfire.

De-regulation allowed some big service companies to diversify. For the first time since the turn of the century, railroads were free to expand into trucking, marine transportation, or warehousing.

In the mid-1970s, a notable business failure occurred. A company called National Distribution Services, which called itself a logistics utility and promised its customers total control of inventory from the end of the production line to final delivery, lasted only a year. It lost millions. Yet today some of the nation's largest manufacturing companies are looking for a business like that. Even with de-regulation, not a single American corporation has fulfilled the dream.

Overnight delivery

No review of the changes in logistics would be complete without noting the passage through adolescence of a corporation that is one of the great success stories in the history of American business. A Yale student named Smith, who earned a 'C' on his term paper describing a new business, used the ideas expressed in the paper to found a logistics empire.

When Fred Smith opened his business in 1973, it began service as the largest single venture capital start-up in the history of American business. To raise the 90 million dollars needed, Smith contributed his personal fortune, as well as 8 million dollars from other members of his family. Without de-regulation, Federal Express might never have achieved success.

The company started by flying small executive jet aircraft, partially because they were less expensive — but primarily because the Civil Aeronautics Board barred the company from using larger aircraft. De-regulation changed that, and by 1983 Federal Express had become the first business in the United States to reach one billion dollars in revenues within ten years and without any mergers or acquisitions.

The company has been acclaimed for excellence of management and for being one of the best employers in America. It has been the most profitable company in the common-carrier industry.

Smith created not just a new business, but a whole new industry by inventing the now famous 'hub and spoke' system of distribution. This system has been copied by both air cargo companies and passenger airlines. The Federal Express concept spawned competition, nearly all of it based in the United States, and these American companies have been highly successful in moving their services overseas. At a time when Americans fret about foreign encroachment on American business, the overnight air delivery industry remains almost exclusively an American game. Few developments have had greater impact on logistics systems.

The ability to receive rapid and dependable deliveries has enabled merchants to operate with lower inventories and react more quickly to consumer demand than ever before.

The revolutionary changes that have characterized business logistics show no sign of ending. The progress to be realized in future decades is limited only by the imagination and creativity of today's logistics managers. ❖

Chapter 2

Improving warehouse productivity

The turbulent business era of the 1990s has created four major changes for warehousing.* These will significantly influence warehouse workers, warehouse managers, and warehouse users. From these changes come four propositions:

- **Time** is one of the most important ingredients in effective warehousing. Therefore, the best warehouse operations are those designed to reduce every aspect of order-cycle time.
- **Quality** is just as important as punctuality, and users of warehouse services now expect performance that approaches perfection.
- The emphasis in using warehouses is to improve **asset productivity**. Three critical functions are to reduce total cost, reuse, and recycle.
- To enter the 21st century, warehouse managers must develop a **new kind of workforce**, and requirements for both management and labor will change significantly.

The critical importance of time

Improved capabilities in computer modeling and communications have enabled today's manager to substitute information for inventory, and to move that information faster and more accurately than ever before.

---

*   From an article by Professor Bernard J. La Londe, Mason Professor of Transportation and Logistics at The Ohio State University. The article was published in *Warehousing Forum*, Volume 7, Number 9, ©The Ackerman Company, Columbus, Ohio.

The best examples of these principles are found in relationships be-tween retailers and their sources. Just a few decades ago, appliance manu-facturers commonly stockpiled huge quantities of finished goods because nobody knew which colors or models would sell. It was important to have inventory available in case somebody wanted to buy.

Today, information systems at point-of-sale allow nearly all retailers to report the sale of a given appliance within minutes of the transaction. This information moves to the retailer's headquarters and back to the manufac-turing resource within minutes. This allows managers to change produc-tion schedules frequently to reflect current transaction activity. The same kind of *real time* reporting exists for many other commodities, even non-durables such as soap.

The result is information that allows warehouse operators to improve order fill and reduce cycle time.

Reduction of back orders and stock-outs saves time for everyone, and better information systems make these improvements easier than ever be-fore. Time needed for order cycle and transit from warehouse to customer has been slightly reduced, and there will be significant additional reduc-tions in the next few years.

The percentage of orders transmitted to distribution warehouses by electronic data interchange (EDI) continues to grow. Many companies ex-pect 50 percent of their transactions to move via EDI.

Emphasis on quality

Improving quality is just as important as reducing cycle time. Bar-code con-trol on outbound shipping has allowed some warehouses to cut their error rate to less than one in ten thousand. This has increased the expectations of warehouse users, creating a growing intolerance of errors and damage.

What would happen to baseball if the rules changed so that a batter was out after one strike? Something similar is happening in warehousing, and those who don't recognize it are out of touch with today's expectations and capabilities.

In warehousing, quality is measured by the operator's ability to deliver product on time, in good condition, and precisely as ordered — without overages, shortages, or any other discrepancy. *On spec, on time, and on budget,* as one logistics executive describes it.

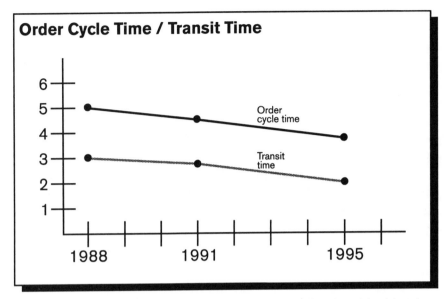

FIGURE 1: Order-cycle time has been reduced and the figure shows the substantial anticipated reduction in the next few years. Transit time is down only slightly, but we expect a more significant reduction in the near future.

Bar coding is part of the quality revolution in warehousing. While a minority of warehouse transactions are controlled by bar code scanning today, by the end of the decade over half will be controlled by bar codes.

Asset productivity

Today's user of warehouse services is forced to place primary emphasis on asset productivity. This drive to improve asset productivity comes from the highest level of senior management as a growing number of corporations rate their success by measuring return-on-assets rather than return-on-sales.

The drive to improve asset productivity is manifested in three areas:
- ◆ Reducing assets or otherwise improving turnover of capital.
- ◆ Re-using materials.
- ◆ Recycling instead of discarding waste.

There are two ways to improve asset productivity. One is to improve the operations to the extent that the same asset investment can be used to handle a significantly greater volume. For example, doubling the throughput of your warehouse with no additional space or lift trucks. The second way to improve asset productivity is to transfer the investment in assets to a third party.

Outsourcing of warehousing is recognized as a way to improve asset productivity. When warehouse services are purchased from a third party, the transaction may be structured to allow the user to *borrow* real estate and materials-handling equipment without creating a balance sheet liability.

Accountants usually require long-term leases on buildings and equipment to be capitalized. However, no such requirement exists for short-term commitments frequently available through public and short-term contract warehousing.

Outsourcing of third-party logistics services has been recognized as an economical alternative, one that will grow in popularity as the facts and figures become more widely known. Additional evidence for this is suggested in Figure 2.

U.S. industry spent nearly 18 percent of its total warehouse cost with third-party providers, but the British claim that third-party firms provide 50 percent of warehousing there.

Figure 2
1991 Estimated Warehousing Costs for Durable And Non-Durable Manufacturing Shipments – $Billion

Component	Manufacturing Durable	Manufacturing Non-Durable	Sub-Total	Percent of Total
In-plant	8.8	6.3	15.1	62.3%
Field-Private	2.5	2.1	4.6	19.2%
Public / Contract	1.9	2.3	4.2	17.6%
TOTAL	13.2	10.7	23.9	

Reuse and recycling are driven both by a desire for improved asset productivity and by pressures from environmentalists. As concerns about trash disposal increase, manufacturers and distributors reduce packaging materials and employ materials that can be re-used or recycled.

In a few urban areas, retailers are required to dispose of the carton when delivering a major appliance to a consumer. As a result, some manufacturers ship appliances without cartons, wrapping them in furniture pads and transporting them in vehicles similar to moving vans. Other materials handling suppliers have designed plastic packages and tote bins that can be collapsed and reused.

The intense search for a new pallet design emphasizes the need for easy recycling capabilities. When a pallet is worn out, how can it be disposed of in an environmentally responsible manner? One brewer ships finished product on plastic slipsheets that substitute for pallets. When the plastic slipsheets are returned to the brewery, they are reground, melted, and molded into new ones.

The new workforce

Senior management must develop a new workforce including managers as well as workers for warehouses. The current logistics executives are younger and more diverse than the traffic managers of a generation ago. They also have a higher rank in the organization.

We asked corporate executives when the first senior logistics executive position was created in their organization. Forty-six percent say this happened in the 1980s. Additionally, we found more than forty-one percent of logistics executives have a graduate degree, and over half of these have some kind of professional certification.

Some workers know more, others know less

The challenge for this younger and better-educated management team is to deal with a changing hourly workforce. Customers are more concerned than ever before about quality of labor. In some cases, the decline of unions in warehouse workforces has been accompanied by a decline of warehouse discipline. The union was a stabilizing influence. When asked to compare private with third-party warehouses, our respondents said third-party providers have fewer labor problems than their corporate warehouses.

Development of high-performance work teams has been a new factor in motivating and stimulating warehouse work crews in the 1990s. Despite this positive influence, management and supervision must deal with a number of negatives.

- ◆ To a greater extent than ever before, available recruits for warehouse work lack language skills, and some may be illiterate. Many others lack basic arithmetic skills needed to check receipts and shipments.

- Warehouse managers report that about half of those seeking jobs have a current problem with substance abuse.
- A growing number of female workers means mechanical aids are needed to replace the heavy manual lifting that still exists in many warehouse operations.

More immigrants in the workforce

With growing numbers of immigrants, managing the twenty-first century workforce will be a challenge in managing diversity. Today one fashion warehouse has a workforce that is almost entirely Haitian, and the prevailing language in the warehouse is French. Supervisors and managers must be bilingual.

Recognizing that they cannot change the labor pool, the best warehouse managers are adapting to it.

The problems are daunting. Reducing order-cycle time will be more important than ever before. Improvements in quality will be equally significant. Improving asset productivity will guide many warehousing decisions. Finally, management will learn to develop a new kind of workforce for warehousing. To an increasing extent, on-the-job training will convert *box kickers* into knowledge workers.

Questions that solve problems

In this and every succeeding chapter of the book, we provide questions you can use to review warehousing challenges with others in your organization. These questions are not an academic quiz to test your recall of concepts presented. Instead, they are designed to help the senior manager review warehousing problems with co-workers.

The answers to most questions will not be found in the text, but only through diligent research within your company or in others — possibly including customers and suppliers. Because often there is no *right* or *wrong* answer we have provided *Comments* instead of *Answers*.

Q **What have we done to shorten order-cycle times in our warehousing operation during the past year?**

C Search for progress in compressing cycle times. These could include transit times as well as order processing times. If a careful search finds no progress, this should stimulate a campaign to improve performance. If there has been some progress, you need to see whether the improvement is slated to continue.

Q **What have we done to improve quality in our warehouse?**

C Make careful note of the answers given. The subject of quality will be explored more thoroughly later and you will find more specific questions in that chapter.

Q **Is our current warehouse workforce properly trained to use computer terminals, bar code scanners, and radio frequency terminals?**

C If you get a negative answer, begin exploring how you will adapt to the limitations of your workforce. Further exploration should concern hiring practices and attempts to upgrade the capabilities of the people working in your organization.

Q **How do our warehousing costs today compare with last year and the year before?**

C Whether these costs are in percent-of-sales, per-ton, or per-unit, you need to know whether you are making progress.

Q **Is our work force improving?**

C This is a general question that doesn't lend itself to quantitative analysis, but you should be able to develop a general feel for the quality of your workforce. The people in your warehouse today should be better than the ones who worked there five years ago. ❖

Chapter 3

Just-in-time – Fad or megatrend?

The intensity with which the just-in-time (JIT) concept swept American industry in the late '70s and early '80s gave it all the trappings of a corporate fad. Dozens of seminars sold the concept, and platoons of consultants offered to initiate their clients into the new religion.

Few remembered that economists had for years talked about the corporate shell game, the practice of pushing inventory back to the supplier and postponing its delivery until the last minute. This had been practiced for years, but under different names. Furthermore, a substantial amount of mythology has become associated with the JIT concept of *kan-ban*.

Kan ban means "signboard" in Japanese, and the term was used because suppliers to Toyota were instructed to place inbound materials beneath posted signs that indicated the appropriate part number. Like many popular business developments, JIT is a product of both fact and myth.

- The first myth is that it is a Japanese idea. JIT is something that the Japanese learned from others. Actually, JIT is a variant of the postponement strategy which has been practiced in business for many decades.

- A second myth is that JIT is a production strategy. In fact, it was used by wholesale and retail distributors at least as early as it was in production. Its use in merchandising is probably more widespread than in manufacturing, and when used in merchandising, JIT nearly always involves warehousing.

- A third fable is that JIT requires that a supplier's plant be close to the user. This is the case in Japan, a compact country where suppliers and customers are pushed close together by geography and culture. In the United States and other large countries, use of air and other premium transportation systems permit JIT to work effectively with a supply line that stretches over hundreds or even thousands of miles.

A Japanese auto builder ordered that tires of a certain size be delivered to a specific spot in the plant at 8 a.m., 11 a.m., 2 p.m., and 5 p.m. Instead of having a tire warehouse adjacent to the assembly plant, the manufacturer relied upon the supplier to have the right tires in the correct location at an appropriate time. Also, instead of the normal rehandling and quality checking, the auto assembler relied upon the supplier to provide tires in perfect condition.

The previous system of storage, rehandling, and checking had generated excessive costs, and the Japanese automaker demonstrated that the *kan ban* concept was one way to reduce these costs.

Because the term *kan ban* was associated with a Japanese company, the phrase 'just-in-time' was adopted as a universal method of describing a timed delivery program.

Postponement

In concept, JIT is a descendent of postponement, first described by Professor Wroe Alderson in 1950. Postponement saves money by delaying to the latest possible moment some final stage of production or distribution.

To delay shipping a product avoids risking its miscommitment. For example, air freight enables some manufacturers to eliminate field inventories. They keep the entire stockpile at a factory distribution center located at the end of the assembly line, and the product is moved into the market at a speed competitive with that of shipping from field distribution centers. This enables the manufacturer to avoid the potential waste of committing the wrong product to a distribution center and later having to cross-ship products to correct an inventory imbalance.

The most efficient distribution point is always at the end of the assembly line, since inventory at the point of manufacture will never have to be backhauled. If air freight is fast enough to allow all inventory to be kept at the factory, a manufacturer may trade off the premium costs of air freight by eliminating inventory losses from miscommitment or obsolescence.

With some merchandise, postponement includes eliminating certain distribution channels. For example, an appliance retailer may have floor samples of each major appliance on the sales floor to show prospective customers. However, when this results in a sale, the actual appliance delivered may not even be in the same city. By using premium transportation from strategically located distribution centers, the appliance distributor avoids committing inventory to each retail store. In this case, postponement is particularly useful because of the cost of handling, storing, and carrying an inventory of bulky and costly appliances. If the customer cannot take the merchandise home in a shopping bag, why move it through the store?

Postponing production

Soft drink manufacturers began using postponement decades ago by producing concentrated syrup. They shipped this concentrate to soda fountains and bottling plants to produce the final product at a point close to the consumer. By postponing the final blending or bottling of the product, the soft drink manufacturer reduced the cost of transportation and distribution.

In the food industry, canners ship product to regional warehouses in bright cans that have no labels. Then, if a private brand order for canned tomatoes is received, the cans are labeled with the distributor's label. In this way, one inventory of unmarked cans can supply the needs of many private label customers. JIT is simply postponement of delivery to hours, or even minutes before the product will be used, creating savings in inventory, handling, and storage costs.

JIT applications

Both wholesalers and retailers have successfully used JIT to provide improved service with less inventory. The pinnacle of success for a merchant is the ability to sell something to a customer before the bill from the supplier is due, thus creating an infinite return on invested capital. Merchandisers recognize that one way to do this is to delay delivery from suppliers to the latest possible moment. One chain grocery company gives grades to its suppliers based upon timing of delivery, and early delivery is considered as harmful as late delivery. If goods are sent in too soon, they increase the space needed to store inventory, they slow the turnover, and they create the probability that the company will have to pay for the goods before they are re-sold.

Because of this emphasis on turnover and reduction of capital investment, merchants constantly seek ways to push the inventory investment
back to the supplier. One way to do this is to delay receipt of goods until
they are about to be sold.

Knowing where the inventory is

One auto parts retailer has a goal of providing service that will always save
the sale and keep the customer from going to a competitor. Yet the typical
store of 5,000 square feet cannot carry the 30,000 stockkeeping units that
are maintained in the product line. So the retailer keeps a master warehouse in its headquarters city to stock all items. If a customer cannot find a
part, store managers have three options:

- ◆ See if another nearby store has the part in stock. If so, the
  customer is asked to go to the other store where the part is
  held in reserve for him.
- ◆ Ship from the master warehouse overnight by air, with a
  promise to the customer that the part will be available on
  the next day.
- ◆ Resupply the item overnight by air directly from the supplier.

This policy has contributed to rapid growth of the company as a chain
retailer. The prime goal is to save the sale by providing next-day delivery to
the customer. Sometimes the cost of saving the sale exceeds the profit, but
the company realizes the ultimate value when the customer makes future
profitable purchases.

Using JIT for service and repairs

Sometimes JIT is used to eliminate parts and service centers in many locations around the country. One health-care supplier, for example, produces
an appliance used in hospitals. If it fails, the company uses a premium air
service to fly in a new unit and to return the one that has malfunctioned.
Technicians repair the malfunctioning unit at one central location, rather
than in scattered repair depots. Furthermore, the service is usually better
than it would be in field repair stations.

Similarly, a computer service company maintains detailed records on
the equipment used by each customer. If a computer breaks down, the service company isolates the problem through telephone consultation. In

about one third of the cases, a technician is able to solve the problem by providing advice over the telephone. When this cannot be done, the failing component is replaced rather than repaired, again using air freight to deliver the replacement unit and return the one that has malfunctioned.

Using JIT in warehousing

While early writings about JIT suggested that this was a strategy to eliminate warehousing, JIT has created more warehouses instead of eliminating them. However, the newer JIT centers are flow-through terminals more than they are warehouses. JIT is a method of increasing the velocity of inventory turns, but that increased velocity is not accomplished by eliminating warehousing, but simply by changing the way in which the warehousing function is performed.*

Both merchant and manufacturer may use a warehouse as a staging point to increase inventory turnover through strategic placement of stocks close to the point where they will be used. For example, a local distributor might stage the inventories of several resources at a convenient public warehouse.

Rather than receive small quantities direct from the source by common carrier, the distributor receives a full truckload of product from a variety of sources at the last moment, and the product is immediately sorted and redistributed for outbound shipment.

Cross docking

The ultimate in fast inventory turnover is cross docking, a distribution system in which freight moves in and out of a distribution center without ever being stored there. Cross docking involves the receipt, sorting, routing, and shipment of products in a minimum amount of time. On occasion, some value-added services may be included in a cross-dock situation. Usually these are limited to repackaging or kitting.

---

*   This chapter is based on information from *Warehousing Forum*, Volume 3, Number 5,
     ©The Ackerman Company, Columbus, Ohio.

The movement of freight from one vehicle to another is nothing new. For many years, shippers assembled pool boxcars and sent them to distributors. Pool car distribution involved the unloading and reshipment of segregated loads consigned to smaller customers. The difference in freight costs between full-car or truckloads and small shipments exceeded the cost of handling pool distribution.

Cross docking is different because the warehouse operator receives bulk shipments and then assembles smaller orders on the warehouse floor. The results are dramatic compared to the cost of conventional warehousing operations involving receipt, stowage, order picking, and shipment. For example, one grocery products distributor saved seventeen cents a case by changing from conventional warehousing to a cross-dock operation.

Cross docking works best when it is limited to the relatively small number of SKUs that are most popular. These items typically sell on the basis of fast and precise delivery.

Questions that solve problems

Q Are we using JIT anywhere?

C The warehouse operation is the tail, rather than the dog, on most JIT applications. If your warehouse is part of a manufacturing organization, use of JIT will probably originate elsewhere in the company. Third-party warehousing people usually get into JIT only when a customer requests it.

Q Are our competitors using JIT in a way that puts our organization at a disadvantage?

C A positive answer should cause you to become actively involved in stimulating the use of JIT within your own company.

Q Has anyone in our company considered the use of JIT for service or for repairs?

C This relatively little-known application for JIT is one that is worth considering in many operations.

Q Are there any opportunities for postponement in our company?

C Be sure to consider every type of postponement, including brand or label assembly and commitment. ❖

Chapter 4

The growing role
of information technology

T he greatest source of savings in today's warehouse is the ability to trade information for space and labor. While space and labor costs tend to increase over time, the cost of computing and transmitting information has decreased — both in relative and actual terms. Consider:

- ♦ The pocket calculator, which weighs a few ounces and fits in the palm of your hand, has more computing power than the $900 mechanical desk calculator used in the 1950s.
- ♦ Because of automation and increased competition, the cost of long-distance calling is less expensive than it was a few decades ago.
- ♦ Telefax machines have made it easy for us to transmit hard-copy information over telephone lines.
- ♦ Bar coding in the warehouse enables us to turn the readable code on each package into words and numbers that identify the product and provide some information about it.

When we can learn something quickly and accurately in the warehouse, we can avoid work that would otherwise be required. A computer terminal at the receiving dock or a radio-frequency terminal on the lift truck can update computer files to show information about goods just received. The information is transmitted to a host computer that recognizes those items needed for immediate shipment. These items can be directed to a shipping dock so that they never move into storage.

Technology and forecasting

While improvements in handling of information have created many changes in the warehouse, the most important is an improved ability to forecast. Accurate forecasts provide one of the best ways to improve productivity in storage and handling.

The forecasting needs for a warehouse manager are primarily short term and are needed for scheduling purposes. Five commonly asked questions could be answered through forecasting:

◆ What will the warehouse workload be tomorrow?

◆ How many workers should we call in for next week?

◆ Do we have enough warehouse space to handle the peak requirements of a current inbound surge?

◆ If we build or buy another building, will we have enough warehousing volume to keep it full?

◆ If we change locations, how big should the new building be?

Every warehouse manager has problems that could be solved or alleviated by an accurate forecast. Think how much easier it would be to manage a warehouse if you had a reasonably clear idea of what the volume of shipping and receiving would be tomorrow. And the job would become even easier if you had an accurate idea of what was going to happen next week. Short interval scheduling of labor in a warehouse is based upon such a forecast. As forecasts extend further into the future, it is natural for them to become less accurate.

Forecasting strategies

Three basic strategies exist for forecasting: deterministic, symptomatic, and systematic.*

The **deterministic strategy** assumes that the present situation causes changes. In the warehouse, you know how many orders were received today. Therefore, you should know how many picking tickets will be generated tomorrow. As you look at forecasting in the warehouse, it is essential to

---

* From *Warehousing Forum*, Volume 2, Number 4, ©The Ackerman Company, Columbus, Ohio.

question whether the apparent determinism is actually functioning as you expected it would. For example, are there conditions when the ratio between orders and picking tickets changes for explainable or unexplainable reasons?

A **symptomatic strategy** assumes that present signs show how the future is developing, but do not themselves determine the future. The symptomatic strategist watches leading indicators that accompany business changes. For example, a summer heat wave reduces activity for some items while increasing activity for others. Just as the deterministic strategy may have exceptions, so can the symptomatic approach. Perhaps your warehouse is distributing toys that move dependably each year at the holiday season. But toys have a product life. When they approach the end of that life cycle, the holiday movement may slow because they are no longer popular.

A **systematic strategy** is based on the assumption that there are underlying regularities or laws that affect movement even when other indicators seem chaotic. Pareto's Law, the 80/20 Rule, is an example of systematic strategy. Nobody knows why 80 percent of the activity involves 20 percent of the items, but major exceptions to this law are rarely found in warehousing. In many inventories today, the principle of Pareto's Law has only been accentuated. Rather than an 80/20 relationship, it is becoming more common to find a 90/10 or a 95/5 ratio.

Forecasting techniques

While there may be two dozen techniques for forecasting, all can be divided into four general methods: judgment, counting, time series, and causal.

The **judgment method** relies upon the opinions of key individuals as they describe their view of the future. To apply the judgment method, one interviews those people whose opinions are critical. One third-party warehousing executive interviews key contacts at his twenty largest customers twice a year. The purpose of those interviews is to obtain information about future business levels or other changes that might influence the warehouse operation.

The **counting method** involves the collection of a much larger amount of data from many sources. A market survey typically uses the counting method. Such a survey might ask hundreds of people their opinions about a product or service, and the number of people expressing each opinion is carefully measured.

The **time-series method** requires the use of moving averages to extrapolate trends from past figures. A typical moving average might compare demand in twelve periods and then forecast demand three months, six months, and nine months. Forecasting accuracy diminishes as the forecaster extends the prediction range.

The **causal method** uses equations based on historic patterns of correlation between two variables. For example, there is often a correlation between the commodity price today and the future cost of grain. If your warehouse handles commodities, causal methods are a likely predictor of future activity.

Practical forecasting applications

Consider some practical applications and how they might work in your warehouse. You would like to know tomorrow's workload, and you might be able to forecast it by seeking a correlation between the number of tons to be shipped tomorrow and the number of mail and telephone orders received today, yesterday, or the day before.

The toughest part of this forecast is to find the correct lag between receipt of orders and the time they move out of the warehouse. Some investigation and experimentation will be necessary. What will the demand be for our warehousing services next year? What will be the probable workload in our warehouse next June? Is there some likelihood that June of next year will be substantially different from this past June?

The ability to obtain reasonably accurate answers to questions like these can have a great deal to do with the success of your operation. Forecasting is neither simple nor easy, and most warehouse operators use very little of it. Your ability to develop and refine a workable forecasting system could facilitate improvements by providing an edge shared by few of your competitors.

Information as a means of control

Information can cut costs and reduce errors, but validating the data is essential. When bar-code control systems are part of an order picking program, it becomes almost impossible to make a mis-shipment. If the code on the box does not match the code on the pick list, the system provides an audible error warning to the order picker. Warehouses using such systems report an error rate of less than one hundredth of one percent.

Information systems can be used to minimize travel through the warehouse, to pull merchandise in accordance with pre-arranged selection priorities (FIFO, LIFO, or lot number), and to select items of similar size for a stable outbound shipping unit. An information system can also track the productivity of individual workers. Each employee has an identification number, and those numbers may be bar coded on identification badges. Every time workers begin a new activity, they use a scanner to read the code on their badges. This transmits the start-of-the-job time to a computer. The computer lists the time the workers start each job and when they finish. This is quicker and easier than punching a time clock, and it allows the quick personalization of every job done in the warehouse.

Management not only knows that the job was done and how long it took, but also who did the work and how productive that individual was. If a pattern of errors or damage should occur, it is easy to determine whether one or a few workers have contributed disproportionately to the discrepancies.

Best of all, this productivity information is recorded on a real-time basis, enabling management to monitor productivity and to detect potential bottlenecks as they are happening.

Information systems can improve the communication among warehouses and the production and marketing groups. They can also improve communication between warehouses in a chain. By using a real-time information system, your production people can determine the ability of each warehouse to accept new product moving out of a factory. Marketing people can verify that critical orders have been shipped.

When the information system links the warehouse to a carrier, you can even determine whether the product has been delivered or how far it is from point of delivery. In effect, the information system allows warehouse users to get a constant and accurate update of the status of every warehousing job.

Information for effective sequencing and JIT

Information systems can control the sequencing of product to supply an assembly line. For example, if automobiles of various colors are on the assembly line, the brown seats must match the brown car, the red ones the red car, and so on. Therefore, the warehouse supplying the assembly line must sequence the colors in the correct order. An error could be costly to correct, but good information technology makes such sequencing virtually error-free.

Information technology can also support JIT. When something breaks down on the quick-response delivery system, the receiver will need to find a substitute product that can be delivered quickly. A few truck lines offer an information system that allows them to identify which trailer contains the needed product. They can then stop or divert the trailer so that the needed part arrives when and where its needed. Once again, information is substituted for inventory because the transportation company can quickly find and divert a critical shipment.

Today we see bar-code scanners strapped to the wrists of warehouse workers so that a natural hand motion points the scanner at the product. While the use of scanners may reduce errors from illiterate or learning-disabled order pickers, the use of such technology also requires higher skills from warehouse workers. These workers will no longer be 'strong backs with weak minds' capable only of handling boxes. The warehouse employees will be knowledge workers who handle automatic identification equipment and computer terminals.

Questions that solve problems

Q Does the information system now used in our warehouse provide all of the control capabilities described in this chapter?

C This question should be the subject of a discussion with your people. Recognize that you may not need all of the *bells and whistles* an information system can give to you. On the other hand, be open-minded about the possibilities of changing things in the future. Examine carefully the motivations and opinions of those in the organization who try to tell you it can't be done. Perhaps the best answer for the doubters is to find another warehousing organization that is already doing the job that supposedly cannot be done.

Q What are we forecasting in the warehouse today, and how well do our forecasts work?

C Don't be shocked if you find little or no forecasting used. If nobody knows how to do it, there are ways to learn — both within the academic world and through management seminars.

Q What tasks are being done in the warehouse today that could be modified or eliminated through the use of available information technology?

C While related to the first question, this one might help your people zero in on specific modifications that are appropriate to bring your warehouse up to today's state-of-the-art in information technology.

Q How does our error rate compare with that of our competition?

C A primary function of the information system is to increase accuracy.

Q Is our order cycle time superior to that of our competitors?

C Better information technology will reduce cycle time. ❖

Chapter 5

Union or union-free warehouses?

Until a few years ago, the great majority of larger warehouses, particularly those in major cities, were unionized. Frequently the union was the same one that had organized the factories of the warehouse operator, but sometimes the organizing union was one associated with transportation, such as the International Brotherhood of Teamsters.

Even when unionization was the norm in warehousing, many warehouse operators worked hard to maintain a warehouse operation that was either union-free or at least organized by a union that was different from the one that had organized the company's other plants.

The risk of strikes or other labor disputes is a key consideration in warehousing. In some industries, work stoppages or other disputes among production workers are likely, and therefore it's important to have a strategy for continuous distribution of finished products, even when one or more production plants are on strike.

This strategy may be carried out in many ways. Some companies keep distribution facilities far from manufacturing locations to cushion the effect of work stoppages. In some cases, the distribution center is located in a rural area with a favorable labor climate so that its non-union status is easier to maintain.

Although such distribution centers can legally be picketed by manufacturing workers engaged in a lawful strike, cost and distance often make such picketing impractical. As a result, orderly distribution continues during a strike. And if the distribution centers are not unionized, there is little danger of a strike by their employees — either out of sympathy for striking manufacturing employees or in support of the workers' own economic demands.

How one company shuts out the union

One medium-sized retail organization has a chain of small shops throughout the country. The organization is vertically integrated and owns plants that manufacture some of the products it sells. Many of its production facilities are unionized, as are some of its retail stores.

In spite of the presence of a union, the company has carefully preserved the independent status of its distribution operation. Some of its products are distributed by private trucking, but the company retains a stevedoring company to hire and control the truck drivers. The company also maintains a group of private non-union distribution centers.

Some time ago, the company endured a long strike to keep its largest distribution center non-union. After this event, workers at one of the company's regional distribution centers voted in a union. The union won by just a few votes and the company signed a one-year labor agreement. The employees subsequently petitioned for a decertification election. At the expiration of the contract, the union was rejected by the great majority of the distribution center workers.

Management of this company feels that distribution is the one branch of their business that can and should be kept non-union. Yet they accept the presence of unions at the manufacturing level, and even at the retail level.

Public warehousing alternatives

Many manufacturers use public warehouses because the third-party operator insulates them from the impact of labor disputes.* To use a public warehouse as part of a strike hedge, the manufacturer must observe three ground rules:

- ◆ Rule 1. The manufacturer should enter the warehousing relationship well before the strike begins. Any agreement entered into shortly before a strike and terminated when the strike ends would be viewed as legally suspect.

---

* The author is indebted to Theodore J. Tierney, a partner in the law firm of Vedder, Price, Kaufman & Kammholz, Chicago, for extensive research and advice.

- ◆ Rule 2. A manufacturer should avoid using more than a limited percentage of a public warehouse's total capacity. In one case, the court ruled that picketing was justified because the strike-bound company occupied 85 percent of the total available space in a warehouse. In contrast, picketing was stopped by court order where the employer's goods occupied only 5 percent of total warehouse capacity.
- ◆ Rule 3. The warehouse's management must have full control over the placement of goods in the facility. To avoid lawful picketing, the customer should not rent any particular physical space at the site.

Public warehouse strikes

What happens if workers at the public warehouse go on strike? In most states the user can remove goods through the picket line by filing an action for replevin — a legal move to recover goods unlawfully withheld from their rightful owner. Under this action, the court issues an order to the marshal or sheriff compelling removal of the goods from the warehouse and their placement in the owner's hands.

Subcontractor warehouse services

A warehousing subcontractor arrangement involves the use of an independent warehouse operator's personnel within the manufacturer's facilities. In using the subcontracting option, the user must beware of creating a *joint-employer* relationship with the subcontractor's employees. To avoid this possibility, the warehousing contractor must be in full and sole charge of determining how many employees are needed, who they will be, and the method used to perform the work. A subcontractor must also be in sole control of hiring, training, disciplining, and discharging workers, as well as all other aspects of the employment relationship.

Transportation strikes

The transportation industry has a long history of union activity and many warehouses are designed to deal with strikes by carriers. For example, a distribution center with a railroad spur can be used during trucking strikes. From a practical standpoint, strike activity at a warehouse seldom impedes rail movement of goods in and out of the facility. Railroad companies will usually provide switching service with supervisory personnel and it is often physically impossible for pickets to block industrial railroad tracks because they are on private property. Rail movement is frequently an effective hedge when a strike disrupts trucking operations.

Creating a participative environment

Whether or not your warehouse has a union, effective management can create an environment in which the influence of union officials is minimized. In practice, you do not need to be union-free in order to submerge union influence. What is required is an atmosphere that builds loyalty to the company, not interest in the union. In some unionized warehouses, grievances are virtually unknown. Union officials are consulted only for renewal of the contract, and there is no discussion of union contracts and union affairs.

Others have created an environment that is simply not conducive to unionization.

One retailer provides a dignified and relatively luxurious setting for warehouse workers. In that company, every worker — from president to trainee — enters through the same front door and lobby. Furthermore, everyone on the payroll uses the same cafeteria for lunch.

This egalitarian environment is even more pronounced in a non-union manufacturing plant where everyone, president and factory worker alike, wears a white shop coat when on the production floor. The white uniform hides the pinstripes of the corporate executive or the blue collar of the factory worker. The result is a removal of the 'we-they' symbols of business dress.

For most warehouse workers, the line supervisor or foreman symbolizes management. Therefore, labor problems are often the result of weak or highly authoritarian supervision. Workers who are treated fairly tend to respect both their supervisor and senior management. They are not attracted by the appeal of a union organizer, and they are not interested in the union if it is already present.

Many managers believe compensation is the prime motivator for hourly workers, yet repeated surveys show that money is relatively low in the priorities of most American workers, including warehouse people. They are more interested in prestige, security, respect, and a feeling of belonging. These desires can be frustrated by insensitive, authoritarian, or unfair supervisors. While low pay may be stated as the cause, the true motivation to unionize is typically non-financial. The worker who supports a union organization drive is reacting either to the reality or to the perception of unfair treatment in the workplace.

The role of the supervisor

In many respects, an employee's supervisor is the company to that employee. A supervisor often has more impact on morale and perceptions of the company than any other single factor. So the selection and continued training of supervisors is vital.

Selecting supervisors should involve more analysis than merely promoting the most efficient workers. While a worker's productivity certainly should be considered, it does not guarantee that he or she has the qualities necessary to be an effective supervisor.

The credibility of your supervisors is critical. It is essential that you do all you can to enhance and maintain that credibility. Supervisors should be kept well informed and, in turn, should be the prime source of information for your workers. Supervisors should also, whenever possible, be given credit for working-condition improvements.

The two-tier wage alternative

Over the decade of the 1980s, one significant development in union-management relations in the warehousing and transportation industries was the introduction of two-tier wage plans.* The introduction and modification of these plans received considerable publicity. Two of the high-visibility industries in which the introduction and modification of two-tier plans received the greatest attention are warehousing and transportation.

Under a two-tier plan, the union agrees that the employer can set the wages and benefits of newly hired employees at a rate at or near the rate

---

*   From "A Report Card On Two Tier Wage Plans" by J. Michael Kota, *Warehousing Forum*, Volume 6, Number 1, ©The Ackerman Company, Columbus, Ohio.

paid by a non-union competitor. In exchange, the unionized employer agrees that the wages and benefits of current employees will be maintained at a higher level.

Prior to the 1980s, in most logistics industries, most employers had been unionized. Wage rates were usually uniform (often under multi-employer master contracts), so competitors did not compete on labor costs, and increases in labor costs were uniformly passed on to customers. The customary result: High wage rates, even though many occupations in those industries did not require high levels of education or skills.

During the 1980s, several external factors combined to place unionized companies under pressure:

- ◆ Previously regulated transportation firms were de-regulated, making it easier for new competitors to enter those industries.

- ◆ Many new competitors, including foreign companies, took advantage of that ease of entry and entered those industries.

- ◆ The supply of available employees increased because of general business declines. Moreover, in many areas, new immigrants added to the entry-level labor pool. New competitors could find plenty of available employees who were happy to work for lower wage rates.

- ◆ The unions representing employees in these industries either did not attempt to organize, or were unsuccessful in organizing, employees of the new, lower-cost competitors. For example, the growth of the Teamsters through the 1980s was in industries other than its warehousing and trucking base.

What did unionized logistics firms do in response to this pressure? Some did nothing and went out of business. Others sought major concessions in pay and benefits to meet their new competition.

During the 1980s, employers sold unions on two-tier wage plans with the argument that they represented the least painful way for an employer and a union jointly faced with low-cost competition to meet that competition.

Relatively few two-tier wage plans remain intact after five years have passed, most having been changed to meet new conditions in the workplace. Common changes include:

- ◆ Eliminating the lower-tier or pay scale.

◆ Merging the lower-tier employees into the upper-tier.

◆ Refining the two-tier plan. For example, some employers have eliminated two-tier wage programs and have substituted a two-tier benefit plan.

In warehousing, changes in the supply-demand equation have varied by region. Some communities have a shortage of labor, so there is no point in negotiating a lower-tier wage rate. Moreover, if your competitor has been forced to increase wages to keep people, that company's cost advantage has been reduced and so has the need for a two-tier wage plan.

Further, the supply-demand equation may have changed with respect to a particular job because the content of that job may have changed. For example, as warehouses have become more automated and computerized, the skill level required in many entry-level positions has increased significantly, and the pool of qualified prospective employees for those positions has shrunk.

Through the 1980s, a number of alternatives to two-tier wage plans have developed:

◆ **Lump-sum payments**: Sometimes the employer may wish to provide a single payment as a substitute for a regular wage increase. The payment provides extra money to workers without changing their base rate. Many collective-bargaining agreements covering warehouse operations have provided for such lump-sum payments, which may provide the stimulus to settle a labor contract without establishing two classes of employees.

◆ **Profit-sharing (especially when coupled with a wage freeze or concessions)**: Profit-sharing has the same objective (moderation in base wage rates) as lump-sum payments, and also provides a productivity incentive.

◆ **Increased productivity of current employees, through technological improvements, work-rule changes, et cetera**: Greater productivity, whatever the reason, serves to justify a higher wage rate.

◆ **Use of temporary employees**: Some unionized warehouse operations have successfully negotiated for flexibility in the use of temporary employees so long as no current employees are laid off. This strategy is more prevalent where the warehouse's workforce naturally fluctuates. From a union's perspective, this strategy can avoid morale problems.

A temporary two-tier plan may be used to reflect the training curve for newly hired workers. Used in this fashion, the two-tier plan is little different from wage scales with lower starting rates that are common in many industries.

A 1991 Bureau of National Affairs survey of employer bargaining objectives showed that a majority of employers wanted to retain the two-tier wage programs that they had then. However, among those who did not have such plans, only five percent indicated that they would seek to establish such a plan within a year.

The experience of the 1980s has placed warehouse employers in a much better position today to judge the advantages and pitfalls of a two-tier plan in their operation.

Planning for the impact of strikes

As the first step in preparing to face a strike, be fully briefed on contract deadlines.* It should not be hard to keep track of such deadlines in your own firm, although it is easy to miss them in the case of your suppliers. Many purchasing agents require each supplier to list contract expiration dates, and keep this information as part of the master purchasing file.

A strike at your company

Every distribution operation has traditional alternatives for dealing with a work stoppage. These include the use of public warehouse facilities, non-union transportation companies, or even non-union private distribution facilities.

If your firm is preparing for a strike, the company's main objectives in bargaining should be outlined since they are likely to affect decisions made during the work stoppage. If public warehouses are used as a strike hedge, the manufacturer should begin the public warehousing operation before the strike starts — dispersing the product so that it represents only a small

---

*   Adapted from an article by Dr. Bernard J. Hale, McGaw Laboratories. The article first appeared in *Warehousing & Physical Distribution Productivity Report*, Volume 14, Number 3, ©Alexander Research & Communications, Inc., New York, NY.

fraction of the total capacity of each warehousing supplier. These precautions allow the warehouse operator to file a secondary-boycott charge with the National Labor Relations Board should illegal picketing of a public warehouse occur. In selecting a public warehouse as a strike hedge, it is important to appraise the labor stability and operational flexibility of the warehouse supplier. Properly applied, the strike-hedge inventory can be a powerful bargaining tool in contract negotiation.

A strike that affects one of your suppliers

The effect of strikes directed at other companies can be as disruptive as disturbances within your own organization. A first step in planning for this contingency is to determine which suppliers are essential to your operations. This may depend on whether they are sole sources or whether they supply a critical percentage of the purchasing volume.

Having identified the critical suppliers, the next step is to learn if those companies are unionized. If so, what is their labor relations record over the past decade? If there is a contract, when does it expire? Some information on contract expiration is publicly available, including the Negotiations Calendar issued by the U.S. Bureau of National Affairs. The risk of a supplier's strike can be mitigated by developing an inventory hedge in the form of advance stockpiling of the critical items. Interim purchasing arrangements, such as the import of similar items, may also be a source of relief.

Strikes that affect customers also affect you

A strike against your customer also can have a serious effect on warehousing operations. It is advisable to follow closely the contract expiration dates and negotiations affecting companies with which you have important business relationships. If a customer's strike seems imminent, consider accelerated deliveries or such special accommodations such as direct-store delivery to bypass a strike in a retailer's distribution center.

Planning is essential

Transportation strikes require particular resourcefulness in planning. The traffic manager must find alternative sources well in advance of the strike. The problem should be discussed with customers and suppliers, who may be able to use their own private trucking to move products in or out of your warehouse.

In times of trucking strikes, some small carriers will make a side agreement to settle on the master contract and agree to keep working during the general strike. The traffic manager should locate such firms and arrange to use them. Owner-operators of trucks also frequently ignore strikes. In addition to using trucks from customers and suppliers, your own firm may have private transportation that can be used.

Non-union transportation companies also can be used, though such firms naturally will serve their regular customers first.

Questions that solve problems

Q Is our warehouse now union free?

C You should frequently question your people about what they are doing to maintain this status if it exists.

Q What steps do we take for proper training and orientation of our supervisors?

C If your company does not have a training program for supervisors or a program to review their performance, your union-free status could be in jeopardy.

Q What procedures are in place to resolve complaints made by hourly workers?

C Don't consider just the statements made by your managers and supervisors. Ask the hourly employees in the warehouse as well.

Q If the warehouse is unionized, ask your people about grievance records and frequency of visits by union organizers.

C Your goal is to learn whether or not your management has been successful in submerging the union.

Q What steps have we taken to plan for the contingencies of strikes against outside firms as well as against our own company?

C Look for a reasonable number of detailed options to counteract strikes against suppliers, strikes against customers, or strikes against the transportation companies serving your warehouse.

Q Have we explored a two-tier wage plan? If so, how did it work?

C The answers may tell you whether a two-tier wage plan is appropriate for your company, or whether it was put in for sensible reasons. ❖

Chapter 6

The challenge of returns

The traditional management of logistics systems, including warehouses, has emphasized the movement of materials from sources of supply to points of consumption. Warehouses are part of the flow process, but we usually assume that the flow goes only from source to consumer.*

Until the past few years, concerns about the flow of materials from consumer back to source were almost unheard of. However, recent years have brought new challenges, including the need for reversing the traditional logistics flow. Hence a spotlight on the challenge of returns.

Three reasons for returns

The first of these new challenges was improvement of consumer protection through quick and accurate product recalls. A production error, a design failure, or even a case of deliberate sabotage may cause the need to isolate and return all units of a given production lot in order to ensure the safety of the consumer.

Perhaps the best-known example was the case of deliberate poisoning of Tylenol®. The manufacturer, Johnson & Johnson, immediately recalled every bottle of Tylenol. All bottles were returned to a central point and destroyed.

Similar incidents have taken place with contaminated food items, faulty automobiles, and chemicals that have a production defect. When the

* From *Warehousing Forum*, Volume 8, Number 1, ©The Ackerman Company, Columbus, Ohio.

fault or defect is discovered, the manufacturer usually isolates the problem to given production lots and limits the recall to those lots instead of recalling the entire inventory.

Some food manufacturers make test recalls in order to verify the capabilities of warehousing and trucking supplies to handle a recall correctly. The need for speed and precision in the process is obvious, particularly when the defect could threaten the lives of consumers. In this situation, the prime stimulus for product recall is consumer safety.

Environmental issues at work

A second major motivator for returns is avoiding the degradation of the environment. Within the United States, there is grave concern about the depletion of landfill sites and the consequent rising cost of solid-waste disposal.

A proven way of reducing the volume of waste is to recycle and reuse certain packaging materials. This may involve the sorting of recyclable material by product type — plastic, ferrous metals, other metals, and paper. Once sorted, the recyclable material moves via various routes until it is returned to a manufacturing point where it can be remanufactured into new packaging or other similar products.

Precision is less critical in this kind of return, since consumer safety is not involved. However, the concerns of environmentalists have created almost as much public pressure for recycling of packaging as for the recall of defective consumer goods. In a few cities today, laws require that a vendor of a major appliance return the carton when the appliance is delivered in order to relieve the consumer of the substantial disposal problem of the large box. The problem of course is not eliminated, but only transferred from consumer to vendor.

Economic concerns are a factor

The third motive for returns is conservation of assets. For years before we had environmental concerns, pallets were exchanged rather than donated to the buyer. The exchange reflected the fact that the vendor simply couldn't afford to give away an expensive pallet with each unitized load. Similar motives caused the development of refillable beverage bottles decades before anyone worried about landfill capacity. The bottles were expensive and, in fact, there was a time when soft drinks came in a bottle that had a higher value than the fluid inside. The consumer could not be forced to return the bottle, but was penalized for failure to do so.

Railroads use boxcars with reusable dunnage. The successful use of DF (damage free) cars depends on the willingness of every user to return the reusable dunnage to the boxcar after it has been unloaded. Not all shippers are dependable, and policing dunnage returns has become a major problem for the rail carriers.

In a similar fashion, the auto industry has reusable packing techniques, such as steel racks to hold engines, metal bins and cages to hold a wide variety of small auto parts, and several devices to unitize tires. In each case, the warehouse, the trucker, or any other party in the logistics process has an obligation to return this permanent packaging material so that it can be used again. The auto industry has been notably successful in imposing the discipline needed to protect reusable packaging so that it can be used many times before being discarded.

Handling returns

Warehouse managers, both third-party and private, are key players in the return process.

Consider first the safety recall. The speed and accuracy of the warehouse manager in identifying, isolating, and returning production lots that are potentially dangerous is of critical importance. The warehouse manager who fails in the process is likely to be disciplined, even if the failure is only in a test recall. Manufacturers who face this kind of safety risk have little tolerance for lack of accuracy in a product recall. When faced with a recall, the warehouse manager must approach it with all the seriousness and concentration of a fire or disaster. Done wrong, the consequences could be just as grave.

The warehousing professional can be particularly creative in the case of environmental returns, since some warehouses are able to provide value-added services such as compacting, bailing, shredding, grinding, or other disposal processes. These will lower the cost of storing and transporting the material that is to be recycled. The economy of performing such services as close as possible to the origin of the material flow is obvious. Early compaction lowers transportation costs. Therefore, we can anticipate that a growing number of warehouses will have equipment to compact material being returned for recycling.

The most important thing the warehouse can do in handling returns is to perform the function at the lowest possible cost. Since the motive for the return is conservation, the manufacturer seeks to minimize costs in all phases of the return process. Sometimes the material could be stored outdoors at a lower cost, but outdoor storage is an eyesore, and such storage also exposes the materials to contamination. The best way to reduce costs may be not to store the material at all, but to be sure that it is promptly moved in an otherwise empty vehicle that is returning to the recycle point.

Reconfiguring for efficient handling of returns

New layouts and new equipment are likely to appear in warehouses that are involved in handling returns.

In some cases, returns will involve disposal of waste materials by burning. Then the warehouse operator will need to acquire and operate incinerators.

Other types of equipment may be needed to process or to temporarily store recyclables and waste materials. These include bailers, shredders and compactors. The arrangement of this equipment within the warehouse or on the warehouse grounds must be carefully considered to avoid problems of odor contamination, spillage, or other housekeeping problems.

The layout should be designed to provide optimal layout and flow of materials to and from the machines. This flow should include adequate areas for segregation and sorting of waste materials.

Dissimilar materials must be isolated for recycling purposes, and the facility should be designed to facilitate the sorting process. In some cases, warehouse facilities will be redesigned or reconfigured to handle recycling and waste management in the receiving areas.

Security may be an issue

Sometimes a product return is required for stock balancing or to allow minor repairs. One small-appliance manufacturer has allowed dealers to return unsold merchandise to a central warehouse on a periodic basis. This good-will gesture is done in order to remove some of the retailers' inventory risk and encourage dealers to adequately stock the product line. In other cases, slightly damaged merchandise is moved to a central collection point for refurbishing or repair. Stock balancing and repair returns may involve costly merchandise, and sometimes the merchandise is not returned in original containers. When this happens, it is not easy to obtain an accurate count and prevent pilferage.

Therefore, a warehouse handling such returns must be configured to provide maximum security for the returned products. Goods in makeshift packages should be reconditioned immediately so proper count of the merchandise can be maintained. The handling of valuable returns represents a significant security risk, but it can be controlled through careful storage practices.

Reconditioning and repackaging

One of the consequences of handling returns is the frequent necessity to repair, clean, recondition, or repackage the returned merchandise. Accomplishing this may require the establishment of a small assembly operation within the warehouse. Packaging, cleaning, or repair may be accomplished by moving the product down an assembly line that contains the appropriate materials. This may require significant reconfiguration of warehouse design.

Keeping it simple

A valuable series of scholarly works deals with the concept of reverse logistics. Some of this writing makes the process appear more complicated than it is. Logistics people have handled certain kinds of returns, such as beverage bottles, for many decades, so there need be no mystery about the process.

In essence, returns are primarily common sense. Worries about the environment and consumer safety have created a new degree of urgency about the process, often because of the involvement of government and consumer protection agencies. Despite this, the essential components of the process have changed remarkably little. The next time you see some ponderous writing about reverse logistics, just compare it to the return of soft drink and milk bottles.

Questions that solve problems

As you discuss returned goods processing with managers, your questions should focus on environmental changes or business changes that may force you to handle returns. Here are some points for discussion:

Q Are we handling any returns today? If so, are we handling them effectively?

C The answers will provide a good review of your current status in returns handling. This review should also uncover opportunities for improvement.

Q Are there any environmental considerations with our product that may cause us to process returns for the first time?

C Look beyond the immediate future and consider projections within your industry for long-term changes. In some cases, these changes will require substantial planning. Now is the time to start.

Q Do we have any equipment for recycling or processing of returns in the warehouse now? If so, are the layout and flow efficient?

C In looking at layout and flow, you may also want to consider reconditioning and repackaging, both of which are enhanced by effective product flow.

Q Do our people have proper training and rehearsal in the handling of product recalls?

C Recalls are not an issue in every business, but if they are critical in yours, you cannot go too far in training and rehearsing. This insures that the process will be handled properly when it must happen. ❖

PART

21

Warehouse Control

Chapter 7

Quality and productivity

Some say that if high quality is established and emphasized, productivity will take care of itself. Quality may be defined as *precisely conforming to requirements*. The performance standard is usually one hundred percent conformance, or zero defects. In warehousing, as in many other activities, the best people are perfectionists. They maintain the attitude that every error is avoidable, and every defect should be inspected with the goal of insuring that it does not happen again.

Applications in the warehouse

How do we measure quality in a warehouse operation? You will have a few measurements specific to your operation, but here are some that nearly all warehouse managers use:

- ◆ Housekeeping, maintenance and appearance of the facility.
- ◆ Shipping accuracy.
- ◆ Order fill rate.
- ◆ Scheduling — both inbound and outbound.
- ◆ Number of accident-free days and reduction of injury claims.
- ◆ Employee turnover.
- ◆ Equipment down-time.
- ◆ Reduction of product damage, both warehouse damage and carrier damage.
- ◆ Supplier performance.
- ◆ Compliance with government regulations.

As you look at the list above, it is important to note that each criterion is measurable, each is relevant to generally perceived notions about quality warehouse operations, and each should be the subject of continuous improvement by everyone in your workforce.

When failures occur, the causes should be identified so corrective action can be taken.*

Housekeeping has always been considered the primary barometer of management effectiveness in warehousing. Whether your level of housekeeping is inspected by an important customer, your boss, a customer's truck driver, or a casual visitor, the impressions made by excellent or atrocious housekeeping are not soon forgotten.

An often overlooked aspect of housekeeping is personal appearance, which is important for every professional. In warehousing, this includes hourly employees. Some of the best-managed warehouses use uniforms to create a neat personal appearance for every worker.

Sloppy personal appearance is a symbol of a lack of self-esteem, and is usually accompanied by a lack of concern for quality. Therefore, we react positively only to a person with a neat personal appearance.

Shipping accuracy is deceptively easy to measure. Conventional wisdom says that you simply relate the number of reported errors and complaints to the number of shipments made to create a ratio that reflects shipping accuracy. But a few unscrupulous receivers report non-existent discrepancies. Their motives may be to correct a purchasing error, to unload damaged merchandise on a carrier, or even to steal merchandise from suppliers by claiming false shortages.

Study your complaint file carefully. If most reported errors are concentrated with a few consignees, you should check the reliability of the people who are receiving the freight.

Order fill rate is a simpler measure. Either you were able to fill the order completely or you weren't. Set a standard for order fill rate, and once the standard is met, consider raising it a bit.

Scheduling both inbound and outbound shipments is the best cure for chaos at a truck dock. The success of a scheduling program is not easily measured, but most common carriers prefer dealing with shippers and receivers who make appointments and stick to them.

---

*   From an article by D. F. McMillan, Shell Oil Company, *Warehousing Forum*, Volume 6, Number 3, ©The Ackerman Company, Columbus, Ohio.

If you require appointments from your carriers, you assume an obligation to live with the appointment schedule you create. The carrier who receives a firm appointment for a 2 p.m. delivery and is then told to wait will
be quick to charge you for detention time.

Measurement of injuries and accident free days is relatively simple
and is an effective way to communicate to your people that safety is a high
priority in your company.

Unusual turnover of employees is a sign of difficulty in any business,
and unfortunately it can be a common problem in warehousing. While
some turnover is normal, losing more than 15 percent of your employees
annually is a likely indicator of problems with compensation, supervision,
quality of work life, or some combination of these.

Equipment down time is a simple and non-controversial measurement. All machinery breaks down occasionally, and a measurement of actual break-down time will show whether or not the warehouse operation is
above, below, or at the norms.

When measuring **product damage**, consider both the damage caused
by warehouse errors and that caused by carriers. In making this measurement, it is critical to insure that no one in your warehouse operation is permitted to fraudulently blame damage on carriers or shippers when it was
actually caused in your warehouse.

When a warehouse operator measures **supplier performance**, the simplest measurement is the timely delivery of inbound shipments at the receiving dock. Another measurement checks the accuracy of shipments and
the amount of damage.

At a time when **government regulations** are an increasing burden on
many businesses, the ability of your warehouse to remain free from OSHA
and FDA citations is a measure of quality.

Quality distinguishes the best operations

Some managers see warehousing as a means of creating a distinctive image
of quality. An image of quality can distinguish one warehousing operation
from others.

The ability to reliably provide and consistently maintain high service
(error free, fast cycle, value-added activities) is challenging. Some companies are able to achieve reliable performance for a short period but find
maintaining consistent performance is another challenge.

Quality experts such as Deming, Juran, and Crosby have developed specific philosophies and approaches to quality management. These approaches involve a number of common principles, including these:

◆ **Strive for continuous improvement.** An operation, function, or *management system* should set continuous improvement as its goal and work to achieve better system performance.

◆ **Understand the full cost of poor quality.** Your warehouse people must understand the full cost of non-conformance to standards. The cost of *doing it right the first time* is always less than the cost of finding and correcting quality problems and doing the job again.

◆ **Focus on causes, not symptoms.** Find and correct the causes of poor quality in your warehouse. Do not try to achieve quality by inspecting after the fact. Instead, alter the system that causes the errors to occur.
  For example, inspecting outgoing shipments is a costly way to assure order accuracy. You must identify the sources of stock-picking or labeling errors and correct them through training, workload balancing, work simplification, data-entry automation, and identification.

◆ **Monitor system performance.** Use statistical tools to monitor the performance of the system to maintain control.

◆ **Use a team approach.** Quality is not just a management or a quality-control department problem, but a company-wide concern. Warehouse managers who are able to remove fear of change, encourage participation, reward innovation, and involve all employees in problem solving are the leaders in quality.*

---

*   From an article by William C. Copacino, Andersen Consulting. It appeared in *Warehousing Forum*, Volume 6, Number 10, ©The Ackerman Company, Columbus, Ohio.

Quantity versus quality

Warehousing people, by the nature of their jobs, deal in quantity-based activity. They calculate pounds-per-man-hour and other quantitative measures to show how well they are doing.

It is important to avoid confusing quantity with quality. A highly productive warehouse operation that has high error rates, poor housekeeping, and poor service could deteriorate to a point where the quantity output is less significant than poor quality.

In manufacturing, product quality results from eliminating defects. In warehousing, product quality is measured by the loyalty of customers and workers.

How to increase productivity

Only your imagination will limit the ways you can improve productivity in a warehouse.* Of the eight that will be considered, five are critical:

♦ Establish improvement targets
♦ Reduce distances traveled
♦ Increase the average size of each load handled
♦ Seek round-trip movements within the warehouse
♦ Improve cube utilization

Establish improvement targets

In warehousing, as in athletics, workers perform better in a competitive atmosphere. Because warehousing involves random operations more than manufacturing, the development of work standards is more difficult. Yet the use of productivity goals, based on predetermined engineered standards, is feasible in a warehouse operation.

Warehousing is often a hedge against uncertainties. Therefore, an accurate forecast may eliminate the need to store materials. A good forecast will prevent the deployment of items in Chicago when they are needed only in Miami. Better forecasting also reduces two prime sources of waste: the cost

---

*   Adapted from Making Warehousing More Efficient, by the author and Bernard J. La Londe of The Ohio State University, *Harvard Business Review*, March-April 1980.

of *reserving* space the user thinks will be needed and the *hoarding* of workers that may be needed when volume increases.

A few companies give the estimating and planning responsibilities to logistics managers. This means that logistics people are responsible for market forecasts and the scheduling that follows them. Consider the advantage of concentrating this responsibility in a department that must both forecast the future and fulfill its own forecasts.

Forecasting should include a prediction of variation in flow. Most companies have rush seasons based on demand peaks or responses to sales incentives. Such peaks can waste storage space and increase labor costs.

There is a way to control such waste. Smoothing the flow usually involves cooperation with marketing personnel. Can we give customers an incentive to do their own warehousing during the off-season? If a sales contest is involved, must the goods be shipped immediately? Entering the order at the warehouse might permit it to be counted for incentive purposes, but the shipment could actually be made later to smooth the work flow.

Reduce distances traveled

In controlling the distances traveled in moving material between storage bays and shipping or receiving docks, the warehouse manager finds one of the easiest ways to cut costs.

First, examine the layout. One of the best tools in reducing travel distances is a rule called Pareto's Law, or the 80/20 rule. This law states that in most enterprises, 80 percent of the demand is satisfied with only 20 percent of the stockkeeping units. Clearly, if management identifies this 20 percent of the items and locates them near the shipping and receiving doors the effect on distance traveled will be dramatic. Yet in most warehouse operations, goods are stored by product family. A grocery product operation, for example, may have all canned goods in one section, all paper items in another, housewares in another, and so on. In some cases, storage characteristics require such a separation, but often they do not.

The planner who desires to change the layout to conform to demand, must first determine the demand pattern. In doing so, recognize that your target is constantly moving. In any dynamic business, a study of Pareto's Law must be repeated to reflect changes.

Are your order pick lists designed for maximum efficiency in the warehouse? A document that lists items in the same order they are found in an order-pickline, allows the stockpicker to start at the top of the sheet and at the head of the aisle, and move down the aisle and down the document at the same time.

Reduction of distances traveled is a function of planning, data processing and materials handling. The planner can use Pareto's Law or some procedure to design aisles and staging areas to reduce unnecessary movement. Then data processing personnel can design a locator system that functions effectively with random locations and order-pick lists that conform to the physical layout.

In materials handling, inbound movements offer good opportunities for trip economy. In some warehouses, the responsibility for finding a location for inbound loads rests with the material handlers. In the absence of instructions, they will put the incoming load in the first empty slot. The result is a needless proliferation of stock locations for the same item.

Look at the location and use of dock doors. Many warehouses have dock areas dedicated strictly to receiving, while other docks are used only for shipping. But time can be saved through use of the same doors for both shipping and receiving.

If you allow any dock door to serve either purpose, you reduce travel by assigning inbound loads to the door closest to the area where the items are to be stored. Do the same with empty vehicles arriving for outbound loads.

Unlike our national highway network, the warehouse 'highway system' of aisles can be changed without substantial cost. The layout of aisles should be constantly fine-tuned with a goal of reducing travel distance.

Increase unit load size

The warehouse that supplies convenience stores frequently may open cases of tomato soup and ship individual cans because the small store cannot justify ordering in full case quantities. While the cost of breaking cases is high, the distributor is meeting the needs of the convenience store. Contrast that situation to the harbor scene where a 40-foot marine container carrying whiskey from Scotland is unloaded. Handling large units greatly reduces the opportunities for breakage and pilferage, as well as the cost-per-ton of handling.

As you examine your own warehouse, ask whether the average size of units handled could be increased. Doing so may require changes in marketing policy. Some grocery product companies offer customers an incentive to buy in pallet-load quantities, with the discount offered only when the order calls for an exact pallet load — 50, 100 or 150 cases.

Seek round-trip opportunities

Because most fork-lifts carry a payload in just one direction, the truck travels empty half of the time.

In contrast, high-rise facilities equipped with stacker cranes include a computer control with a memory unit. This memory is used to maximize round-trip travel opportunities.

When the crane is putting away an inbound truckload containing item F, the computer already has determined the best storage address.

Meanwhile, the computer remembers that item J, stored in a nearby slot, is wanted for an outbound order being staged. Under instructions from the computer, the crane takes item F to its storage address, then moves to the address for item J and returns with this merchandise for the outbound order.

The opportunities for reducing one-way travel are not limited to computerized stacker cranes, but moving payloads in two directions requires effective communication. Equipping each fork-lift truck with a radio helps. If the driver advises the dispatcher that item C is being moved to a given storage address, the dispatcher can instruct the driver to return with a pallet of item N.

Admittedly, maximizing round-trip hauling adds some complications. For one thing, it requires precise planning by supervisors. Moreover, involving the lift driver in both shipping and receiving creates new opportunities for errors. Also, the shipping and receiving docks will require larger staging areas to accumulate a bank of work to support roundtrip movements.

While the process is complex, your supervisors can control the complications if they are given reasonable lead times to plan and control round-trip travel.

Improve cube utilization

The cheapest space in any warehouse is that closest to the ceiling. If you were constructing a warehouse with 22-foot clear stack height, you might develop a cost figure of 20 dollars per square-foot, or 91 cents per cubic-foot ($20 divided by 22). However, if you raise the clearance from 22 feet to 24 feet, the total cost of the building will increase only slightly, to about $20.30 per square-foot in the example. This means a drop in the cost per cubic-foot from 91 cents to 85 cents.

While packaging strength limits the practical pile height, management can do something about the packaging problem. The most obvious solution is to improve the package. If you can't change the package, consider high-density storage racks, such as drive-in racks to permit higher stacking of products with weak packages.

As cube utilization improves, travel distance in the building can be reduced. But there is always a trade-off in using overhead space. Elevating the product to the roof takes time. The most economical storage plan is influenced by the speed of turnover. The fastest-moving product should be stored not only close to the door but also close to the floor.

There are limits to cube utilization. To allow effective functioning of sprinkler systems, fire insurance underwriters impose a maximum pile height, particularly of hazardous materials. They also require a buffer between the sprinkler heads and the storage pile. This distance depends on the capacities of the sprinkler system, the pile height, and the type of merchandise stored.

It is important not to overemphasize space utilization. Consider the plight of a grocery warehouse manager who had inherited a system that was the ultimate in narrow-aisle design. As he gloomily surveyed the cramped environment, he made this observation: "One thing about aisles is they cost a little less each year. Aisles don't bargain for pay increases or increased benefits. If we save a few aisles and add a lot of people, we'll never be ahead of the game."

Though maximum use of overhead space may seem to be the cheapest way to get more product into your building, the key to improving warehousing efficiency is to seek the best compromise between storage costs and handling costs.

The next three improvement areas may be less critical, yet they will significantly change warehouse productivity.

Free labor bottlenecks

Bottlenecks are always at the top of the bottle. Since management is also at the top, it's your responsibility to correct the situation.

A typical bottleneck occurs in unloading a floor-loaded boxcar. Two laborers may be assigned to the boxcar to palletize cases for a fork-lift truck driver who removes loaded pallets. If the laborers' speed exceeds the driver's, they wait until he returns to remove a load. Changing the crew size will clear the bottleneck.

Another approach is the *one man, one machine* technique, which gives each worker a lift truck, so that worker has no need to wait for anyone else. As you tour your warehouse, look for workers who are waiting and find out what has caused the bottleneck.

Reduce item handling

In a typical factory warehouse, products are each handled 16 times. Many of these handlings can be eliminated and they should be. Each movement of a product is an opportunity to damage it. Each lifting further fatigues the package.

As you examine your warehousing operation, ask why it is necessary to stage every inbound load on the dock before moving it to a storage bay. Ask the same thing about the staging of outbound loads. In trying to reduce the number of product handlings, pay particular attention to temporary storage locations and see if they can be eliminated.

Improve the packaging

From the warehouse operator's point of view, the perfect package is made of cast iron and filled with feathers; it is indestructible and can be stacked 50 feet high with no artificial support. Such perfection is non-existent, of course, but the warehouseman is justified in showing concern about packages that won't permit use of the available space in the warehouse.

Warehouses built in the last few decades have ceiling heights that exceed the free-standing stacking capabilities of packages going into them.

The packaging engineer wants a container that is light and cheap — just strong enough to get the item to the consumer.

The manufacturer must consider the trade-offs. The product manager should ask whether it would pay to spend more money on packaging, and achieve savings through avoidance of product damage in warehousing and distribution.

A new look at productivity

In the race to improve productivity, it is easy to overlook the real reasons we are interested in it, and the ways productivity measurement can be helpful to us.

The Puritan work ethic

In the North American culture, being productive is a means of fulfilling the Puritan work ethic. Even for those who do not have an Anglo-Saxon background, this legacy is deeply embedded in our culture. The patron saint of the Puritan ethic was Benjamin Franklin, the colonial printer who realized that one of the most popular book purchases of his day was an almanac. To fill his own almanac, Franklin borrowed heavily from the Puritan culture of his native New England. Historians argue about whether 'early to bed and early to rise...' was actually invented by Franklin, but no one argues that he created lasting popularity for this and other proverbs.

The Puritans have their prophets today, including C. Northcote Parkinson, the British philosopher who formulated a law stating work will expand to fill the time available. Americans have been taught that hard work is good and that most of us improve ourselves by intensifying our efforts on the job.

The Puritan work ethic has its traps, and one of these is a tendency to confuse *activity* with *accomplishment*. The *activity trap* catches those who become extraordinarily busy without increasing their productivity.

In the warehouse, we often see a supervisor who delegates poorly, doing tasks that should be done by hourly employees. Some managers fail to delegate simply because they can't give up old tasks, which are comfortable and familiar.

Failure to separate the critical tasks from the less critical ones will cause people to fail in business not because they did not do things right, but because they did not do the right things.

Our productivity prejudices

In our pursuit of productivity, we tend to overlook those who work closest to us. Some managers monitor the productivity of hourly workers while ignoring over-staffing in the office. The presumption is that these knowledge workers will always work hard and be productive. This is a sort of class chauvinism — people like us are okay, but those *other people* must be watched.

There is national chauvinism connected with productivity, also. Americans have felt that they were world productivity leaders, boasting that we had the world's largest supply of telephones, cars, refrigerators, and other material comforts. Surely this was our reward for working hard, the payoff for being true to our Puritan heritage.

In recent years, we've seen an invasion of high-quality products from Europe and Asia. Suddenly we fear a foreign peril from other cultures where people seem to be working harder than we do and gaining in productivity at a faster rate than the United States.

Today experts ask whether we can save American industry from decline. Surveys show that the biggest recent change in industry has been a reduction in employee loyalty. We see the results of downsizing and the destruction of morale when a stable company is dismantled to liquidate the debts of a leveraged buyout.

Having considered the motives and the symptoms, we need to consider why we need to measure productivity at all. Traditionally we measured work so that we could get everyone to perform better. Productivity was a way to get non-Puritans to conform. The unstated theory was: *If only everyone would work just as hard as we do, the world will be a better place.*

Much of this folklore came from the *efficiency experts* of the 1920s and 1930s, who taught that the stopwatch and time standards would save companies from going soft as they matured.

The real reasons for measuring productivity

Perhaps the most important reason to measure productivity in a warehouse is to insure that you have properly charged for services rendered. If you learn the actual time taken and then discover that a proper charge for that time is non-competitive, then — and **only** then — should you conclude that you have low productivity. If workers understand the prime reason for measuring productivity is to be sure that charges are properly made for services, they will cooperate with you in maintaining the measurements.

One public warehouse has a cost committee made up of supervisors and hourly workers. When a prospective customer requests a price quotation, the prospect's specifications are given to the cost committee. The committee might be asked to estimate the number of man hours needed to unload a truck and the number of minutes needed to fill each order. Estimates made by the committee are the basis for a rate proposal. The man-hour estimate is multiplied by a standard cost per hour to develop a price the company quotes to the customer.

Productivity standards enable us to communicate our expectations. A foreman who knows a reasonable time to fill each order can give a warehouse worker a stack of orders and say, 'I'll see you back here at four o'clock' knowing both he and the worker understand the time estimate is reasonable. Both also know there will be good days when the worker will finish early with considerable pride, and there will be bad days when something goes wrong and the task takes longer than estimated. But on average, the performance time will nearly equal the estimated time.

Most thinking about productivity emphasizes measurement, and warehousing productivity can be easy to measure. When you know how many pieces of freight were received and shipped, and you also know the number of hours worked today, simple arithmetic will show productivity in pieces per man hour.

Of course there are many ways to complicate the measurement task. Order picking takes longer than bulk transfers, and broken-case order picking takes longer than full-case picking. Which hours should be counted — only those devoted to moving freight? Or should janitors, supervisors, and clerical workers be included? These variables must be handled **consistently** to get an accurate measurement.

Because progress in warehousing has changed the ratio of knowledge workers to box kickers, evaluating productivity is more challenging.

Some feel the need to bring in an outside consultant to solve a productivity problem. While the management consultants may teach productivity improvement, what will you do when they are no longer present? Consultants should be considered teachers, but no teacher can function without good students. Do you have an *internal* consultant who will take over?

Some hope the consultant will do the distasteful — identify and fire those who are not working as hard as they should. This use of a *hatchet man* is an abdication of management duties. Maintenance of productivity requires daily attention by line supervisors and management.

As you look at productivity, keep your eye on the bottom line. The goal of your company is to produce steady profits with a stable work force. That result is generally based on customers who are happy with your product or service and willing to come buy more of it tomorrow.

Questions that solve problems

As you audit the quality and productivity performance of your warehouse, here are some questions you might ask your warehouse managers:

Q **Does the housekeeping and appearance of the warehouse meet our standards? Is there any part of the building that you would be ashamed to show our most important customer?**

C Ask this question only after you have conducted your own inspection of the facility and have formed your own answer.

Q **Is our accuracy and control of damage better or worse than our competitor's?**

C No one may have a precise answer to this question, particularly the first time it is asked. If your people don't know, is there a way to create a new measurement so they will know next time you ask?

Q **Is our fill rate better or worse than the competition's?**

C This is also likely to be unanswered the first time you ask, yet asking the question will stimulate new investigation and measurement.

Q **Have we created a work life that is relatively free of accidents and gives our people an incentive to stay with the company?**

C Quantity of accident-free days and measurement of employee turnover have a lot to do with the morale of any organization.

Q **How do we currently measure the quality of our operation?**

C Having read this chapter, you have many answers. Your operation won't improve until your people know the answers as well. Asking this question provides a good look at the skills of your organization.

Q **What steps have we taken to increase productivity in our warehouse during the past year?**

C We have described a number of ways to improve warehouse productivity. Have your people used some of them? Have they used others that you never thought of? The answers to this question will demonstrate both the creativity and the competency of your warehouse operations people.

Q **If our productivity is better (or worse) today than it was, why did this happen?**

C The answer to this question will tell a lot about your management's attitude toward productivity improvement. ❖

Chapter 8

Third-party or do-it-yourself warehousing?

When you start or alter a warehouse operation, should you control it with your own people or hire a third party to manage the warehouse for you? Before considering the question, it's essential that we agree on some definitions.

In the United States, a wide variety of third-party warehouse operations exist. Most are commonly referred to as *public warehouses,* and much of the business they do is on a thirty-day agreement, which offers great flexibility for users. But a growing portion of third-party warehousing is *contract warehousing.* The primary distinction is that a longer agreement applies for contract warehouses.

Among the wide variety of providers are specialists, both in warehouse functions and customer types. You may find a specialist with extensive experience in handling products similar to yours. These functional specialists may concentrate on temperature-controlled storage, fulfillment, or bulk warehousing.

While the majority of third-party providers operate in just one facility or a group of facilities in a single community, an increasing number have become multi-city operations. A few have national and international coverage and though most of the enterprises are small, a few are large and are part of publicly traded corporations.

In making the decision to manage your own warehouse or to hire outside expertise, it is advisable to survey carefully the number and quality of third-party providers who are qualified by location and experience to handle your products.

Reasons to *make or buy*

The make-or-buy decision has long been used by managers to decide whether a certain component should be manufactured in-house or procured from outside. To some extent, the decision to hire a third-party or do-it-yourself is a classic make or buy decision.

In warehousing, the decision is driven by five primary factors:
- ◆ Management: availability and philosophy.
- ◆ Capital: cost and availability.
- ◆ Labor.
- ◆ Flexibility.
- ◆ Control.

Management

Does your organization currently have sufficient management to operate a new warehouse operation? If the answer is no, what is the risk of a start-up with unknown and untested managers?

On the other hand, if your corporation is over-supplied with management, the warehouse start-up could provide a means of offering a job transfer rather than the pain and cost of management layoffs. As you look at this alternative, consider whether the transferred managers would have the experience and the skills needed to manage a warehouse. While such skills can be learned, consider where and when this will occur.

Management philosophy has much to do with the manufacturer's decision to make or buy. Today, a growing number of companies reward managers for reducing personnel and assets under their control. *Down-sizing* or *right-sizing* are popular in today's corporations.

Yet there remain many bureaucratic organizations where power is measured by people and assets. If a manager perceives that the path to success is to increase the number of people and assets under control, it is natural to favor a private warehouse rather than a third-party supplier. After all, the private warehouse represents a new source of employment and a growth in number of people in the organization.

Warehousing is asset intensive, and most new operations require millions of dollars for new facilities and equipment. If your enterprise rewards empire builders, warehousing could be part of the process.

Capital

Financial strategy has a major influence on the make-or-buy question. Most companies measure their success by examining the ratio of net profit to sales and emphasizing 'the bottom line.' But a growing number of corporations place equal or greater emphasis on their ability to receive a return on assets, which is a blending of profit margins and capital turnover.

Capital turnover is the ratio of total assets to sales revenue, and this ratio can be improved either by increasing sales or reducing the number of assets under your control. When a corporation concentrates on improving return on assets, managers are rewarded for reducing inventories and minimizing the quantity of fixed assets.

How does this influence the make-or-buy decision? If you can acquire warehouse facilities through a third party, you may avoid the need for either long- or short-term real estate leases, and thus avoid the necessity of capitalizing leases to meet public-accounting standards.

In a few cases, the third-party warehouse can be a vehicle to obtain financing of the inventory. Public warehousing companies are branches of banks in many Latin American countries. As such, they routinely offer negotiable warehouse receipts and financing of inventory based on its value.

In the United States, field warehousing is a term used to describe a similar function. While field warehousing is rare in the United States today, a growing number of third-party operators advertise the ability to avoid or delay taxes or customs duties by using third-party warehouses located in free-trade zones. While these operations accommodate private as well as third-party warehousing, taxing authorities sometimes provide preferential treatment for goods held by a third party.

Labor

A key factor in the make-or-buy decision is cost and availability of warehouse labor. Existing practices may cause your labor to be more costly than that of sources available on the open market. On the other hand, some companies find they can hire and maintain a workforce at a lower cost than third-party operators quote for a similar service. In making this judgment, don't hesitate to do some comparison shopping with third-party operators. All are accustomed to quoting an hourly sales price for labor services.

Labor relations policies may influence the warehousing decision. For example, some manufacturers who accept unionization in production plants strongly resist unionization of the distribution system. This happens when management views the distribution system as a safety valve that must function if production is disrupted.

For whatever reason, the distribution manager who intends to stay non-union is likely to make a different decision about using third-party warehouses than one who is unconcerned about unions.

In one non-union chain of retail stores, a relatively luxurious environment is provided within the distribution center because management feels it is a valuable fringe benefit for the workers. In that situation, buying outside warehousing services is not considered because no warehouse contractor could duplicate the environment offered by the company in its own facility.

In other cases, the user may choose to buy services from a non-union third-party warehouse, recognizing that the contract will not be renewed if the labor situation deteriorates.

Flexibility

The most frequent cause for a decision to use third-party warehousing is a need for flexibility. If you knew that you would always need storage space for 10,000 pallets every week and that you had sufficient labor requirements to keep twelve workers busy every day, a private warehouse operation might be economical. But few users have stable requirements for either space or labor, and it is this instability that can make the use of a third-party attractive.

Since public warehousing arrangements can be canceled in thirty days, the risk of empty space is controlled by the warehouseman's ability to share the space needs of many users.

The typical user of a public warehouse occupies 10,000 square feet or less of space. This means a building of 100,000 square feet might have ten occupants. The public warehouseman hopes that as the space needs of one user decline, those of another will increase.

Recognizing the importance of sharing to reduce risks, some public warehouse operators decline to quote a prospective customer who requires huge amounts of space. The rationale is that if the customer should decide to leave, the amount of space that suddenly becomes empty is greater than the warehouse operator can absorb without serious losses. For this reason, a user requiring large amounts of space is frequently unable to find an operator who will provide it without a long term contract.

Sometimes the location creates a risk. Large metropolitan areas represent the safest market for industrial real estate, since they usually have many potential users. On the other hand, the market for a big warehouse in a small town in South Dakota will be limited.

A significant difference between public and contract warehousing is the degree to which the user is free to select a strategic location. The warehouse user may need a facility in South Dakota to gain competitive advantage. When he contracts the building and removes the speculation on space, he can find third-party operators willing and able to run the warehouse no matter where it is located.

The contract operator may assist in site selection, building design, or lease negotiation. Alternatively, the user may build and/or lease the space, and then negotiate with a contract operator. The relationship can range from the user owning or leasing to a sub-lease arrangement from the operator. The real estate contract can be as simple as one paragraph that indemnifies the operator from financial loss resulting from vacant space.

Usage may determine selection

The nature of your use is a consideration for selecting operators, and particularly for deciding whether to use public or contract warehousing.

Bulk and seasonal items are prime candidates for public warehousing because space costs may be more important than labor costs. The traditional public warehouse operator is more likely to offer low-cost space than the typical contract operator.

But contract warehousing may be necessary if your inventory has unique handling or storage characteristics, or if you require special handling equipment or customized information systems.

The user's business outlook is an important factor in choosing between the two kinds of third-party operators. If your industry is declining, and your corporate philosophy is to *cut costs at all costs*, you may choose the reduced-risk exposure of public warehousing. If your needs are short term, then public warehousing is appropriate because it avoids any long-term commitment.

If your goal is to cut fixed assets or to reduce head count, then contract warehousing represents a better alternative than private warehouses. Contract warehousing is often most attractive to a growth business because it creates a partnership that can be expanded.*

Whenever quantities of space and labor needed are unknown, or whenever the probability exists that the location needed for warehousing may change, a purchase of warehousing service from a third party provides a flexibility that can be measured in dollars saved by avoidance of risk.

Control

The strongest argument for doing it yourself is control. If an error could cause the loss of a customer, or — in the case of health-care products — the loss of a life, you may well conclude that control of warehousing cannot be delegated to any third party, regardless of the quality of the supplier.

While few will admit it, the control issue is an emotional one. Some managers are unable to accept the risk that a third party might do an unsatisfactory job. Major warehouse failures can cost managers their jobs, and the manager who has been damaged by a bad experience with a third party will face the prospect of losing control again.

The emotional factor aside, electronic monitoring allows users to achieve greater control over third-party warehouse operations than ever before. If something goes wrong, it can be detected quickly. However, detecting a problem is one thing and fixing it is another.

For those with a substantial fear of the consequences that might result from a loss of control, the do-it-yourself method may be the only answer.

Picking public warehouses

You should adopt a structured approach to the selection not only of public warehouses, but of any third-party provider of logistics services. Once the relationship has started, there are ways you can maximize its benefits.

You should segregate the process of picking and retaining logistics suppliers into the following steps:

---

*   "Public vs. Contract Warehousing", by William G. Sheehan, *Warehousing Forum*, Volume 4, Number 5, ©The Ackerman Company, Columbus, Ohio.

Steps to take before beginning the search

- ◆ Determine resources that will help you identify qualified bidders.*
- ◆ Write a request for proposal.
- ◆ Evaluate the bidders.
- ◆ Establish a plan to implement the new relationship without disturbing your present clients.
- ◆ Manage the relationship to be sure it is a long lasting one.

The preparatory steps

Look inside your operation to define your company's logistics goals. For example, is your company trying to be the service leader or the price leader? If your growth has been via the low-price route, you may need a different kind of supplier than if your goal is to provide the highest level of customer service. Other considerations:

- ◆ Will you develop new products that are different from the present line, and how will the new products affect volume, seasonality or warehousing requirements?
- ◆ Will your distribution channels remain as they are today, or will you open new channels? For example, if you sell through department stores today, is there a chance that you will some day distribute through mail order?

The type of third-party provider you pick will depend on the answers to these questions and others like them. Certain providers are specialists in serving particular distribution channels, while others have made their mark by providing superior service or rock-bottom costs. Knowing your own objectives will prevent you from wasting time with a potential supplier who does not fit your needs.

As you explore your own objectives, be sure to gain opinions from the appropriate people in your company. As you seek opinions, be sure the other managers understand the process you use to select third-party resources. Consider the completion of an in-house customer-satisfaction sur-

---

*   From "Picking Public Warehouses" by Mark Richards and Jim Potochick, *Warehousing Forum*, Volume 7, Number 3, ©The Ackerman Company, Columbus, Ohio.

vey to answer these three questions:

- ◆ What do you like best about the current distribution system?
- ◆ What do you like least?
- ◆ What capabilities are necessary, which ones are nice, and which are superfluous?

Once you have drafted results, review them with each of the people involved to obtain a consensus on the objectives.

Identifying qualified bidders

Once you have clarified the internal objectives in using a third-party provider, you need to determine who the potential bidders are and then develop a short list of highly qualified providers. Several sources of information about third-party warehouses are readily available.

Trade and professional societies are a neutral source since they list members but do not promote any one member more than another. Two such trade organizations are the American Warehouse Association and the International Association of Refrigerated Warehouses. Leading professional societies include the Council of Logistics Management (CLM), and Warehousing Education and Research Council (WERC). CLM and WERC members who use or operate public warehouses are often good references concerning potential suppliers.

Talk to your peers. Those who are in similar industries will be particularly helpful, but you can also learn about potential suppliers from peers in unrelated businesses. Ask these people who they are using and how they feel about the performance of each supplier. They will share this information with you because they expect you to reciprocate when they have similar questions.

Publications are an easy way to obtain lists of suppliers. Trade associations and professional societies all publish their membership directories. There are at least two national directories of third-party warehousing: *American Public Warehouse Register* and *Chilton's Distribution Directory*. Some warehouse users refer to the business-to-business section of phone directories.

Other public warehouse operators also are a good source of references. Most companies in this industry will not hesitate to recommend a respected firm operating in another city. They typically will not 'knock' an industry colleague and, if they do so, consider this to be a danger sign.

Information from your own customers may be the most important reference of all. Presumably those customers will be served by the public warehouse you hire, and they should be asked to compare the service offered by the various public warehouses that ship to them. If more than one of your customers points out that one public warehouse has given outstanding service, this could be a good reason to use that particular supplier.

Writing the RFP

The next step is the development of a Request for Proposal (RFP). The most important thing about the RFP is that it provides identical information to every potential bidder. Some bidders try to gain an unfair advantage by obtaining information not available to the others, and you should prevent this.

It is essential that your RFP present the precise format bidders must use for the quotation. Failure to do this could result in a variety of pricing formats that are impossible to compare. If you are looking for a price quoted per-hundred-weight, then you must say so. Each bidder should state the estimated total annual cost.

Second, you should list the general information you want to receive from each potential bidder. In return, you provide general company information about your own operations. The more information you provide, the more accurate the proposals will be.

This information should include details about shipping requirements of your key customers. It should provide the characteristics of storage as well as a profile of the materials handling operation. Details about transportation can influence warehousing costs and should be provided.

Be sure to provide ample details about your information system.

If you need special value-added services, be sure you stipulate this and encourage the potential supplier to describe any unusual services that are available.

The RFP should ask how long the rates will be guaranteed.

As you seek general information about the warehouse, it is appropriate to ask for a corporate organization chart and background information about the owner and key executives.

Make your own financial investigation, including a Dun and Bradstreet report. Some buyers ask for a list of the operator's major customers.

Consider how long the supplier has been in business and how long each manager has been with the organization. The work hours are important, as is the union affiliation or lack of same.

Tell the bidders who your major customers are and what order lead-time you have negotiated with each. If certain customers have peculiarities, be sure to share this information with the bidder. If you have a minimum-order size, be sure the bidders know that.

Your data on storage should include the number of inventory turns per year, the number of SKUs to be stored, special storage requirements (such as temperature control), a description of how the product will arrive, the weights and dimensions of each model, the pallet patterns for each product, details on a pallet exchange program, and stacking patterns for each item.

Provide details on handling costs. These include the average order size, the number of SKUs per order, the case weight of each item, a description of your return policy, the average number of orders shipped each day, and the peaks and valleys in the shipping season.

Transportation information should include the mode in which in-bounds will be received, particularly whether by motor freight or rail. If it is important for you to have a 'house carrier' (delivery service controlled by the warehouse), be sure to bring this out since some warehouses don't provide this service. Describe the delivery area to be served. State the desired transit times for each delivery. Be sure that you specify the percentage or amount of product that customers pick up rather than have shipped.

As you investigate computer information services, determine whether the warehouse is using WINS (Warehouse Information Network Standards), the most established information network. If you intend to furnish the warehouse with communications equipment, be sure to provide details. Tell the supplier what reports you require and how quickly you need them. Identify the person who heads the information services section.

Increasing numbers of warehouses have value-added services such as packaging, shrink wrapping, assembly, display creation, and kitting. If you need such services, determine how much experience the supplier has in providing them.

Analyze the bids

Once you have listed all of the proper information in the RFP, you should receive relatively consistent bids from the firms on your list. Prices that are unusually high or low should be questioned. As the bids come in, it is important to establish the criteria for evaluating the potential providers.

Most users recognize that quality is more important than price. They also recognize that good people make good warehousing happen. If the people at the warehouse don't give you confidence today, they probably won't inspire your confidence as the relationship matures.

As you evaluate warehouses, look at the stability and training of the workforce. If the public warehouse has high turnover and no training program, your operations are likely to suffer. If inventory velocity is important to you, seek out public warehouses with technology that reduces order-cycle times.

Since the third party warehouse will be an extension of your company, your comfort level is the most important point in the decision. That comfort level should exist with both the facility manager and the company's chief executive. If **both** fail to inspire your respect and trust, then it is best to keep looking.

Final selection

As you proceed through the selection process, you will reduce the field to a few finalists. To evaluate the bidders on their own home ground and to meet those people who do not normally make sales calls, you must visit each of the finalists. The field interview should include a general review of the bid package, a request for explanation of the company's pricing philosophy, and information about any major customers they have lost and the reasons.

If your RFP did not request them, now is the time to ask for an organization chart and a financial statement. Both the people and financial stability of the company will become your concern as well as theirs. Since cost will be the basis of later renegotiation, it is appropriate to ask about pay scales and whether or not a union represents any of the work force. Ask about the average length of service for warehouse employees. Real estate costs may be important, particularly if the buildings are leased.

Take a look at how the office is organized. Interview your customer service representative. Would that person handle your account exclusively, or a number of other accounts? What kinds of back-up systems exist in the office operation?

A walk through the warehouse is critical. Housekeeping is a prime barometer of quality, so be sure you compare cleanliness and storage efficiency of the finalists. The condition of the equipment is a reflection of housekeeping, and you should be particularly observant. How does your tour guide interact with the other employees in the warehouse? If the relationship seems less than cordial, you need to know why.

Every warehouse has areas that are awkward to show, such as a rework area. Be sure your tour includes these parts of the operation.

Ask whether certain order pickers will be dedicated to your account, and what hours they will work.

Plan to devote two or three hours to this field visit. Afterward, ask yourself whether the individuals you have met possess a management style and service orientation that are in harmony with your own.

You should make the final selection of a vendor only after you have carefully considered both the prices quoted and your comfort level with each of the finalists.

Managing a successful transition

Whether you are starting a new third-party relationship or moving from one supplier to another, it is important not to disturb your customers. The transition is of great importance. A smooth transition depends on the development of a good implementation timetable, ample communications (internally and to customers), and continued follow-up to be sure that everyone is well informed.

Managing a continuing relationship

The most important step in maintaining a good relationship with the new supplier is to constantly communicate your expectations. One RFP contained a first page that was titled *What We Expect of You and What You Can Expect of Us*. Many third-party relationships that fail are the result of inadequate communication of expectations.

Since the consequences of misunderstanding are so critical, it is best to communicate your expectations in more than one format. You should do so through correspondence, personal visits, and phone calls.

An operations manual is a formal way to outline your expectations, but the right people won't always read it carefully. You may wish to use checklists, which are shorter and easier to control. A personal visit is the most effective way to communicate, but this is expensive and time consuming.

Because visits should not be just in one direction, ask representatives of your supplier to visit your operations so they can meet your people and see how you run your own warehouses.

Ongoing performance evaluations

After the decision is made and the new warehouse is in operation, you should measure the performance. As you look at those measures you use to gauge the performance of a warehouse, consider five rules:

- ◆ Keep it simple. A complex procedure is hard to understand and expensive to administer.
- ◆ Be sure the thing you are measuring is critical to the operation. Measuring trivia wastes time and causes people to get lost in detail.
- ◆ Be sure that the measurement is up-to-date. Stale information is a waste of time.
- ◆ Be sure to measure quality as well as productivity. Sometimes one is achieved at the expense of the other.
- ◆ Consider multiple variables when you measure either quality or productivity. For example, consider both the number of pieces shipped accurately and the dollar value of merchandise shipped correctly. A single error involving very expensive merchandise could be more serious than normal statistics would reveal.

Once you have done the measuring, be sure to provide regular feedback to the warehouse supplier. This feedback can be a motivator or a demotivator. If you emphasize the positive and encourage competition with other warehouses, your warehousing people will be favorably motivated.

Managing for maximum efficiency is an on-going process. It is enhanced by periodically meeting and setting new objectives. Any operation that is not continuously improving is actually losing ground, since the competition is presumably moving forward. It is valuable to meet at least once a year with management at each third party warehouse to agree on attainable goals for the year ahead.

By making the right start, building and maintaining excellent communication, and periodically reviewing objectives, you can make the selection of warehouses into an orderly process.

Questions that solve problems

If yours is an organization that used to be bureaucratic but is now dedicated to reduction of assets and management, much of your questioning should be designed to be sure that the people who report to you share your philosophy and are not addicted to empire building. Here are some questions that can help you discover whether your people share a consensus on this issue:

Q Do you see any reason why we should run the warehouse ourselves?
C Listen carefully to the answers — if they seem illogical, the respondent may be reacting from an emotional desire to maintain or expand an empire.

Q Can you think of any good reasons why a third-party operator could not handle this job?
C Again, the quality of the answer will reveal whether the opinion is fact based or emotional.

Q Is there any reason why we need a long-term contract to govern this operation?
C This will force your people to look at all the risks involved in either long- or short-term operation.

Q Are there any services we need but could not get from a conventional public warehouse operator?
C Those who do not understand contract warehousing may describe services that are not typically provided by third parties, but might be negotiated with an innovative contract warehouse operator.

You may wish to review and question a pending decision in the selection of third-party warehouses. Here are some questions dealing with this issue:

Q Did we select the finalists because of price or quality?

C Be sure you get details to support the answer.

Q Are we absolutely certain that we accurately described the operation when we wrote the RFP?

C Ask this only after you have initiated a review of the RFP and formed your own opinion about its accuracy and completeness.

Q What steps did we take to check on the quality of the potential supplier?

C This is a due diligence question, and the quality of the answer must be carefully measured. ❖

Chapter 9

The critical role of planning and scheduling

Planning and scheduling are critical to warehouse operations. Competence in planning distinguishes an *exceptional* manager from a manager.*

Defining and justifying a plan

A *plan* is a detailed scheme, program, or method worked out beforehand for the accomplishment of an objective or project. A plan becomes a schedule when the certainty of implementation is such that specific times are added. Plans are often categorized as strategic, managerial, and operational.

Long-range, strategic plans require the setting of overall objectives, allocation of resources to attain those objectives, and policy-making. Planning involves asking questions such as: What part will warehousing play in the future of the organization? It is often restricted to establishing direction and guidelines rather than to making everyday operational decisions.

Because long-range warehouse planning relates to the organization as a whole, it involves compromise, trade-offs, and the resolution of conflicting objectives among divisions. For example, expansion into new marketing areas could bring up the question of whether you should commit capital to build a new warehouse or pay for the services of a local public warehouse. In either case, the decision affects other departments, including

---

*   Adapted from an article by Leon 'Bud' Cohan, T. Marzetti Company.

sales, marketing, customer service, production, personnel, and finance.

Short-range planning includes procedures to achieve the organization's strategic objectives. In warehousing, even short range plans involve trade-offs with other divisions. Absent adequate planning at the senior level, the process of compromise and trade-off could result in bickering, turf fights, and conflicts.

Operational planning includes plans for everyday management of warehouse tasks, and this is the level where plans are most likely to become schedules. A list of operational plans and schedules might include disaster and emergency plans, product recall plans, equipment maintenance plans and schedules, training plans, vacation schedules, master plans, job- and task specific plans, regulatory compliance plans, inspection plans, daily work schedules, carrier appointment schedules, and organizational plans such as restrict shipping to morning hours and receiving to afternoons.

There are at least two good reasons for planning: To achieve higher productivity, and to train and develop managers.

Achieve higher productivity

As a general rule, planning and scheduling of warehouse operations improve productivity. Planned and scheduled operations are inherently more productive than random ones. Following this line of reasoning, make two assumptions:

- ◆ Senior management wants productive warehouse operations.
- ◆ Whether a warehouse is or is not productive is not self-evident.

While few would quibble with the first assumption, some might take issue with the second.

Assumption two is based on several observations. First, some senior managers are less than intimately familiar with warehouse operations. Second, though cost accounting systems are the primary tool for measuring warehouse productivity, they rarely contain adequate warehouse-specific costing categories. They tend to lump the numbers together, thereby hiding many indicators of non-productivity. Third, even if a cost-accounting system is warehouse-specific, the numbers indicate only that an operation was more or less productive during one period as opposed to another. This, of course, is not the same as determining productivity in the first place.

Without a rock-solid means of quantifying warehouse productivity, senior management's next-best tactic to ensure productive operations is to insist that warehouse managers adopt productive management techniques. These techniques include planning and scheduling, and follows the 'duck' principle: *If it walks like a duck, quacks like a duck, and has feathers on its back, it is a duck.*

Additionally, the extent to which warehouse operations are planned and scheduled may be objectively observed. Planning and scheduling, therefore, are not only effectiveness indicators for middle and junior management, but, by extension, may be used to evaluate warehouse operational productivity.

Train and develop managers

Having managers (especially junior ones) think about tasks and operations in a logical, stepped sequence is intrinsically valuable in that it trains and develops them to be better managers. Not infrequently, this is planning's primary benefit. These managers must ask and answer *What if?* questions. Answering the questions accurately allows a manager to act promptly should the *what if* event occur. This builds confidence while minimizing damage and loss.

How to plan by using a format

Drafting plans in an orderly fashion — by using a format — helps ensure that the finished plan *covers the bases*. The following format has been adapted from the Marine Corps' *Five Paragraph Order*. Drafting a plan according to this or a similar format is a particularly good approach for inexperienced planners:

- ◆ State the current situation and what must change or occur for the plan to be invoked.
- ◆ It is often helpful to amplify this by listing assumptions. For example, a plan to operate the warehouse during a strike might assume that the hourly labor force has walked out, certain management personnel will be available to pick orders, some carriers will cross the picket lines, others will not, and so forth.

Be sure to identify the sources of the assumptions so they may quickly be (re)validated and updated when the plan is implemented. Plans must be sufficiently flexible to allow for quick revision should the assumptions prove inaccurate.

♦ State the plan's purpose. What is the objective, mission, or goal to be achieved?

♦ It's always a good idea to review the mission of the warehouse and determine whether the plan is consistent with it. Will implementation of the plan conflict with objectives of another department? Will another department be charged with the same task?

♦ List those who will be expected to execute the plan and make specific task assignments to each.

Task assignments must be clear and understandable. They should also include controls, limits, and provision for feedback and mid-course revision.

Even though the planned-for situation may be extraordinary, assigned tasks must be realistic. For example, if ten experienced order pickers are normally required to pick 10,000 cases, don't expect ten 'warm bodies' from the sales department to match that, even if all of them have college degrees.

♦ Define the control and communication channels. Specifically, who is in charge of what, and how are those charged with executing the plan to control their activities?

♦ Include decision rules: a given event calls for a specific response or action. Include norms and standards that will allow measurement and define tolerant limits. Plan to provide enough guidance, tempered by flexibility, to avoid knee-jerk reactions or constant tinkering in response to random variation.

♦ List the resources that are required or available, and fix responsibility with regard to who will obtain them and how they are to be used or distributed.

Planning techniques and tools

Dock schedules
All docks, inbound and out, must be scheduled. This doesn't mean that a late-arriving or unscheduled carrier must be turned away, only that appointments are required and that a daily schedule is published. A certain percentage of carriers will always be unable to honor their appointment times and dates.

Bad weather, accidents, and unavoidable delays at earlier stops happen; usually they are not within the control of the carrier. Warehouse managers must allow for this and create flexible scheduling that avoids idle time. Should a carrier's missed appointment truly result in extra cost to the warehouses, then those costs should be documented and billed to the offending party. On the other hand, this policy must be balanced against the warehouse manager's willingness to pay carrier detention charges when the warehouse is responsible for the delay.

Computers
Personal computers (PCs) are tools warehouse managers can use to centralize data from the corporate mainframe or mini-computer. Because of this, managers and supervisors should have ready access to a PC.

Spreadsheet programs such as *1-2-3* or *Improv* by Lotus or *Excel* by Microsoft permit the manager to manipulate work standards and labor hour data to prepare or revise daily work schedules. Attempting the same task manually is too time consuming. Supervisors who are tied to their desks making these calculations lose valuable time when they should be on the floor supervising.

Commonly available scheduling tools such as pads, wall boards, charts, and document handling devices to reduce office clutter and facilitate handling paperwork (files, baskets, collators, ad infinitum) should be made available to the warehouse manager.

Backlog
Another important value of scheduling is the ability to calculate current backlog. By using measurement techniques, the warehouse manager can calculate the number of hours of work needed to perform all of the tasks as-

signed.

When these are compared with hours remaining in the normal work day, the manager can determine whether some of the current work should be put off until the next day, scheduled for overtime, or possibly reassigned to another distribution center.

Scheduling for peak demand

In some businesses, the scheduling problem of the warehouse is compli-cated by uneven demand. For example, in the retail grocery business Thurs-day is usually a peak day that follows three days with abnormally low demand. As a result, the food-chain warehouse will probably have too much work for Monday and Tuesday to supply the Thursday peak and not enough for Friday. Such unbalanced workloads can be partially balanced by delaying work that has a minimal penalty, such as unloading of inbound boxcars.

Real-time information and scheduling

Real-time information systems record and deal with events and conditions as they occur, or as they are recognized. In most warehouses, particularly those with fast movement, substantial savings can be made with the timely transmission of information to receiving docks. This allows precise replen-ishment while it avoids unnecessary product movement.

If the receiving manager knows when to expect certain merchandise, plans can be made to speed up critical inbound shipments. This reduces handling requirements. For example, if the receiving department knows that stock number 123 is urgently needed to fill current orders, it expedites handling of an inbound load containing stock number 123. Then instead of putting that stock number in an assigned pick slot, today's outbound orders are picked directly from the merchandise staged at the receiving dock. This eliminates double handling of that stock number — from receiving dock to pick line and back to shipping dock.*

---

*   From *Warehousing and Physical Distribution Productivity Report*, Volume 16, Number 10, ©Marketing Publications Inc., Silver Spring, MD.

Aids to scheduling

Warehouse scheduling can be improved by a variety of commonly available scheduling tools. One of these is a pad or schedule board to assist the planner in tracking the schedule.

Another is a record of work schedules during comparable earlier periods so that management can predict probable seasonal workload peaks.

A building layout diagram is essential; it should show stock locations, pick lines, staging areas, and other data to facilitate scheduling.

Planning and scheduling are critical to warehouse operations because they contribute greatly to increased warehouse productivity. Scheduling is nothing more than the implementation of three points:

* Smoothing the flow variation.
* Eliminating labor bottlenecks.
* Improving forecasting accuracy.

Most warehouse operations have some variation in workload and flow. This variation usually cannot be eliminated, but it usually can at least be reduced. The scheduling problem is simplified if the variations between peaks and valleys can be minimized.

The military term for a labor bottlenecks is *hurry up and wait*, and this phenomenon is observed in most warehouses at least occasionally. It happens because of an imbalance among people, machinery, and workload.

Both the bottlenecks and the flow variations can be dealt with most effectively when you are able to see them coming. Therefore, forecasting is a critical factor in reducing the waste that occurs with poor scheduling.

Eliminating delay

Scheduling to reduce delay is possible once the manager knows the time needed for each element of each job as well as the likelihood of delay or interruption.

How does one determine the time required to unload each truckload? Maintenance of historical time records is the best way to cut the guesswork. The process does not need to be complex. Once a history of unloading times for different kinds of loads has been assembled and analyzed, supervisors can accurately predict how long it should take to load or unload each vehicle. With this knowledge, truck appointment times can be set to reduce waiting time and congestion.

The importance of locator systems

Scheduling can be either eased or complicated by the accuracy and effective use of stock locator systems. If the locator is in poor condition, the same stock number will be scattered around the warehouse, hampering fast movement of merchandise.

Scheduling is always improved when the fastest-moving items are close to the floor and close to the door.

Above all, when the scheduler accurately knows exactly where each item is located, the items can be picked and shipped with a minimum of travel time. Locator system effectiveness is equally important for the scheduling of inbound loads. The best storage location for each inbound load should be designated before the load arrives at the receiving dock.

Questions that solve problems

The presence or absence of planning is not always obvious, so here are some questions to ask your managers about their planning practices:

Q How does the warehouse plan fit into the strategic plan for the corporation?
C If nobody knows, it might not be their fault. If warehousing is not included in your strategic plan, see that it becomes a part of the next plan revision.

Q Do we run a scheduled truck dock?
C If the answer is no, you need to find out why. It is difficult to imagine a good reason not to do this.

Q Who is responsible for planning and scheduling in our warehouse operation?
C Learn how your planners do their job and whether they feel that they get results.

Q How do we use computers to facilitate planning and scheduling?
C The answers will tell you whether your people have learned to use PCs or other tools to leverage their own effectiveness.

Q What steps do we take to meet peak demand?
C Look for some creative answers on this one, including the use of part-time people and the delay of certain work that does not have time priorities. ❖

Chapter 10

Warehousing costs

As you consider the true cost of controlling space and operating your warehouse, look both at costs related to function and at the concept of *opportunity costs*.

If you own a building that your company constructed in the 1960s, your occupancy cost is probably low because the construction cost was low compared to today's rates and the mortgage debt on the building has likely been paid in full.

But what would it cost to replace this building if it were destroyed? Alternatively, what would a third party pay in rent if you elected to close the building and put it on the market?

Real estate, like any other product, has an opportunity cost as well as an accounting cost. If the value of your warehousing facility is substantially higher or lower on the open market than the rent that is currently charged for the space, you should anticipate a change as you adjust to the realities of today's market.

Costs related to function

The first function of warehousing is storage, and one group of costs are those associated with *goods at rest*, or those expenses that would occur even if the stored products were never moved.

The second group of costs are those related to *goods in motion*. These are the handling costs that occur only when materials are moved.

To understand and control overall warehousing costs, it is best to make the distinction between goods at rest and goods in motion. Because the allocation of these costs is always a matter of judgment, there can be reasonable debate about whether any cost item should be applied to one function or another. Some warehouse operators assign all fixed costs to goods at rest because these costs cannot be reduced, even when materials-handling activity decreases.

Developing a cost for labor

What is a realistic cost for each hour of work in the warehouse? Figure 1 shows how a base wage rate of $7.50 per hour is converted into a total cost per employee of $11.00 per hour. Note that allowances are estimated for time lost to vacations, paid holidays, and paid sick days. Fringe benefits are shown as a lump sum. Another allowance is for the cost of supervision.

As you examine labor budgeting, you should look critically at several factors. Is the supervision burden realistic? If you use part-time workers who do not receive fringe benefits, has this saving been calculated in developing a total cost?

Sometimes the accounting people who develop a standard labor cost have scanty familiarity with warehouse operations. As a manager, you should question the standard costs in the light of current experience. In this situation, the standard cost is 147% of the base labor cost. Does this ratio seem realistic as compared to those used in other operations?

If your internal warehouse labor cost is higher than hourly prices charged by third-party providers of contract warehousing service, you might ask why your company is charged warehousing costs that are higher than services available from outside suppliers.*

---

*   From a seminar presented for Warehousing Education and Research Council by Professor Joseph L. Cavinato of Pennsylvania State University and Professor Thomas W. Speh of Miami University.

Figure 1		Total Cost of an Employee		
Cost area	Days	Hours /Day	Wage Rate	Annual Cost
Days on job	223	8	$7.50	$13,380
Plus: Paid vacations	10	8	7.50	600
Paid holidays	10	8	7.50	600
Paid sick days (avg)	7	8	7.50	420
Total days paid	250	8	$7.50	$15,000
Fringes				$2,500
Supervision				
Cost	$17,000 per year			
Span of control	8 people			
Total supervision per employee				$2,125
Total Annual Cost				$19,625
Actual Rate of Pay				
Effective cost	Total Annual Cost / Hours on Job			
	$19,625 / 1784 hours = $11.00 per hour			

Courtesy of Joseph L. Cavinato

Justifying purchase of equipment

For most equipment purchases, the price is only a part of the total cost of ownership.* In the case of a lift truck, maintenance over the life of the equipment may be greater than the cost of the vehicle. Also, be sure to include the cost of training people to use a piece of equipment, particularly one that is substantially different from anything now used in your facility. While people are learning, there will be waste or damage. In many companies, management overhead must be factored into the cost of any new asset.

Against these costs, you must measure the benefit.

♦ What benefit will you realize from purchasing another lift truck? Additional equipment may reduce overtime, and the overtime savings should be calculated.

---

*   Ibid.

◆ Perhaps the new truck will operate in narrower aisles than an old one, allowing you to change the warehouse layout to place an additional number of pallets in the same amount of space. What is the value of this increased storage as compared to the cost of the new truck?

◆ If the new truck is faster than an old one and will therefore save time, how much time? What is the value of that time?

As you perform this analysis, look at the danger points. If the proposed new lift truck breaks down, how will you operate the warehouse until it is repaired? Does the selling dealer have the ability to keep the new lift truck running? What is the financial stability and service reputation of the dealer?

As you review an appropriation request, beware of common pitfalls. If you omit costs, you may delay the project. Try to think of every cost related to owning the new asset. Be sure the cause-and-effect relationships that you describe are accurate. Avoid creating detailed tables that represent a degree of measurement that does not exist in your warehouse operation.

In any capital commitment, there are at least three common risks. These are the chances that:

◆ The business environment might change.

◆ Operating situations might change.

◆ Project estimates might be wrong.

If any one of these should occur, the need for the equipment could disappear. What is the resale value of the equipment on the open market if this happens?

Establishing a value of inventory

While some warehouse managers have no control over the inventory they store, others have some degree of influence — possibly even total control. Even if you do not have full control of the inventory, you can be a better warehouse manager if you understand the real and hidden costs of inventory.

The purpose of a finished-goods inventory is to afford an opportunity to make a sale by having product in the right place at the right time. When inventories are in your warehouse and are not moving, it seems evident that they are not filling their purpose. There are four general costs of inventory: capital costs, opportunity costs, risk costs, and administrative costs.

As a warehouse manager, how will knowledge of inventory costs affect your operation? First, you will get a better understanding of when the use of high speed transportation is a good investment.

Consider the situation illustrated in Figure 2. In this case, management had the option of moving a shipment of machinery from the United States to Europe by air freight or by ship. Even though the line-haul costs more than doubled, the *total cost* by air is less.

The air freight cost is less primarily because the shipment has a value of $50,000, and the capital to buy that inventory costs thirteen percent per year, or nearly $18 per day. Saving 19 days by air, as opposed to marine transportation, represents a saving of $198 in the cost of inventory. This would be lost if the product cannot be used because it is sitting in the hold of a ship.

This cost analysis presumes the merchandise will be put to use as soon as it arrives in Europe. If the inventory will be stored while awaiting a future sale, the assumptions about inventory value would be different.

Figure 2	Total Cost Analysis	
Task: Transport machinery from Marietta, Georgia, to Rome, Italy		
Activity	**Air**	**Ship**
Transit time	2 days	21 days
Transportation		
Linehaul	$2,200	$900
Plant to terminal	0	260
Terminal to customer	0	180
Packaging/crating	100	350
Insurance	220	650
Documentation	110	150
Inventory cost*	36	374
Total	**$2,666**	**$2,864**
* $50,000 at 13% times days in transit		**Savings by air: $198**

Courtesy of Joseph L. Cavinato

As you make decisions about transportation modes, as well as other warehousing decisions, your knowledge of the value of your inventory can and should play an important part in the process.*

Cost of goods at rest

Most warehouse operators measure storage by using the cube of the item. In some operations, product cube is not the best way to make the allocation. Space required by the product is not always a function of the cube, but instead may be defined by the size of the storage rack space it occupies, or by the amount of floor space taken up by floor-stacked product.**

When product is stored in pallet rack, floor rack, shelving, or cantilever rack, the rack fixture itself is a constraint because we cannot mix product in a fixture. Once the product occupies any part of the fixture, the entire space is unavailable for any other use until that product is gone.

Because of this, the fixture opening is the space for which storage is charged. How the product fits into the fixture opening determines how efficiently the space can be used. The more units stored in the rack fixture, the lower the cost per individual unit stored.

For floor-stacked product, the space is calculated based on the product's footprint — the amount of floor space used by a stack of product. Space is charged based on the number of square feet occupied. The higher we can stack the product, the lower the cost per individual unit stored.

Storage might be thought of as charging rent for a square foot of floor space, or the use of a fixture. Then the cost allocated per unit of product is a measurement of how efficiently the product fills fixture or floor space.

The cost is also influenced by how much time the product spends in the fixture or on the floor. Therefore, product turn must be calculated. The faster the product turns, the less time it spends in the fixture or on the floor, and the lower its share of the annual rent.

To start the calculation process, identify the type of storage fixture you will use for each item. Then calculate the number of units that can be

---

*   Ibid.
**   Adapted from an article by Kenneth E. Novak, W. W. Grainger, Inc., *Warehousing Forum*, Volume 5, Number 11, ©The Ackerman Company.

stored in each fixture. In the case of floor-stacked product, determine the number of square feet that the stack will require and then how many units high the product can be stacked. Divide the total number of units in storage into the occupancy costs to find the cost for each item presuming it remains in storage for an entire year.

The figure you just calculated would be the storage cost if the inventory turns once per year. Use the actual turn rate of the item to calculate that portion of annual occupancy cost you should charge to each item.

The influence of inventory turns

Storage costs may be calculated as a unit cost per month, or possibly per year. However, within that storage period, the same spot in a warehouse may be occupied by more than one unit of a very fast-turning inventory. Because of this, calculating the number of turns requires relating throughput inventory to average inventory.

An inventory that turns faster is less costly to store than one that turns slowly.

Throughput is generally defined as the total of units received and units shipped divided by 2. The average inventory is defined as the total of beginning inventory plus ending inventory divided by 2. The relationship of throughput to average inventory indicates the speed of product turn.

The influence of warehouse layout

Warehousing costs are influenced by factors that affect the ability to store and handle a product. These factors include stacking height, which is limited both by the clearance available in the building and by the strength of the package being stored. If you have a 20-foot building and you are storing product that can be stacked only five feet high, you must purchase storage racks to use all the overhead space. In these cases, an amount must be allowed for the cost of pallet rack or other storage equipment.*

---

*   From an article by Robert E. Ness, Ohio Distribution Warehouse, *Warehousing Forum*, Volume 2, Number 5 ©The Ackerman Company.

The computation shown in Figure 3 illustrates a method of determining a cost per hundred weight (cwt) for an inventory consisting of 115 SKUs, 50 of which are fast movers. The inventory is stored on pallets, with 100 cases on each pallet. The warehouse operator has selected a layout with deep rows on one side of a 12-foot aisle, and shallow rows on the opposite side.

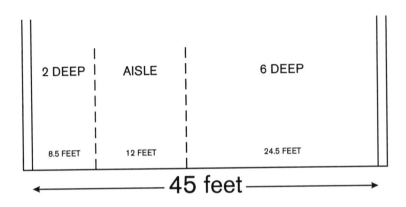

The total square feet needed in this layout is increased to allow for a honeycomb factor, the lost space in front of partial stacks. There is an additional 20 percent added as an efficiency factor, which is actually the allowance for docks and staging area.

Line 21 of Figure 3 shows the rate calculation that multiplies square feet used by cost to develop a dollar cost for storage. Total storage cost is divided by tonnage throughput, which is shown in the computation as billing units. Note that product received is reduced by half to reflect the fact that goods flow in at a steady rate throughout the month. On average the inventory is in the warehouse only for half a month.

This calculation was used by a third-party warehouse in developing costs that are converted into storage fees. The same kind of calculation is valid for any warehouse operator who wishes to convert gross warehouse cost into a cost per unit.

Figure 3	Storage computation

Volume / Criteria

1. Average inventory: 6 million pounds   300,000 Cs   3,000 Pallets
2. Monthly throughput: 4 million pounds   200,000 Cs   2,000 Pallets
3. 50 SKUs are fast movers   65 SKUs are slow movers

Layout

4. 3,000 pallets divided by 3-high stacking = 1,000 spots.
5. 1,000 spots divided by 80% honeycomb factor = 1,250 storage spots.
6. 1,250 storage spots times 80% fast movers = 1,000 deep-row spots.

   1,250 storage spots times 20% slow movers = 250 short-row spots.
7. 1,000 deep spots = 3,000 pallets with 50 SKUs.
8. 1,000 spots divided by 50 SKUs = 20 spots per SKU. (Fast movers.)
9. 250 spots divided by 65 SKUs = 3.8 spots per SKU. (Slow movers.)
10. 45 feet - 12-foot aisle = 33 feet storage
11. 33 feet divided by 4 feet per pallet = 8 pallet rows per bay

Space calculations

12. Deep facings = 167
13. (6 pallets times 4 feet deep) times 4 feet wide = 96, plus
    (4 times 12-foot aisle divided by 2) = 120 square feet per facing
14. 120 square feet per facing times 167 facings = 20,040 square feet
15. Short-row facings = 125
16. (2 pallets times 4 feet deep) times 4 feet wide plus
    (4 times 12-foot aisle divided by 2) = 56 square feet per facing
17. 56 square feet per facing times 125 facings = 7,000 square feet
18. 20,040 square feet plus 7,000 square feet = 27,040 square feet
19. 27,040 square feet divided by 80% efficiency = 33,800 square feet

Rate calculations

20. 33,800 square feet times $0.195 per square foot per month = $6,591
    Beginning inventory   = 60,000 cwt
    Product received   = 40,000 cwt times .5 month (20,000 cwt)
    (mid-month)
    Total billing units   = 80,000 cwt
21. $6,591 divided by 80,000 cwt = $0.082 per cwt cost

Cost of goods in motion

Per-unit handling rates are simply an expression of time devoted to handling each unit multiplied by total labor cost. Observation of handling procedures will allow reasonable calculations of the time involved. Here are the results of some typical observations:

◆ In unloading, the time required depends on whether the product arrives floor-loaded, palletized, or slipsheeted. For each of these shipping methods, a different unloading time per pallet was created. For this and subsequent full-pallet activities, the time required to handle a unit is calculated by dividing the handling time per pallet by the number of units stored on a pallet.

◆ The time required for checking, identifying the product, and validating the quantity against the vendor's packing list is a flat rate per pallet.

◆ The time for put-away and picking line replenishment will vary, depending upon the location of the product. This time is determined by the travel time required to move the product from one area to another.

◆ In picking, the total time is a function of both the travel through the picking line and the time to handle the product at the picking station. All products in the warehouse are assigned to a predetermined storage and picking type classification. The travel cycle is a constant for each classification of picking. The handling for a particular product is related to the product cube and reflects the time required to select and transfer the product onto a picking vehicle.

◆ Outbound trailer loading is a function of the cube of the product. The bulkier the item, the more time is needed to move it onto a trailer. This is true up to the point at which the product should no longer be hand loaded, but instead would be loaded with a fork truck. At that point in time, a mechanical loading rate is applied.

◆ If strapping is required, the time is based on the cost of moving the product through an automated or manual strapping process.

Figure 4 shows a sample of times calculated for a roof vent. The times calculated, or characteristics selected, will of course be different in your warehouse.*

Figure 4		Roof Vent Handling Time		
Activity	Driving characteristics	Handling per pallet	Units per pallet	Handling per unit
Unloading	Palletized	2.8		
	Floor-loaded	5.7	+2	2.9 min
	Slipsheeted	3.8		
Checking	**Automated**	0.4	+2	0.2 min
	Manual	1.2		
Strapping	Unstrapped	0.0		
	Automated	0.0	+2	0.0 min
	Manual	0.7		
Put-away	Bin	5.2		
	Cantilever	3.7		
	High bay	0.5		
	Low bay	6.3	+2	3.1 min
	Tier	3.7		
Picking line replenishment	Bin	2.4		
	Cantilever	6.3		
	High bay	0.5		
	Low bay	4.0	+2	2.0 min
	Tier	2.6		
		Handling time	Cube of product	
Order pick	**Fixed travel**	.11		0.1 min
	Pick/Rate/Cube	.04	x 16.35	0.7 min
Loading	**Handling/cube <20/cube**	.17	x 16.35	2.8 min
	Handling/cube >20/cube	.10		
Total handling time for seven activities: 11.8 minutes				

---

*   Novak, op. cit.

Questions that solve problems

You need ask only a few questions to learn whether your warehouse people have a reasonable understanding of costs.

Q Do we know a cost per unit for moving our products through the warehouse?

C If the answer is no, your people need a tutorial on developing warehousing costs.

Q What are our costs per unit?

C These costs might be compared to quotes from third-party warehouse operators.

Q Describe to me how we developed our per unit costs?

C Compare the answers to this question with the methods described in this chapter. Don't assume that there is only one valid procedure. There is room for innovation in the development and control of unit warehousing costs. At the same time, be sure that you are satisfied with the reasonableness and precision of the costing method that is used in your operation.

Q How do our unit costs compare to the same time period last year?

C When you get the answer, be sure you also get an explanation of why things changed.

Q How do unit costs at X warehouse compare with Y warehouse?

C Be sure to find out why. ❖

Chapter 11

Asset utilization

As merchandise moves through the logistics channels from source to customer, one party is accountable for goods at any point. Materials move from source to carrier to factory to distribution center and finally to the customer. There is always a risk of loss and when losses occur, accountability becomes an issue. For that reason, it is necessary for the responsibility of each party who handles the goods to be clearly defined.

As the goods move through the distribution system, the title may be transferred many times. The precise point at which a transfer has occurred can become important if loss or damage occurs. Traditional selling terms for freight shipments define the owner of in-transit goods at different points in its movement. Various selling terms are used. These sale terms define when title passes from seller to buyer.

- ◆ When sales terms are 'F.O.B. Origin', the buyer assumes title to the goods from the time they leave the seller's premises.
- ◆ The seller has title to the goods while in transit if the transaction is 'F.O.B. Destination.'

Third-party accountability

The law does not treat all third-party freight handlers in the same fashion. Under the Uniform Commercial Code (UCC), common carriers are legally responsible for any losses to their cargo. Motor and rail carriers should carry cargo insurance that pays for losses regardless of cause.

Both the UCC and common law have treated third-party warehouses differently. The warehouse operator's liability for goods is limited to *reasonable care* as defined in Section 7-204-1 of the UCC:

A warehouseman is liable for damages or loss or injury to the goods caused by his failure to exercise such care in regard to them as a reasonably careful man would exercise under like circumstances, but unless otherwise agreed he is not liable for damages that could not have been avoided by the exercise of such care.

Where the public warehouseman's responsibility for goods in his care begins and ends is not always clear. The point of transfer of responsibility varies by operation. For example, warehouse operators who provide delivery trucks will retain custody of cargo until it is delivered. If goods are received by rail, responsibility begins when the railcar enters the warehouse property. A question may arise concerning freight that is still on common-carrier trucks when those trucks are parked on the warehouse company's property.

The creation of a public-warehouse receipt is a legal acknowledgment of responsibility for care of goods. The signing of a bill of lading transfers responsibility from the public warehouse to the carrier.

Goods consigned to a public warehouse should always be addressed to the owner of the goods *in care of* the public warehouse company. This is the legal way to show that title to the goods remains with the owner, and that the public warehouse is acting as an agent.

Protection standards against theft and vandalism have become more stringent. Increasing crime rates have affected warehousing practices as much as they have other aspects of life. Burglary protection systems believed adequate in the past must be constantly reevaluated by warehouse management.

Effective security against fire and theft is partially a matter of attitude. The finest systems in the world are worthless if interest in loss prevention has not been instilled in your people.

Using warehouse space effectively

Many warehouse managers are unable to measure accurately the capacity of warehouses they manage, and an even larger number either cannot, or do not, calculate the percent of capacity currently held in the warehouse. For many, the only way to know when the warehouse is full is when a visual inspection shows that there seems to be no space left. For a few, the first awareness of the problem is when forklift drivers complain that they have no place to store today's inbound loads.

An overstuffed building is a warehouseman's nightmare — trying to put too much material in storage is one of the worst things that can happen to any operation. When a warehouse is over-full, one item may be blocked by another. In extreme cases, material is stored in aisles, staging areas, and docks, where it is damaged by forklift traffic. When aisles are blocked, or one item is stored in front of another, workers must waste time re-handling items to retrieve and ship a desired product.

Given the serious consequences of overcrowding, surprisingly little attention is paid to achieving a workable capacity measurement system.

Some feel that a measurement system is impossible. If you are storing 3,000 SKUs and these range in size from a loaded pallet to a pencil, how can you possibly make a warehouse capacity measurement?

One approach is to divide the inventory into product classes based on storage characteristics. Objects in pencil-sized boxes are not stored the same way as other cartons the size of a pallet. So the warehouse might be divided into sections or departments, each designed to handle a different class of freight. A typical warehouse might be divided into three departments devoted to three classes of inventory.

One portion of the warehouse is open space designed for free-standing stacks. This space is designed to hold loaded pallets or other units that can be stacked without artificial support.

A second portion of the warehouse is devoted to rack storage. Pallet racks capable of holding full or partial pallets are used to store products that cannot be safely stacked without artificial support, or low-quantity items (one or two pallets).

The third type of storage is shelves or bins, and these should hold the pencil-sized items. Any product that is too small to be effectively stored on a pallet is in the bin storage area.

Which product goes where? Size, storage characteristics, and volume will all guide the decision. If the product can be safely stacked in high bay areas, and if there is sufficient volume to fill normal storage rows, then the item should go to the open area designated for free-standing stacks.

Let's look at a case example:

A warehouse has a clearance that allows pallets to be stacked three high. It is designed with storage bays that hold four pallets of depth on the north side of each aisle and with short rows just one pallet deep on the south side of each aisle. This layout assures that space will be wasted whenever any storage row contains less than twelve pallets (three high by four deep) on the deep rows, or less than three pallets on the short rows. This waste is called honeycombing, which is illustrated in Figure 1.

Figure 1

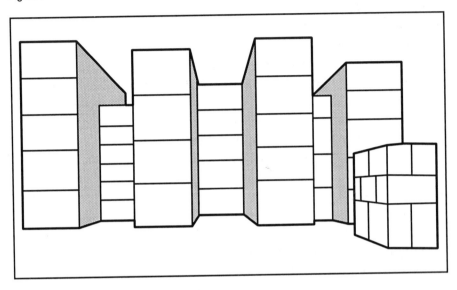

If you are using a warehouse with these characteristics, any stockkeeping unit that does not always have at least three pallets in inventory might be consigned to a rack storage area rather than a free-standing storage area.

Many warehouse operators set up both an order selection area (sometimes called a pick line) and a bulk storage area. A small quantity of each item is kept in the selection area so pickers can fill orders easily, while backup stocks are stored in other parts of the warehouse. If your warehouse is designed this way, your calculation of storage capacity must include both the capacity of the pick line and the capacity of the reserve storage space.

Once the storage characteristics are understood, assignment of each product line to the appropriate areas follows a logical pattern. If you have a pick line, its rack and bin positions must contain a sufficient quantity of merchandise to support a reasonable number of hours of order picking. In the bulk-storage area, items with sufficient volume and the ability to be stacked are assigned to free-standing storage. Items that have low volume or cannot be stacked are placed in pallet racks. Items that are too small to be efficiently stored on a pallet are assigned to bins.

After these divisions are made, consider a storage space calculation for each *department* of the warehouse.

Start with the free-standing storage area. The layout plan shows 40 percent of the warehouse is used for dock, aisles, and staging areas. This leaves 60 percent available for storage. From this 60 percent, an additional 20 percent is lost to honeycombing.

Assume that the prime product for the free-standing area is packaged in cartons measuring 20 by 24 by 10 inches, and the cartons are received in highway trailers containing 1,000 items, with just one stockkeeping unit in each trailer.

The product can be stacked 15 feet high. Using a 48 inch by 40 inch pallet, the cartons can be stacked in layers that are 2 units by 2, and 5 layers can be placed on each pallet. With this configuration, the warehouse ceiling limits stacking heights to three pallets high, or 15 layers of cases in the 3-pallet stack. Each storage pile, allowing for a normal overhang on the pallet, occupies 15 square feet.

Figure 2 illustrates a storage space calculation that shows that each carton will require a little more than one-half square foot. Similar calculations can be made for each additional carton to be placed in the free-standing stack area.

Figure 2   **Storage Space Calculation**

Assumptions:

1.   A portion of gross space must be dedicated to aisles and staging, leaving 60% net space.

2.   Honeycombing losses further reduce net space, leaving only 80% of the net space (48% of gross) available.

Calculations

A.   Each pallet of product contains 5 tiers with 4 cases per tier, or 20 cases total.

B.   Each stack of 3 pallets contains 60 cases.

C.   Each stack is the size of one pallet plus one inch overhang on each of the 4 sides: 42 times 50 = 2,100 square inches or 14.6 square feet. Round this to 15.

D.   Each stack consumes 25 gross square feet, or 15 divided by 60%.

E.   Each stack, after honeycombing, requires 31.25 square feet, or 25 divided by 80%.

F.   Each case takes up .52083 square feeet, or 31.25 divided by 60 cases.

Alternatively, storage capacity in the area can be expressed in pallet loads. By examining the pallet rack layout, as well as the characteristics of each type of pallet, a simpler calculation will show how many pallets will fit in the space.

If you know that the free-standing storage area has a capacity of 4,500 pallets (300 rows of 12 each plus 300 short rows of 3 each), a daily physical check can show how many pallets are in stock at the end of each day. By dividing the actual number of pallets by capacity, a percent of capacity is calculated.

Storage capacity for a rack area should be expressed in terms of pallets. Some pallets may be partially empty as cases are removed, one at a time, in the order selection process. However, the partially empty pallet will take just as much space in the rack as it did when it was full. Therefore, a capacity calculation based on cases will be distorted whenever there are partially full pallets.

Express the storage capacity of your rack area by counting pallet positions. The storage rack is designed to hold 3,000 pallet positions, and each of those positions will contain either a full pallet, a partial pallet, or no pallet. Once the total number of pallet positions is known, you can calculate rack capacity use by dividing the number of pallets in storage by the total number of pallet positions available.

The same procedure is used to calculate bin capacity, which is usually expressed in number of lines because only one product is usually stored in a bin. If you have 1,000 bins, you have room for 1,000 different lines or stockkeeping units. Line capacity may be reduced if you determine that more than one bin should be devoted to certain fast-moving or high-volume items.

The easiest way to calculate bin capacity is to count the number of empty bins and show a ratio of empty bins to the total number of bins available. The calculation may show an imbalance between the storage areas if rack storage is full while ample space remains in the free-standing area and, if this happens frequently, the problem should be corrected by acquiring additional storage racks.

Using the calculations just described, you can determine the capacity of each area of the warehouse. The capacity measurement should be done daily.

Controlling the lift truck fleet

The most important tool for monitoring and controlling industrial trucks is the hour meter. While some users believe the purpose of the engine hour meter is to show when the truck needs maintenance, it has a more important purpose: to measure the amount of time that the lift truck is actually used.

Measurement can reveal uneven use of these trucks, and sometimes lack of use can be traced to poor discipline. Perhaps an individual operator may not enjoy driving one particular unit. Without such controls, your warehousing people may request new forklift trucks when you already own one or more machines that are seldom used.

While the best way to determine usage is the hour meter, these meters are not an accurate indication of the time that a lift truck is dedicated to a given function. In the process of loading or unloading the engine may be turned off which stops the hour meter; yet the truck could not be removed from this task without disrupting the process. The meter reading does not cover all of the time when the machine is dedicated to a single project.

For this reason, some users have adopted a rule of thumb that the practical limit for lift truck usage is 75 percent of the time, or about 5.5 hours of a 7.5 hour shift. Therefore a truck that is used for 5.5 hours in a normal work shift might be operating at full capacity. You can examine the productivity of your materials handling fleet as a whole first, and then by individual truck. See Figure 3.

Figure 3

1. **Data**

Number of days worked	23
Number of active lift trucks	5
Total hour-meter readings	362

2. **Base calculations**

   Base = Number of days times number of trucks times 5.5 hours per truck
   23 days times 5 hours times 5.5 hours per truck = 632.5 hours

3. **Use ratio calculation**

   Use ratio = Total hour meter readings divided by Available base hours
   362 hours divided by 632.5 hours = 57%

Figure 3 looks at the fleet as a whole. Assume that hour meter readings have been kept on each of the 23 work days of the month, and you have found that five lift trucks accumulated 362 metered hours of usage. When this number is divided by the number of hours that were available based on the capacity assumption described above, we find a fleet that is used at just 57 percent of capacity. This is clearly a sign of trouble, and the next step is to see how much each individual truck is used.

Figure 4		Usage per truck	
Truck #	Capacity (hrs.)	Used (hrs.)	Use (% of capcity)
1	126.5	126	99.6
2	126.5	130	102.8
3	126.5	90	71.1
4	126.5	14	11.1
5	126.5	2	1.6
	SUMMARY	362	Average: 57.2%

Figure 4 shows a typical individual truck analysis. It is common to find that 'favorite' machines are heavily used, while others are nearly idle.

How should you respond when warehouse supervisors request a new piece of materials handling equipment? When you have utilization records, you can ask why trucks number 4 and 5 are so lightly used. If both are obsolete, then just what is wrong with the design? Without such investigation, you might buy a new truck that has the same design problems that have caused units 4 and 5 to be neglected.

A close look at Figure 4 shows that truck number 3 might be able to absorb all of the jobs handled by 4 and 5 without reaching 100 percent of capacity. In this case, perhaps no new trucks are needed, just better assignment of the work between three trucks that are heavily used now. If this is true, trucks number 4 and 5 should both be sold, or if some spare capacity is desired, one should be sold and the other retained as a backup.

Because demand for equipment can fluctuate with the season, it is wise to consider the alternative of using short-term lift truck rentals versus the alternative of keeping an older vehicle in the fleet for seasonal or temporary use. When one or more machines is a backup, its individual usage record should be considered separately from trucks that are in full-time use.

Sometimes management faces a capital shortage together with an overused lift truck fleet. When this happens, consider using the trucks on second or even third shifts.

Materials handling equipment is a major budget item for most warehouses. When controls are lacking, the fleet will grow. It is easy for managers to retain old equipment that should be sold or traded for newer vehicles. Unlike automobiles, there is no antique value for old industrial trucks. Therefore, there seems little excuse for keeping a vehicle that is not being used.

Controls based on meter readings will show when there are too many lift trucks as well as when there are too few. For operators of more than one warehouse, these records are especially valuable because an under-used truck can be moved to another warehouse that needs more lift truck capacity.

Buying versus rebuilding

If you compare the specifications for a new forklift truck with the specifications for a five-year-old model, you will find that the most significant difference between the two is the price. Yet heavily used equipment will wear out, and an old truck may be both expensive to maintain and unreliable.

The obvious answer is to trade it for a new one, but some warehouse operators extend the life of forklift trucks through a rebuild program. Most trucks have 10,000 hours on the meter and show substantial wear when they are seven years old. This is the time to consider whether a rebuild would be preferable to purchase of new equipment.

A rebuild is more than major repair — it involves dismantling and inspecting every operating part in the truck. Parts that show any discernable wear are replaced. Engine work includes the reboring of cylinders or the installation of a new block. Worn parts of transmissions and differentials are replaced, as well as steering mechanisms, brakes and all electrical wiring. Chains, cylinders and hydraulics are repaired or replaced. The truck is equipped with a new seat, pedals, meters, tires, knobs, handles, and decals. The truck is completely repainted so that it looks like a new vehicle.

If this rebuild is done by a dealer or repair shop, the cost is usually about 50 percent of the price of a new truck. Some operators have developed rebuild capabilities in-house, and they may reduce the cost to approximately 35 percent of a new truck.

Detailed maintenance records should be in place before you make decisions on rebuilding. If you track hourly maintenance costs, you have the tools to know whether repair, rebuild, or disposal is most appropriate. For example, if one vehicle has a major failure after 8,000 hours, its maintenance history will show whether it is economical to schedule a complete rebuild at 8,000 hours rather than to fix the failure and then rebuild just 2,000 hours later.

A study of both maintenance costs and usage records will show which periods of the year are best to take machines out of service for rebuilding. One warehouse operator developed a five-year plan for rebuilds.

Nothing lasts forever, and even the best lift truck reaches a stage where it is no longer economical to keep it in the warehouse. However, the decision is often made on the basis of changes in technology rather than the current condition of the equipment.

While the industrial truck has changed little in the last decade, some of these machines have been replaced by specialized vehicles with advanced features. You may wish to raise the storage capacity of your warehouse by replacing existing trucks with vehicles that will operate in narrow aisles, thus adding usable space to your building.

Consider trucks with higher masts, better order-picking capabilities, or heavier lifting capacity. Since it is almost never practical to modify an older truck's lift height or lift capacity, a prime reason for replacing an old truck is a need for improved storing or picking capabilities.

Questions that solve problems

If you want to learn how well your warehouse managers are protecting corporate assets, here are a few questions to ask:

Q As our finished goods move through the various distribution channels, can you describe to me exactly who is responsible for the product at each stage in the distribution process? How have we protected ourselves against loss of the product in each stage?

C Don't settle for a generalized answer. Insist that your managers trace an actual movement and describe in detail your insurance coverage, and protection standards.

Q Exactly how full is our warehouse today, and how have we measured its capacity?

C Whether or not your manager gives you a detailed answer, go to the warehouse and ask for specific demonstrations of the measurement system.

Q How many lift trucks do we have? Is this too many or not enough? Why do you feel this way?

C Regardless of the answers received, follow-up by asking whether every power unit has an hour meter and whether those meters work. Then ask if these meters are used to track operating hours. If your truck fleet is not controlled, now is the time to establish a process. ❖

Chapter 12

Reducing errors

In many warehouse operations, errors are the worst problem management faces. Errors mean lost customers, or worse — sometimes an error can be deadly. As long as human beings work in the warehouse, there will be some errors, and management's job is to reduce them to the greatest possible extent. In some warehouse operations, a decrease in errors is the best way to increase productivity. 'Zero defects' is now widely regarded as a reasonable goal.

The cost of an error

Cost of errors varies widely, but you should try to get an estimate of the cost in your operation. If the wrong item is shipped, you will have an unanticipated stock-out when inventory is exhausted, with a corresponding overage in some other item. The undetected stock-out can cause customer relations problems when you are unable to deliver an item that showed on your book inventory.

Correcting the error not only includes the cost of receiving the return, but also of shipping the proper item. In some industries, the shipper allows the receiver to keep a wrong item to avoid the cost of the return. The cost of taking back the wrong item and returning it to stock is many times the cost of a normal warehouse receipt. Part of this cost is the administrative burden of correcting a shipping error and handling a receipt of just one or a few packages.

But the most devastating cost of warehouse error is the creation of an unhappy customer.

Preventing warehouse errors

Many steps can be taken to minimize the possibility that an error will be made. One cause of errors is a misunderstanding of what was ordered when the order is taken by telephone. Such misunderstandings are minimized if the order taker repeats the order to the customer. Consider the procedure used by one fast food company that makes home deliveries. This firm asks for the caller's number, then the operator calls back to repeat the order. Besides eliminating prank calls, this second phone call catches a high percentage of errors.

A locator system prevents errors

Warehouse locator systems are used primarily to cut search time, but they have a second advantage—that of preventing shipping errors. If you have an accurate locator system, the order picker will be asked to go to a given location to pick a given item. If the picker finds that the item is not in that location, there is either an error in the locator system or an error in the item specified. Order pickers who always question a mismatch between the locator system and the item provide a second chance to find errors in the selection system.

Markings as a source of errors

A surprising number of warehouse errors are made because the labels or markings on packages are confusing or even misleading. Eliminate nonessential markings and be consistent in the marking or labeling system.

Any marking system should have the trade name first, then size, color, and item number. Some markings are too small to be read in normal warehouse light. Others are in a color that does not show up under high-intensity lighting systems. If you have a high error rate, consider whether the marking on the packaging could be improved.

Another source of labelling error is the use of packages within a package. You may have a shipping case that contains inner packs, each of which contains three bottles. When terminology is unclear, the warehouse order picker may not know whether the customer wants one case, one pack, or one bottle. Confusion can result in unreported overshipments which create a loss, or an undershipment which causes a customer claim. Be sure that your system is absolutely clear in stating how many pieces the customer really wants.

Picking documents

When multi-part forms are used, the picking document is frequently a copy that is fuzzy and difficult to read. Preventing errors requires picking documents designed for the order filler. The document should be as legible as you can make it, using the minimum letters and numbers required to identify the product.

Eliminate unnecessary information that might distract the order picker.

A picking document might have four columns. The first shows the location of the product. The second contains the identification numbers for the product. The third column is left blank for the order filler to place a check mark after picking the item. The fourth column lists the quantity to be selected. Any changes in the order should be marked only in the third column.

Use of bar coding

Bar coding will reduce handling time and errors. Consider the receiving process as an example.

Without bar coding, the warehouse worker writes a receiving report while unloading each inbound shipment, then carries the receiving report and the accompanying packing list to the office for entry into the inventory system. A clerk compares the documents for discrepancies and then enters the information on the receiving report. After entry, the clerk might obtain the appropriate storage location for the merchandise. The report is then returned to the worker who stores the stock in the assigned location.

With bar coding, the work performed by the clerk is eliminated. The warehouse worker scans a label on each item received and then downloads the information to the computer system. The system reveals any discrepancies by comparing what was scanned to the advance information transmitted by the client to the warehouse. A screen then displays the appropriate storage location for each unit scanned. After downloading, the process takes just seconds. Furthermore, the warehouse worker is faster and more accurate because there is no longer a need to write information by hand.

Physical factors in the warehouse

The environment of your warehouse can invite order picking errors. The most common problem is lack of sufficient lighting. While minimum lighting may be adequate for bulk storage locations, an order pick area should have illumination of at least 50 foot candles. Items that are most popular and most frequently picked should be at levels that eliminate reaching or stooping by the order picker. These fast-moving items should be at least 16 inches above the floor, but no higher than 6 feet, to minimize stretching or stooping.

Some products invite errors because of similar markings or similar appearance. Do not store such confusing items next to each other.

Personnel factors

The way you deal with people affects error reduction. Communicate your expectations so your people will know what you expect and will work to live up to those expectations. Your expectations may be in a written procedure, or they may be expressed in meetings dedicated to reduction of errors.

The first place to communicate your expectations is in the training of new people. Your trainers should review written procedures and discuss them with new hires. When you train new order pickers, use dry runs to teach them the importance of doing the job right the first time.

One controversial practice is the elimination of full-time checkers. Many warehouse operations have done this with success. While others feel it is impossible. Your decision will be influenced by the quality of your work force and the nature of the merchandise being selected. In many cases, elimination of checking is economical because error costs are less than the cost of the checker. This option is available if your people accept the responsibility and understand that the only checker is the customer. When worker literacy is low or product value is high, a checker may be necessary.

Identification with work

People who identify with their work usually do it better. One method of doing this is to have each order filler sign each page of an order document after completing it. If the worker doesn't complete the page, he or she initials each line handled.

Another means of encouraging worker identification is to insert a picking ticket in every order filled. This ticket should include the picker's name, not anonymous numbers. One picker's ticket reads: *This order was picked by Thomas E. Jones. If you find any discrepancy between the ticket and your order, please call 614-406-7890. Ask for the Claims Department and give my name when reporting the error.* A further refinement is to put the order filler's name and photograph on the ticket. This personalization has resulted in improved order accuracy. Using peer pressure to encourage more accurate order picking is often effective, listing each worker's error rate on the warehouse bulletin board. The individual making the most errors is at the top of the list — those making fewer errors follow. Always be sure that workers are graded on errors as a *percentage* of total lines picked. The fastest order picker may appear to be the worst error maker, when this may not be the case. If you post an error-rate list, be sure to provide recognition and praise for those workers who achieve the lowest percentage of errors.

Questions that solve problems

Since error reduction is a key step in quality improvement, you should question your warehouse managers frequently on this subject.

Q What was our error rate last month, and how did it compare with the same month of last year and with prior months of this year?

C If nobody has an answer, there is work to be done!

Q Can you think of anything that we could do to reduce the error rate?

C Look for some creative answers and take careful note of the manager who says that nothing else can be done.

Q Have you read or heard of any new technology that would help us to lower our error rate?

C Keep an open mind when you hear the answers. New technology is likely to go beyond anything described here since written descriptions of state-of-the-art devices are usually obsolete before the ink dries. ❖

Chapter 13

Measuring performance

Every manager is concerned about quality, and particularly about whether the warehouse is improving or falling behind. No single set of benchmarks could apply to every warehouse operation, but a common framework will enable you to design your own procedure. Using this framework, you can create an audit format based on history, projections and goals.

The first step is to separate performance items that are *quantitative* from those that are *qualitative*.

On the quantitative side, every warehouse manager has control over three elements: Space, equipment, and people. Use the ratios described in Chapter 11 to compare the actual versus the maximum possible use of warehouse space and materials handling equipment. You can also compare the quantitative output of workers to established benchmarks.

Qualitative measurements are just as important as the quantitative ones. First on the list is customer service — How well has management satisfied the needs of customers? A second measure is human relations. How successful is management in maintaining a harmonious workforce? Overages, shortages, damage, and errors might all be referred to as 'claims,' and used as a barometer of management's success in preserving the inventory. Safety is another measure of quality in warehousing.

Quantifying warehouse space

Every warehouse has a capacity, measured in square feet, cubic feet, or their metric equivalents. From the theoretical capacity you can deduce a practical capacity by subtracting space dedicated to aisles, staging, and support. Since management can influence the amount lost, the simplest way to measure capacity is to compare actual space used to theoretical capacity.

You have a warehouse containing 100,000 square feet and you store pallets. The pallets are all standard size 48 inch by 40 inch, each of which occupies 13.33 square feet, which we round to 14 square feet to allow for overhang.

The product you are storing can be stacked three pallets high. By dividing 100,000 square feet by 14 square feet per pallet, we find that over 7,000 pallets could be stacked on the floor. At three high the theoretical capacity of the warehouse is 21,428 pallets.

The theoretical capacity can never be reached, but a measure of your efficiency is the ratio of actual usage to theoretical capacity. If there were actually 10,000 pallets in the warehouse on the first day of January, your efficiency would be 47 percent of theoretical capacity (10,000 / 21,428 = 47%).

By maintaining such ratios over time, you can track one warehouse's performance or compare different warehouses storing the same product.

But what if the inventory is more complex? Where different kinds of cargo are involved, divide the warehouse into departments. One department will store palletized freight on standard pallets. Others might be used to store spare parts in bins, major appliances, bulk containers, or other categories of items with distinct storage characteristics. Once you have established these departments, you can develop an individual rating for each department. You may be able to convert the individual categories into a composite rating for the entire warehouse.

Quantifying equipment use

Every powered lift truck should be equipped with an hour meter that records the time that the engine was running.

For a one-shift operation, the theoretical maximum running time is 2,080 hours per year, based on 52 five-day weeks at eight hours per shift. A use ratio for each truck is calculated by dividing the hours actually shown on the meter by the theoretical number of hours available. Calculate the overall fleet use by averaging the individual results.

Management has the ability to move actual capacity closer to theoretical capacity, and to identify under-used vehicles in the fleet.

Quantifying worker productivity

Measuring the productivity of people is more difficult than calculating space or equipment utilization. Benchmarks are rarer and less reliable. Start by developing some historical data.

Last year our 100,000 square foot warehouse moved 72,800 pallets. We employed five people, so each worker handled 14,560 pallets. Dividing this by the number of work hours in the year (2,080) shows the average productivity was seven pallets per hour.

If we use seven pallets per hour as a benchmark, we can compare this year's productivity with last year's. Management will know at least whether productivity is improving or deteriorating.

For warehouses with different kinds of cargo, separate benchmarks will be established for palletized products, single case order picking, binned parts, and other categories. Just as storage was departmentalized, materials-handling hours are separated into various departments.

The scoring systems for space, equipment, and people, are tools the manager uses to determine progress in controlling the three essential elements of warehousing. Past improvements in productivity can be evaluated and future improvements can be estimated before a change takes place. The calculations should be repeated following a change to find out if the desired end has been achieved. Comparing all results to theoretical capacity, rather than practical capacity, eliminates the guesswork involved in rules of thumb for aisle loss, equipment maintenance, and lost time.

Monitoring several locations

A multi-city warehouse operator should compare the performance of each warehouse with that of the others.* (See Figure 1). The most obvious way to track service performance is to count the number of reported errors. However, those errors should be compared to the volume of orders, since a warehouse with low volume of orders should also have a low number of errors. Calculate the service rating by dividing the number of errors by the to-

---

*   Adapted from an article by John T. Menzies, Terminal Corporation, *Warehousing Forum*, Volume 3, Number 8, ©The Ackerman Company.

tal number of orders, but consider the order volume compared to a six-month rolling average. If order volume is above normal, a lower than normal rating could be the result of the overload. Tonnage throughput should also be considered. If the tonnage is above normal, the warehouse may be experiencing a different type of overload. Overcrowding frequently causes excess damage and shipping errors.

By using a service performance report, the multi-city warehouse operator can track service ratings and compare them with two measures of volume: throughput and order count.

Figure 1				Service Performance Report				
	Orders	% of 6 Mo. Avg.	Errors	Service Rating Avg.	Throughput	% of 5 Mo. Avg.	Space Use Avg.	Space x 1,000
Boston	1,870	105%	6	99.68%	67,521	101%	90%	78
Atlanta	1,746	85%	11	99.37%	105,879	87%	84%	105
Balti-more	1,571	98%	13	99.17%	95,072	102%	75%	98
Los Angeles	1,412	107%	21	98.51%	140,238	103%	85%	140
Chicago	1,268	97%	18	98.58%	117,816	99%	95%	125
Houston	900	95%	30	96.67%	130,956	89%	77%	127
Total	8,767	96%	99	98.87%	657,491	100%	83%	673

Qualitative measures

Warehouses exist to provide dependable delivery for the end user or customer. Therefore, the most important qualitative measure for any warehouse is customer satisfaction.

The best measure of customer satisfaction is the number of complaints. One quality audit approach measures the number of complaints received for each warehouse every month. These figures are compared over time. Accuracy may be compromised because not every customer will complain about bad service while others may complain even when given outstanding service. Complaints should be tabulated as a percentage of orders filled.

Another way to measure customer service is to log the number of times that orders are shipped behind schedule, or the number of times they are delivered later than promised. These numbers are compared to records of shipping and delivery. Because some customers are not as concerned about on-time delivery as we think they are, this measure may not be a true reflection of customer satisfaction.

Warehouse claims are the result of shipping errors, damage caused either by transportation or warehousing, and inventory overages or shortages. By logging each month's claims and comparing these with the number of shipments made during the month, you can develop a barometer of accuracy. If one month's results are 23 from a total of 7,000 shipments, inventory accuracy is .9967, or 99.67 percent.

Safety is a measurable qualitative goal. Most managers know the number of work days that pass without a lost-time accident.

Since the warehouse operator must protect the products as well as the people, another measurement of success is the ratio between the number of products moved without damage to the total number of items handled. The resulting figure should be over 99 percent, meaning that less than one percent of the products is lost or damaged.

A key qualitative measurement should be people — the measure of a manager's success in human relations. In a union environment, you may log the number of grievances filed. Both union and nonunion operations should measure the longevity of service of their workers. A happy person stays on the job, and high turnover may be a sign of weak management. It may be useful to separate the workers into categories: warehouse workers, warehouse supervisors and office workers. Consider a warehouse that has fourteen employees, seven day-shift warehouse workers, three on the night shift, and four people in the office. In one year, the company replaces two of these workers. The retention rate is 86 percent. However, when we look at departments, we find that the two who were replaced were both in the office, meaning the office has a retention rate of only 50 percent, and each of the two shifts in the warehouse has a rate of 100 percent. Clearly the human relations problem is in the office, which is where management's attention should be centered.

Implementation

Once benchmarks are established for the three quantitative items (space, equipment, and people), and for the four qualitative ones (customer service, claims, safety, and human relations), you can develop an audit form. A sample format is shown in Figure 2.

The audit can be used in several ways. First, managers should be asked to forecast their progress in improving each of the items on the form. Second, the results should be compared over time so that improvement or slippage will be readily noted. Third, where more than one warehouse is being used, compare the results in each operation. Finally, consider refinements and improvements in the audit process.

Once you begin the audit process, you are likely to find ways to refine the benchmarks and improve the measurement techniques. The on-going process of measuring and comparing results with benchmarks will motivate operations people to achieve better results.

Figure 2	Warehousing Audit Score			
Area	Jan	Feb	Mar	Apr
Space	47	52	49	
Materials handling equipment	58	49	51	
People	85	73	76	
Customer service	98	96	99	
Claims	99	99	98	
Safety	98	99	99	
Human relations	83	83	83	

SPACE scores are actual use as a percentage of theoretical capacity.

MATERIALS HANDLING scores are actual equipment hours used as a percentage of theoretical capacity.

PEOPLE scores are actual pieces per working hour compared to benchmark.

CUSTOMER SERVICE scores are the percentage of shipments without compalints.

CLAIMS scores are the percentage of total pieces handled without damage, shortage, or overage.

SAFETY scores are the percentage of hours worked without a lost-time injury.

HUMAN RELATIONS scores are the percentage of time worked without a resignation or dismissal.

Questions that solve problems

An audit of warehouse performance may compare different warehouses, or it may consider the changes within one warehouse over a period of time.

Q How do our warehouse managers compare in the quality of their operations?

C They can be readily compared on the basis of the benchmarks described. There will always be business reasons for unusual performance — good or poor. No two warehouses are alike, even when they are part of the same organization. Yet there are substantial similarities, so the benchmarks should be taken seriously.

Q How effective is my warehouse crew and what can I do to upgrade their performance?

C The quality of the crew is measured by the same benchmarks. Remember that no team is any better than its leader, and your problem might be with supervision. Therefore, look for trouble in both areas.

Q Which warehouse is our best and which is our worst?

C Before you give final grades, be sure that you have considered any external factors that influence performance but cannot be controlled by local management.

Q Which measurements are most meaningful for us?

C Be sure the answers are competently defended and are not a reflection of complacent attitudes.

Q Are we measuring any of the wrong things?

C This could be the opportunity to abolish unused reports. ❖

PART

3

Warehouse Management

Chapter 14

Finding the right people

No warehouse operation can be any better than its employees, so — whether you are starting a new warehouse or adding to the current employee roster — it is impossible to be too meticulous in selecting people. Even if you are not currently adding people, eventually some of your employees will change jobs or leave your employment. Filling these vacancies represents an opportunity to improve the quality of your warehouse team.

Hiring in a tight market

Even when there is not an absolute shortage of labor, you may find a scarcity of the high-quality people you want to work in your warehouse.*

However, you can implement programs that make it easier to find good people in a tight market. There is no single solution to the problem; instead it consists of a number of building blocks:

- ◆ Develop a labor requirements plan.
- ◆ Prepare volume forecasts over several weekly periods.
- ◆ Reward recruiters for quality, not quantity.
- ◆ Work closely with an outside temporary agency.
- ◆ Improve the working environment in your warehouse.
- ◆ Establish schedules to accommodate non-traditional workers: Students, housewives, retirees, or the handicapped.

---

* This subchapter is adapted from an article by Dallas Mulder, in *Warehousing Forum*, Volume 5, Number 7 ©The Ackerman Company.

Labor requirements plan

This plan should specify a benchmark level of people by department for a normal level of activity. Figure 1 shows a labor requirements plan developed by one company.

Figure 1

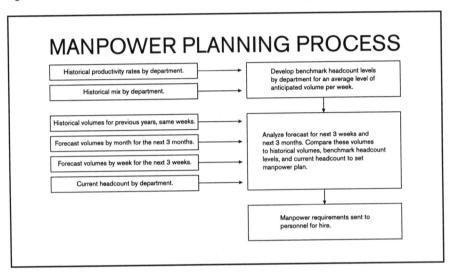

Volume forecasts

Forecasting volume levels is a necessity in finding quality people. You cannot ask the personnel department for five people on Friday and expect five *quality* people to report to work on Monday. Good forecasts provide sufficient lead time to allow personnel or recruiting people to do their jobs effectively. When forecasts are made, both operations and personnel departments should have a chance to react to them and comment.

Quality versus quantity

A critical building block in securing good people is to develop a strong working relationship between operations and personnel. New recruiters should work at various jobs within the warehouse, if only for a few hours, to gain insight into the operation. The recruiter should be encouraged to hire *quality* and not *quantity*. Never force recruiters into a position where they must deliver a number of workers without regard to the job requirements.

Outside agency

Just as you develop a relationship with your own recruiter, it is good to do likewise with an outside temporary agency. There are times when you need both inside and outside help in securing people. Managers from a temporary agency should spend time on-site learning the job requirements, just as your own recruiters have.

Don't go with the cheapest price. You may need to pay more to attract good people, and these better people are likely to stay through the assignment.

Develop incentives so the temporary agency sends you only good people. One such incentive is to not pay for the first day's salary if the temporary doesn't meet your requirements or expectations. Second, don't permit the agency to replace drop-outs during the week. Insist that all temporaries start on Monday. To receive maximum billing, the temporary agency will realize they must send people who will be retained through the week.

Your working environment

The job environment can greatly facilitate recruiting and retaining good people. Design the job so it can be learned easily. Keep the procedures and equipment as simple as possible. Increased automation may reduce the number of people needed, but the skill requirement may greatly increase.

The ideal warehouse has just one job grade for all work assignments. When this is the case, you have maximum flexibility in assigning people to do any work that is needed. Even forklift positions should have the same grade as other warehouse tasks. Many companies require workers to qualify as a lift truck driver by passing rigid tests and receiving a company 'license.' Consider having a ratio of up to five times the number of qualified lift drivers to lifts. This surplus of qualified drivers allows for greater flexibility of re-assigning equipment and coverage for absenteeism and vacations.

When new people are hired, part of their orientation should be to make them familiar with the policy of occasionally reassigning people from one work area to another. When you move people around, it is extremely important that the supervisors receiving these people welcome them and express the department's appreciation. These people will want to feel they are part of a new team, and this requires that someone be assigned to orient, train, and answer questions.

To attract good people, you should create an environment that is equal to or better than your competition's. Can you say *yes* to the following?

- Is the environment safe?
- Is the facility clean?
- Is the workplace temperature comfortable in summer and in winter?
- Do you provide attractive eating and lounge facilities?
- Do you provide lighted and safe parking lots?
- Do you provide security, both inside and outside the facility?
- Do you provide lockers to secure personal valuables?
- Can you provide unusual working hours, such as a four-day work week?

Non-traditional employees

If you have difficulties attracting good people, do you provide flexible or part-time work schedules to attract students and housewives? Do you allow shorter hours for retired people who do not want to exceed a maximum annual earning? If you can provide a work week of four ten-hour days, you will find that many workers will prefer your warehouse because they will have an extra day off. Some companies set up rotating shifts to provide five-, six- or seven-day coverage even though each shift has a four-day week.

Larger companies can develop a reciprocating relationship among divisions. When your needs are high, another division's needs may be low, so you can loan out and borrow workers. Turning workers into 'volunteer fire fighters' does good things for their morale, since they not only get some variety, but a chance to show their talent to co-workers in another division.

While all of these are important, don't overlook the need to provide competitive pay and benefits. Compare your pay scale annually with like companies in your labor market. You can secure this information from your chamber of commerce or from cooperative wage surveys conducted by personnel departments in the area. Your pay range may not be the same as that of higher-skilled or lesser-skilled warehouse facilities, but you need to set a pay strategy that provides the best people for your needs. Because some part-time workers need fringe benefits, you should always offer benefits for part-time employees. Some companies provide the opportunity for the worker to either purchase health coverage or to eliminate the purchase if a spouse has duplicate coverage from another employer. This allows people who already have the insurance to earn a larger amount of take-home pay.

Attracting and retaining good people go hand-in-hand. Attracting good people is not totally the responsibility of your personnel department. The operations and personnel departments must be committed to cooperation. To solidify that commitment, it's essential that you provide opportunities beyond today's job. This is most obviously demonstrated by how higher level positions are filled. Developing people so that you can promote and offer opportunities from within will encourage the best employees to stay.

In altogether too many warehousing organizations, the preferred candidates for hiring are people who have worked in other warehouses. These may not be the best people you could find to work in your warehouse.

One of the biggest mistakes in the hiring process is the lack of a systematic approach. Picking up a resume or application two minutes before the candidate enters your office is not a systematic approach. A system is defined as an established way of doing something, using a set of rules arranged in an orderly form, to show a logical plan of linking the various parts.

The interview process

Your skills as an interviewer will increase by practicing techniques.* It is difficult to imagine a basketball player becoming proficient at shooting free throws by using a different style each time and practicing only once a month. The same can be said for interviewing. The process you use does not have to be difficult, but it must be clearly defined, repeatable, and effective. Figure 2 shows a simple process.

Always begin by defining what it is you are looking for, a profile of the successful person. Education and experience are important, but they are not indicators of success on the job. If they were, any person with a certain amount of education and experience should be successful; and we know this is not true. Knowledge, skills, and abilities determine whether people will be successful, and these should be the keys to the search.

*   From an article by Barry Shamis, Effective Selection Systems, *Warehousing Forum*, Volume 7, Number 4, ©The Ackerman Company.

Figure 2

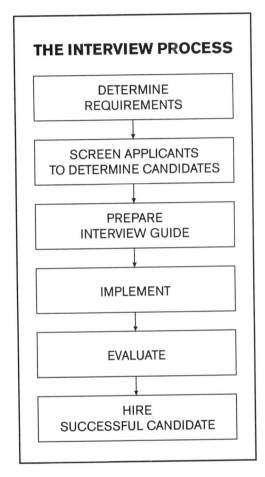

A job is a series of tasks, and successful people accomplish the tasks in an appropriate manner. Ask yourself what tasks a candidate must perform to be successful. Then consider the knowledge, skills, and abilities required to perform those tasks. Finally review how a successful person would accomplish each task.

The first step in developing a list of requirements is to think about the *technical* skills necessary. Consider the tasks and try to determine what workers must know and do to accomplish the tasks. Do they operate any special equipment? What systems do they need to use? Is any special knowledge required? The answers should give you a list of technical requirements.

Next, we need to determine the behavioral requirements. So think about how the tasks are performed. Analyze the environment. What are the specific behavioral traits necessary to accomplish the tasks? Do your employees work in teams or individually? Does the person who fills this position solve problems, come in contact with the public, influence people? How does the person need to act to be successful? The answers should generate a list of behavioral requirements such as problem-solving skills, initiative, and flexibility.

One of the best methods you can use to outline your requirements is to profile a successful person. Think of someone doing the job now or who has recently done the job and been successful. Why is this person successful? What does she do, or not do, that causes her to be successful? How does he react to situations? How does the person deal with people? The answers will help you identify the requirements necessary to build a profile of the successful person.

Once you have established a list of requirements, develop a pool of qualified candidates. This is when the recruitment process begins. In times of high unemployment, recruitment may be primarily a screening process. When prospective employees are scarce, recruitment may become the toughest part of the process.

Whether the process was simple or complex, assume that you now have a group of applicants. From this group you must decide whom to interview. This process converts a group of applicants to a smaller group of candidates.

This screening process is difficult because decisions at this point are made with the least amount of data and are usually irreversible. We seldom go back to the list of applicants ruled out to take a second look. Keep your ultimate objective in mind: To hire a person who will be successful.

Try to screen *in* not screen *out*. Don't look for a reason to throw applicants out; instead, seek reasons to keep them in. Don't risk losing good candidates because of one blemish on the application.

Look for indicators on the resume that the person will be successful in your facility. Review your list of requirements and compare these to the resume. Management skills, knowledge of a specific piece of equipment, and sales skills should be indicated on a resume. Initiative, flexibility, and problem-solving are not as evident and will need to be researched in an interview. Review the resume with the intention of finding indicators that the person has the necessary knowledge, skills, and abilities. To foster this habit, try counting the things you *like* on each resume you read.

Preparing for the interview

Once you have narrowed the list, prepare for face-to-face interviews. Prepare for each the same way. Write an interview guide, your list of questions, in the order you will ask them. This is important for two reasons. First, you can be certain to generate questions that cover all the important information. Second, you can concentrate on *listening*, as opposed to worrying about what to ask next.

Use the application and your list of requirements to prepare a list of questions in chronological order. This format allows you to follow an applicant through his or her career — to see patterns of growth or lack of growth.

This method will help you ascertain whether a person has reached a plateau, whether he repeats mistakes, and how quickly and how often she learns new skills.

Choose the first time period you want to explore and, with your requirements in mind, develop questions that will provide insight into the applicant's knowledge, skill, and ability levels. Make sure you have enough questions to ensure adequate information to assess the person's skills. Advance through the applicant's career. You are taking a journey through the person's background, and determining what they accomplished along the way.

Pay particular attention to the types of questions you ask. The right questions promote a successful interview.

Much of the conventional wisdom is misleading. Avoid open-ended, nonspecific questions, such as, 'Tell me about managing a facility,' and 'What is the best way to control expenses?'

Although these questions do get the candidate talking, they do not garner specific information that will help predict whether the person will be successful.

Avoid theoretical questions such as, 'What would you do if...?' These force candidates to manufacture the answer they think you want to hear. This measures only their ability to second-guess you. Instead of asking 'What would you do if...?,' ask 'What did you do when...?,' which takes the question out of the future and generates specific factual information about past performance.

The two most effective types of questions to ask are factual and action questions. Factual questions require the person to respond with a simple discreet fact. 'How many people did you supervise?' 'What type of equipment did you use?' 'What inventory management system did you use?' Answers to these factual questions help you determine an applicant's knowledge, skill, and ability level.

Action questions require the candidate to describe his or her performance in a specific situation. 'Tell me how you dealt with the last problem employee you had.' 'Step me through how you implemented your quality control program.' 'Explain how you closed your last sale.' Each of these questions requires applicants to explain their actions. The answers will contain information that helps determine how they will act on your job, and to predict whether they will be successful.

Conducting the interview

The face-to-face interview is a critical point in the process. Begin with an opening designed to put the candidate at ease. The goal is to establish rapport and reduce stress and anxiety. Begin with some small talk to break the ice, a current event or something interesting you saw on the resume. You might lead with an issue or event that is hot in the industry.

You are now ready for the body of the interview. Refer to your interview guide and ask your prepared questions in the order you wrote them. Probe for details. Don't assume you know what an applicant means — ask for clarifications and explanations when you need more information.

Once you have asked all the questions, you can begin the closing phase of the interview. Describe the company and explain the job. This is the time to sell the applicant on your company. If you make this presentation at the beginning of the interview, you will waste your time and the applicant's time. Until you understand the applicant's background, you don't know if you need to market the job and you won't know how to market it until you understand the applicant's background.

After you have described the job and company, outline the remaining steps in the selection process. Make sure each prospect knows what will happen next and when. Finally, end the interview on a positive note.

Reviewing your notes

You will have a tremendous amount of information about applicants' knowledge, skills and ability levels. Now you must evaluate the data. This is not difficult if you break the process down to small, manageable parts.

Return to your list of requirements and create a chart similar to the one in Figure 3. List the requirements down the left side of the chart and the candidates along the top. Rate each candidate against each requirement. For each requirement, go back to your notes from the interview and determine if the person meets the requirement.

Candidates must all be measured against the same standard — your list of requirements. Establishing such a standard has two significant benefits. First, it satisfies the major legal requirement of the equal employment opportunity laws, which state that all candidates should have an equal opportunity to compete. Second, it will prevent you from hiring someone who is the best of the worst — a person who looks good compared to the other candidates, but still doesn't *meet* the requirements.

The best candidate will meet or exceed all the requirements. A candidate who is missing an important requirement will probably fail on the job and should be avoided.

Figure 3

MATRIX EVALUATION

Requirements	CANDIDATES			Comments
	A	B	C	

KEY   ✔ Meets requirement.
      − Does not meet requirement.
      + Exceeds requirement.

The last step, hiring a successful candidate, is the reward for your hard work, planning and evaluation. Over time your skill level will increase, as will your odds of hiring a successful person.

Probation

Most labor contracts allow a probationary period of one to three months before the new employee becomes a permanent member of the workforce. Even so, it is preferable to complete all investigations before the new worker is ever put on the job. This prevents the possibility of personal injury or damage caused by an individual unsuited for the job, as well as the expense and pain of dismissing an employee. But no matter how much care is taken with pre-employment investigation, the risk of error always exists.

Management must observe the new employee closely during the probationary period. Pre-employment investigations cannot reveal attitude problems that will show up only in the work place. By eliminating marginal employees during the probationary period, the warehouse operator has a second chance to ensure the highest quality work force.

Proficiency tests

Pre-interview checks may eliminate a high percentage of applicants.* There is no need to waste interview time on applicants who cannot pass your programmed tests or who don't have the appropriate backgrounds. But how do we properly interview the remaining people? First of all, the interview should actually begin before the sit-down phase. Try to observe the applicant from the time he or she arrives on the property. Is the applicant on time? How does she conduct herself during the initial greeting? Does he look you in the eye? How is the applicant dressed? Is he clean, neat, and well groomed? You are probably seeing the applicant at his best during the interview. Tardiness and other bad habits usually do not improve once the person has been hired.

---

* From an article by R. L. Prior in *Warehousing Forum*, Volume 2, Number 1, ©The Ackerman Company.

Figure 4 is a test that will measure basic skills in arithmetic. Since nearly all warehouse workers must count and check the products they handle, some level of knowledge of arithmetic is an essential part of the job.

Figure 4   **TEST NUMBER 5**

Suggested Time – Six Mnutes   **Score**

The following problems require a combination of thought and figuring. Read each one carefully and, here again, do not spend too much time on any particular problem. Do your figuring on the back of test no. 4, scratch paper, or the margins of this page.

1. A store requires a 10% down payment on all merchandise. What would the down payment be on a television set priced at $345.00?

2. If Dr. Jones receives $30 each month from Mrs. Smith, how much will he receive in a year and a half?

3. Mr. Brown pays us $9.47 on one of his accounts and $6.52 on another account. How much change will he receive if he gives us two fives and a ten?

4. Before making the two payments above, Mr. Brown owed us $102.56 on one account and $73.49 on the other. After we apply these payments, what is the *total* of his new balances?

5. Harry's salary is $4,420 per year. How much does he make a week?

6. Mary types 430 words in ten minutes. If she maintains this same rate of speed, how many words will she type in half an hour?

7. If pencils are selling at 4 for 15 cents, how many can you buy for $1.35?

8. Sally has 4 apples. Jane has half as many as Sally and Arthur has two and a half times as many as Jane. How many apples are there?

Post-interview checks

Some people fail to conduct telephone checks because they believe that no one will tell them anything. Sometimes this is true. But if a person has had three or four previous jobs, the chances are good that at least one of the former employers will help you. Here are some good questions for the reference check:

- ◆ How would you describe the candidate's attitude?
- ◆ How did the candidate compare against peers?
- ◆ Was the candidate involved in any significant failures?
- ◆ What was the best way you found to motivate this person?
- ◆ Does the candidate work well with other people?
- ◆ What were the candidate's strengths (or weaknesses)?
- ◆ Why did he or she leave?
- ◆ Would you rehire?

Questions that solve problems

Consideration of these questions will show whether your management appreciates the critical importance of hiring and developing the best people.

Q **Does our company have a manpower plan?**
C If not, consider the plan developed in this text. If you have one, compare yours with what is described here. Finally, have you checked to see if your plan is really followed or just filed?

Q **Are we confident that the quality of work life is as good in our company as it is in other warehouses?**
C If you are convinced of this, are you sure that all your people share that conviction? If you are not, how will you change things?

Q **Does our company offer flexible work schedules to attract potential employees who cannot work on a normal shift schedule?**
C If you haven't done this, ways suggested in this chapter may help. If you have, compare your plan with the one described here and review any alternate ideas that your people might offer.

Q **Are we certain that our compensation program is competitive?**
C Sources to compare are described in this chapter, and you may identify other sources.

Q **Are you a skilled interviewer?**
C If you have chosen to avoid this task, you should then check to see whether one or more of the people reporting to you have developed high skills in interviewing. Compare their approach with the ones described earlier.

Q **What steps do we take during the probationary period to be sure that we have not picked the wrong person?**
C This should cause a careful examination of your initial orientation program as well as your ability to seek feedback from the workforce. Other

workers will not welcome a new person who appears to be inferior in work habits.

Q **What tests do we use during the hiring process?**
C Compare the tests you use with those described here. ❖

Chapter 15

Management productivity

The three most critical jobs for every manager are the selection and recruitment of good people; the training, development, and promotion of those selected for employment; and the dismissal of those who do not make the grade.

A successful manager is able to get things done through others. How do you find people who make your job a success? Some managers have little experience or training in attracting and selecting the people they need for their team.

The qualities you desire should be placed in priority. Some may be absolutely essential, while others could be subordinated if the prospect's essential talents were relatively strong. As you set priorities, remember that it is easier to teach new skills than it is to change an employee's attitude.

Accurate appraisals are essential. Do the people who report to you know how well they are doing, or is your analysis of their performance a secret? Are you too busy to give appraisals, or uncomfortable in giving them? Do you have a format for conducting an appraisal interview? Do you get appraisals from *your* boss?

Some managers start by rating themselves. Whether you're rating yourself or another, you can use the format shown in Figure 1 as a checklist. A successful appraisal emphasizes performance. It provides both positive and negative feedback, recognizing that nobody is perfect and everyone has some good traits. The appraisal interview should include discussion of a step-by-step approach for achieving improvement in future performance.

Figure 1	12 factors to rate yourself as a manager		
	Excellent	**Average**	**Needs Work**
Administration			
Job knowledge			
Planning			
Innovation			
Communication initiative			
Responsibility			
Team player			
Sales person			
Decision maker			
Leader			
Selector & developer of personnel			

Coaching is another aspect of developing better employees. Much of this involves feedback, but an equally important part is your role as a good listener.

The importance of listening

Successful warehouse managers communicate clearly.* Clear communicators have a genuine understanding of what they are trying to convey, use appropriate words to phrase the ideas, choose an effective way to put them across, and listen effectively. Many managers enjoy talking, telling, informing, teaching and judging. Listening — actively attending to what another is saying — is frequently an undeveloped skill, particularly in those who talk a lot. Successful managers who learn to listen effectively often achieve new insights. Sometimes *generous listening* is used as a way to reward others.

---

*   From "Listening: A Warehouse Manager's Tool," by Richard E. Rogala; *Warehousing Forum*, Volume 3, Number 6 ©Ackerman Company.

In a warehouse, the continual movement of material in an efficient, profitable manner requires close cooperation and teamwork. Teamwork is based on good listening skills. Choose a place that is relatively quiet and comfortable to share information. The effective listener minimizes the probability of interruptions. Listening is easier and more successful in physically comfortable surroundings.

One new warehouse manager had been transferred to a new facility by his company. In addition, he was promoted to general manager of the new facility from his position of administrative assistant to the general manager at his old location. He was nervous and highly self-conscious of his age and minimal experience. The people who worked for him — foremen, customer service representatives, and hourly workers — knew nothing about him or his reputation previous to his arrival.

When he arrived, the new manager called everybody together and lectured for forty-five minutes to prove his knowledge and competence. His audience reacted, however, in a noncommittal, reserved manner. They had not been given any opportunity to raise questions, voice concerns, or make observations about the operation. The new general manager's intent was to prove his competence by talking about his experience. In fact, he alienated the people he was trying so hard to please.

Had this new manager taken the opportunity to spend time with individuals, listened to their experiences, heard their observation of how well the warehouse was operating, and then commented on the things he saw they were doing *right*, he would have been in a much better position to elicit their confidence, loyalty, and motivation. The art of listening is a fundamental management tool, but it requires practice. Becoming a better listener will make you a better warehouse manager.

Why warehousing is different

Warehousing creates unique problems for managers because a significant percentage of supervisors and managers are former forklift drivers or checkers. The problems common to managers promoted *from the ranks* are found more frequently in warehousing than in other businesses.

Entry-level work in warehousing has a low image. While this image is not deserved, some managers believe warehousing is a job for a strong back and a weak mind, and that pay scales can be lower than those for manufacturing. The best managers understand that a warehouse employee needs skills in excess of those needed by assembly line workers who are more closely supervised. The very nature of warehousing works against close supervision, so a warehouse worker must be a self starter, a person who will produce high-quality work, and be highly productive without having someone looking over his or her shoulder. The low image stems from management's failure to build community respect for warehousing as an occupational specialty.

The buck stops here

Another peculiar problem for the warehouse manager is the intensity of business pressure at the warehouse level. The shipping dock is the place where *the buck stops* in the corporate *shell game*, which begins with salesmen's promises and ends with the question of whether the order has been delivered.

Such questions, typically handled by warehouse management, must be answered with either a *yes* or a *no*. If the answer isn't what senior management wants to hear, there is scant interest in the reasons why. This creates pressures seldom found elsewhere in the corporate scene.

With this pressure comes risks of failure that are peculiar to warehousing. A late shipment is a failure, but so is shipping the wrong merchandise, shipping the wrong quantity, or even shipping too early. Transportation failures are often blamed on the warehouse, even when management had no authority to select a carrier. Damage, whether caused by the carrier or warehousing people, is a considered a failure — particularly if the damage is not discovered promptly. Theft, from whatever cause, is generally regarded as something good management should have been able to control. Even casualty losses from fire or windstorm are considered to be events that might have been prevented by better management.

It is neither accurate nor fair to blame these failures on management, yet this happens in many companies. Managers in other businesses face risks of failure, but warehouse managers have more risks to cope with than most.

Hazards and sand traps

Failure to delegate is a frequent cause of management ineffectiveness. The cause may be a manager who cannot tolerate work done by the others or the manager who is unwilling to give up an enjoyable task. It is human nature to want to cling to old tasks that are pleasant, but a good manager learns how to delegate even the fun jobs.

Meetings

Meetings are a widely discussed hazard. *The Wall Street Journal* reported that the average chief executive officer spends 17 hours per week in meetings, and middle managers 11 hours. Most managers feel that they spend more time in meetings than they should, but some call a meeting simply to get a group consensus on a decision that should be made by one manager. Show your managerial skill by reducing the number and length of meetings, recognizing that overindulgence in meetings is another hazard to everyone's productivity.

Cost cutting

Pressure to cut costs is a growing hazard for managers. These pressures come from the top, as increasing numbers of corporations are downsizing to become more competitive. Perhaps the best way to deal with such pressures is to develop more awareness of productivity than anyone else in your organization. Nothing can be managed well without being measured. Your measurements of warehouse productivity should be simple, easily understood, and relevant to the task performed. If you can demonstrate that your operation controls productivity and improves over time, you can deal with the cost pressures from above.

Customer service

Another hazard can accompany attempts to improve customer service. Service providers tend to treat customers the way they are treated by their bosses. If managers are characteristically rude or disrespectful to supervisors or workers, this same rudeness moves through the organization. When workers have no one to abuse within the organization, it is natural for them to take out their frustrations on customers. Raising the quality of customer service frequently requires raising the quality of management. It also requires *total* dedication to service, right up to the chief executive. If you do not set the example, your people certainly aren't going to give the kind of service you want your customers to receive.

Your personal life

A common trap for some managers is failure to manage their own life. Many fail to realize the extent to which their actions serve as an example for those reporting to them. First among these is time management. The manager who fails to manage time well, dashing from crisis to crisis, will find these emergencies tend to spread through the organization. The manager who fails to set a fast pace will fail in convincing others to do so. A manager who spends most of the time in the office is likely to allow supervisors to do the same thing. *Management by walking around* (MBWA) has been a popular subject for business writers, but in essence it is management by example.

Do you spend the majority of the day planning, controlling, teaching, directing, developing, and coaching employees? Or do you spend most of your time as the expeditor — ultimate problem-solver? The first step in improving management productivity is evaluating your productivity.

Conflict resolution

Every manager must deal with conflicts, and your failure to do so could be a serious hazard. Sensitive managers understand the origins of conflict and know they can manage it, but they never eliminate it completely. A certain amount of conflict is normal and healthy.

Communicating goals

The successful supervisor informs people about progress made toward established goals. When you let your people know that they have been successful, they will feel better about their work. The successful manager also enforces rules objectively. Consistent enforcement allows everyone to know exactly what is expected.

One of the worst traps is failing to provide feedback. The successful supervisor rewards positive results promptly. Everyone enjoys rewards, even those that are not monetary. Your failure to provide positive feedback is a missed opportunity to provide a reward.

Not all feedback can be positive. Negative feedback is necessary so we can correct our mistakes and grow. However, negative feedback is more readily accepted when accompanied by positive observations and an attitude of trust. When your subordinate knows that your criticism comes neither from anger nor a desire for revenge, the criticism will be accepted. Providing feedback is one of your most important jobs as a manager, and one that too many managers neglect.

New tools improve communications

Improvements in knowledge and technology promise to make being a good manager easier. Some management teams use electronic mail via computer terminals as substitutes for meetings and memos.

Involvement teams, or quality circles, are new ways to get hourly workers involved in decisions that were formerly made only by management. To some extent, they are an improvement on the suggestion box. Some also consider them to be a substitute for a union — a constructive way for workers to communicate their ideas. Successful use of such teams requires a sensitive and fully supportive management as well as training, particularly for the team members. Because some companies have been highly successful in the use of such teams, this is a new management tool you may wish to investigate.

Management and leadership

What is the difference between management and leadership? The best supervisor or manager is also a good leader, though some bosses work in a management role without exhibiting much leadership. 'Management' is defined as the process of planning, budgeting, organizing, and controlling. All of these things are critical to the operation of a warehouse.

Effective leaders, however, continue the process. They set an agenda, build a network, create a vision, and assemble a team that shares that vision. Leadership is expected in top management, but it is needed at all levels of an organization. The best companies have true leaders at the supervisory level.

'Span of control' is the definition of how many people a single leader can supervise. We trace our ideas about span of control back to classical times. The Roman legion was divided into groups of one hundred (the *centuria*), subdivided into companies (*cohorts*), and then into 'handsful' (the *maniples*). A centurion (*centurio*) was in charge of the *centuria*. Today's army has fixed ideas about span of control, with people designed to command units from squads, platoons, and companies through increasingly large units and eventually to the Commander in Chief — the President.

From Roman times through today, the span of control for a military unit has been fixed by formula, without regard to the job being done. This rigid thinking has carried over into many industries, including warehousing. Most of us, without knowing why, have fixed ideas about span of control. It is not unusual to hear a manager say that a well-organized warehouse needs a supervisor for every eight workers, or perhaps one for every twenty or thirty. If the supervisor has more people, he or she is *spread too thin.*

Bureaucratic organizations produce results that are irrelevant in today's business environment. These include the following:

- Over-specialization of jobs. The contemporary warehouse functions best with workers who are able to do any job in the operation. Those whose abilities limit them to one task will always be less valuable.

- Over-dependence on supervisors. As warehousing has developed from small storehouses into huge distribution centers, managers have recognized the inability to closely supervise each worker.

- A commitment to maintenance of the *status quo.* Bureaucrats look for the pre-conceived solution that comes closest to solving a problem. They are not expected to be innovative or to find the best solution — only to find a solution. At a time when warehousing is in a state of unprecedented change, this is not a healthy attitude. Few would argue that the manager must look to the future rather than the past.

- Under-valuing of human resources. The bureaucratic approach tends to depersonalize workers and rely on technical solutions. The individual becomes a cog in the machine. This has been less true in warehousing, perhaps because the work tends to defy automation efforts.

When you think about the nature of work in a distribution center today, the fallacy of the bureaucratic method becomes clear. If the job of a warehouse worker is to put away receipts and select orders in a warehouse of 300,000 square feet, and the forklift-equipped worker roams throughout the warehouse, how can any supervisor oversee the activity? In today's distribution center, the traditional notion of an overseer is absurd. A supervisor can check results, but cannot physically inspect the work as it is done. The landscape is too large, and the work too varied.

Questions that solve problems

As you appraise the management productivity in your warehousing organization, here are the questions you should ask the people who are on your warehouse management team:

Q What is the employment turnover in our warehouses?
C If the turnover is higher than in previous years, why has it increased? Inability to retain people is a sign of ineffective management.

Q How many grievances or complaints are registered each year, and how does that number relate to total employment?
C Substantial unhappiness in the workforce may be a symptom of weak management, but this figure must always be a ratio between the number of stated complaints and the number of people.

Q How much time do our people spend in meetings, and how do they feel about those meetings?
C Quality as well as quantity must be measured in assessing the value of company meetings.

Q Are the hourly employees satisfied with the level of feedback they receive on their performance?
C Getting the answers to this question will not be easy, and random interviews may be the most practical way to gauge feedback effectiveness.

Q What is the current span of control for managers and supervisors, and how has it changed in the past five years?
C In most organizations today, the span of control is broadened by improved leadership and more effective communications. ❖

Chapter 16

Training for excellence

Training may be the most important activity in warehousing. Teaching and training are critical to the survival of any business. Some companies, particularly small ones, fail because no new managers are ever trained. Because those who run the company never take the time to teach younger people to carry on when they retire, there is no one to succeed them.

Whether your warehouse is big or small, never neglect training. What happens when an office employee handling an important account is removed from the scene by unexpected illness? Does anyone else know how to get the job done? The obvious answer is cross-training, insuring that every employee knows at least one other person's job. Many pay lip service to cross-training, but not enough firms actually do it.

One rental car company claims that every manager spends at least one day per year behind the counter dealing with the customers. How many warehouse managers spend a day driving a forklift truck or serving as a customer service representative?

Training goals

Training should not be a pep rally. Workers don't need a cheerleader to shout instructions and wish them luck. They need a partner who works beside them as they go through the process of learning to do jobs that are new to them.

As you look at training programs, consider your goals. Why are we conducting the training program? What results do we expect to get from it? How will we gauge the success or failure of the participants? In other words, how will we give grades? Will those who fail the training course be dismissed, reassigned, or given additional training? Who will be trained and when?

Orientation

Some companies do little more for the new employee than explain who the boss is and where the restroom is located. Since every new employee will be 'filled-in' on the company by somebody, management should see that this orientation is directed by somebody knowledgeable. Orientation is often best provided by the supervisor. This allows new employees the chance to become acquainted with their supervisors, and it establishes them as the best source of information about the job and the company.

In nearly every organization there are three sources of information on how the company operates: the supervisor, the shop steward, and the *grapevines*. Because these information sources are competitive, any evidence of unreliability will discredit that source. If employees are to accept supervisors as the best information sources, they must be most supportive, well-informed, and honest.

First impressions

The most vivid impression that a new employee gets of the company is the one received during the first day on the job. First impressions are made only once. What impression does your company make to a new worker on the first day?

Orientation programs are neglected in many warehouses. Altogether too many companies simply hand new workers the company rule book, show them the time clock, and start them on the job. A 'bull of the woods' foreman may show authority by giving new workers the toughest or dirtiest jobs in the warehouse. Others may over-orient by drowning new employees in more information than they can possibly absorb.

The goal of an orientation program is to make newcomers feel welcome and to communicate your expectations. Here are some features that should be part of every orientation program:

◆ Introduce the company. Tell about the history, the goals and objectives of the organization, and explain the corporate credo.

◆ Describe all company benefits. While this may have been done in the interview process, it should be repeated to be sure that there is a total understanding.

◆ Give a positive introduction to fellow workers. This is a two-way street, and members of a work team should be strongly encouraged to welcome each new worker.

◆ Provide a complete tour. Your goal should be to provide information about everything that goes on in the facility.

◆ Demonstrate your confidence. The orientation is a chance for you to let new employees know that you are confident that they will be successful. The first day on a job is always accompanied by some anxiety, so the orientation should do everything possible to reduce it.

Done correctly, the orientation program creates a positive image that should inspire loyalty and good will. These will last far beyond the opening day and can be the foundation on which you develop effective employees.

Mentoring

Mentoring pairs a new employee with an experienced one as a tutor. The mentor is a leader who is completely familiar with company policies, but is also a recognized *people person*. Each mentor works with only one new employee at a time.

Formal mentoring programs follow a six-month schedule during which the mentor visits the *pupil* every two weeks for three months, then once per month for three months. This formal schedule should not prohibit *informal* visits at any time, since the chance to ask questions on a random basis is an important feature of the program.

Confidentiality between employee and mentor is essential. The role of the mentor is to give advice on company procedures, but to provide personal advice only when asked.

Mentoring is a time-consuming process. It requires frequent interaction with the employee and could result in a short-term drop in productivity. If mentoring is not available to all employees, it could also cause resentment among those not chosen to participate.

Training lift truck operators

Although some employers think no training is necessary, no one is born with the skill to operate a lift truck. Materials handling equipment dealers are required by federal safety regulations to offer training courses. Some of these courses are better than others, and the best have a training center that includes a classroom, audio visual materials, provisions for testing, and a realistic obstacle course. The best training schools are run as a profit center, and the trainer is there to teach safe, productive operation — not to promote a brand of equipment sold by the dealership.

Some trainers offer to hold the course at the customer's facility, using the customer's lift trucks. Classroom learning is confirmed with a tough written test, and some training programs also use an interactive video with an examination.

Trainers emphasize that people on lift trucks are *operators*, not *drivers*. Many feel that operating a lift truck is something like driving a car, but training sessions point out the significant differences between the industrial truck and a highway vehicle.

The training course should include four areas. The first is classroom training, using lectures and video to provide information on safety and proper operation of the truck. The second instructional area is done at the truck, teaching each operator to perform the daily maintenance and safety checks before turning on the motor. The third phase of instruction is actual operation of the truck, moving it through an obstacle course, designed to test both safety and productivity. The fourth phase is documentation through classroom testing and skill tests. Scores are given for both the obstacle course and written tests, and trainers deny a certificate to those who do not earn a passing score.

Accidents are emphasized, both their causes and how they can be prevented. Daydreaming is the primary cause of lift truck accidents. The second most common cause is failure of the operator to sense a potential collision when the mast is extended. Most courses emphasize the operation of conventional forklift trucks, and additional or supplemental training may be needed for specialized trucks.

Every lift truck operator, regardless of experience, should be required to take such a course before being allowed to operate power equipment. Some feel that experienced operators should also take regular refresher courses.

Retraining for new equipment

Many warehouses are changing from forklift and pallet handling to slip-sheets or other palletless handling methods. This transition represents a specific example of how a warehouse training program can function.

Since the handling maneuvers for a truck equipped with either a carton clamp or push-pull attachment are more complex than the conventional forklift, your operator must learn new skills. Furthermore, the probability of hiring people who already possess these skills is slim since specialized attachments are used less frequently than forks.

When palletless handling is introduced to a warehouse, workers may react to the change with fear or uncertainty. The key to a successful training program is the positive motivation of the workers whose skills are needed to implement the new system.

One grocery products warehouseman has devised a simple method to help individuals train themselves in slipsheet handling. A worker takes a stack of eight or ten pallets and uses them as a dummy load. The stack of pallets is placed on top of a slipsheet, and drivers practice picking up and pushing off this load until they gain confidence in controlling the equipment.

The same technique also is used to train the lift driver to handle unit loads high in a stack where visibility is marginal. Using a stack of pallets instead of a real load of merchandise enables the operator to practice with little danger of property damage.

Improving your training

The business of warehousing has always required skilled and dedicated people. In the past, many warehouse operators hoped or believed that someone else would do the training for them. Because they worked under this assumption, many warehouses employed people who had no skills initially and who were able to acquire skills only on the job. At times the cost of this was enormous, particularly if there was a serious accident during the 'training'.

Today people with no opportunity to acquire experience are seeking warehouse jobs. A notable example is female workers, who were almost unknown in warehouses until a few years ago. Many operators have found that female warehouse workers provide superior skills with a very low incidence of accidents.

Warehouse managers have discovered that a good training program for unskilled employees creates operators who do not have to 'unlearn' bad habits acquired in a previous job. The resulting workers are often better motivated and more effective than those who have claimed to have warehousing experience from previous jobs.

Training takes time, and not everyone will be successfully trained. However, a key dividend for a successful training program is that it allows unskilled employees to become effective warehouse operators.

Questions that solve problems

Find new employees — for example, a forklift operator who has been with the company for thirty days or less — and then ask these questions:

Q When you spent your first day on the job with us, what activities took place?

C The answer should include a description of an orientation program. Any response that is either negative or noncommittal suggests either that no orientation exists or that it doesn't have the required impact.

Q Where did you learn to operate a lift truck?

C If the respondent doesn't mention any training offered by your company, you may want to probe further to see whether the employee has received any training since joining your workforce.

Q Do you have any questions about the company that were not covered in your training and orientation programs?

C Ask this regardless of the answers to earlier questions, since it is always advisable to get this kind of feedback from everyone in the workforce.

Q What have you learned working with us that you never had any experience with before?

C The answers will reveal the unique characteristics of jobs with your company and could spotlight the needs for more intensive training.

If the answers to these questions suggest that orientation and training are making little or no impact, it's clear that you have a significant need for change. ❖

Chapter 17

Motivation, discipline, and continuous improvement

Maintaining morale when conditions are turbulent is difficult. If your company or your competitors have endured a financial crisis or a marketing catastrophe, everyone will worry about side effects. Yet the success of any warehouse depends upon the motivation and discipline of the people who work in it. What can you do to build the highest quality team in your industry?

New approaches to work

In a tight labor market, new approaches to work allow employers to attract the best people. Because commuting is a problem in many urban areas, some warehouse managers have modified shifts to begin and end at unconventional hours to avoid traffic delays.

One warehouse attracts the best people in its community by offering a four-day work week with three days off. Longer work days allow each worker to have the same total work hours, but the four-day work week is so popular that the best workers in town seek employment at that warehouse.

Telecommuting is a creative solution to the travel problem for some office workers. Advances in both information processing and communications equipment now make it possible for some people to do office jobs by using computers, modems, and fax machines in their homes.

Some warehouse jobs can be handled by people with physical handicaps. One warehouse has used deaf mute workers for order picking with considerable success. Some warehouse tasks can be performed by people with other disabilities. By tapping the ranks of the handicapped, you may discover workers who try harder because they have a strong motivation to succeed.

At a time when our population is aging, some warehousing companies have recognized the advantage of hiring retired people. One warehouse that distributes clothing uses workers up into their seventies. Absenteeism and turnover is far lower than with younger workers. One firm reports a two percent turnover of retired people as opposed to 70 percent in its younger workforce. The *over-60* segment of our population is now the fastest growing population group in the country, and it will be a growing part of the warehousing workforce.

With more women in the workforce, child care can be changed from a problem to an advantage. Company sponsored child care programs are rare today, but many more companies will provide the benefit to attract working mothers. Company sponsored day-care centers located close to the workplace are likely to be part of the future of many warehouses, especially the larger ones.

Motivate warehouse workers six ways

When the economy turns down or when companies reduce their workforce, everybody is concerned about maintaining or improving motivation of the remaining workers. If you face this challenge, here are six ways to improve the motivation of hourly workers.

Workers are members of your family

The best way to have a well-motivated warehouse crew is to treat that crew as part of the family.

In some firms, the office workers, production people, and the sales group are all respected citizens, but the people in the warehouse and on the shipping dock are considered to be a lower grade of employee. This happens without direction from management, and sometimes without management's knowledge. The effect on morale is devastating. Marketing people blame all customer complaints on the people in the warehouse, and the warehouse workers feel they get no respect from anyone else in the company. This attitude feeds on itself and, once established, it can be difficult to correct.

A large retail organization emphasizes the importance of its warehouse crew. By touring the warehouse frequently and periodically attending warehouse meetings, the chief executive sends a clear message that warehouse workers are as important to the company's success as any other group. By constantly reminding warehouse workers that they are key people on a successful team, the company maintains high morale in the warehouse.

Seek the best workers

Standards for hiring warehouse workers should be at least as high as those established for other departments. When *rejects* from other departments are reassigned to the warehouse, the effect on morale is severe. Skills needed for order picking are at least as great as those found in production work — and there is no excuse for suggesting that the warehouse will be a safe haven for incompetents.

In selecting warehouse employees, don't think about just the job opening; consider future promotion as well. One company uses two criteria in selecting employees:

- ◆ Do we know anyone who can do the job well?
- ◆ Do we know anyone for whom the job would be a good developmental assignment?

But it isn't just enough to just pick the best — it is equally important to pluck out bad apples. If you have someone in the warehouse who is not performing, or who shows evidence of substance abuse or a poor attitude, the mechanism must be in place to urge that person to shape up or get out. When management demands the highest standards, everyone on the team will recognize that only the best can stay. While some feel that this will lower morale, a selection process that emphasizes quality will raise spirits rather than lower them. Nobody likes to work next to a loser, and warehouse workers are no exception.

Measure and appraise

Conduct an appraisal interview at least once a year with everyone who reports to you. Keep this meeting separate from any review of compensation. The appraisal process is difficult, and some managers avoid it because they fear the delivery of negative feedback. Yet everyone needs to receive grades, and good managers give them — positive or negative.

When you hire workers, and at regular intervals, tell them what you expect and the criteria you will use to evaluate their performance. Recognize success when they meet your goals, but also point out the times when they fail. Regular feedback will avoid surprises and help everyone on the team to improve and develop. Those who cannot, or will not, meet the goals should not be surprised when you take the necessary action to remove them from the team. The performance appraisal should not be considered as a chance to reprimand an employee, but your chance to give a worker recognition and feedback.

Promotion from within is a constructive way to track success. Advancing from worker to supervisor is common in a warehouse yet it is not always successful. Sometimes star workers fall short as supervisors because they do not possess needed people-management skills. However, such skills can be taught, and it is worth the effort to provide leadership training.

Empower your employees

In the warehouse, each worker must be given the power to serve customers. This means that an hourly worker might have the right to work overtime to finish an order that is urgently needed by the customer. Management must back the decision even if it is occasionally made in error. While the consequence of an error might be some excess overtime pay, the consequence of rigidity may be an angry customer — or possibly a lost one.

Empowerment could mean that you involve workers in the planning process or even the pricing process. One public warehouse has a cost committee made up of hourly workers as well as supervisors. When a rate is calculated for a new customer, the cost committee is asked to estimate the time necessary to unload a typical inbound shipment or to ship an average order. The price is based on the committee's estimate, and the warehouse has achieved notable success in basing prices on these estimates.

Celebrate success with recognition and rewards

Developing incentive pay for warehouse workers is difficult. The constant variance in work content makes a fair incentive system virtually impossible. However, there are many informal ways to recognize a job well done.

The size of a reward is less important to workers than most managers think. Recognition is more important than the number of dollars involved, as is illustrated by one warehousing organization's suggestion system in which the maximum reward is $250. The whole program costs less than $10,000 per year, but the effect on workers is positive. This suggestion system emphasizes frequency of rewards rather than size, and people feel that management is listening because they receive a check and a letter of thanks.

Make supervisors coaches, not traffic cops

The good supervisor is a source of training and counseling. Workers need to bring their problems to a sympathetic leader, but they also need to feel that the supervisor will get something done. A person who dispenses 'tea and sympathy' without achieving any change will soon lose respect. At the same time, a foreman who drives, rather than leads, will experience heavy turnover as workers look for a job with less pressure and a happier environment.

Warehouse supervisors are in a delicate position — serving as a bridge between workers and management. The successful warehouse supervisor must have a good relationship with both those above and below. Communications with management must be clear and effective, and yet the supervisor must have the ability to listen to hourly workers and to support them.

Almost without exception, a well-motivated warehouse work crew is also led by outstanding supervisors.

As you re-examine your own warehouse operation, consider your ability to use the six steps outlined above to improve motivation in your workforce.

Maintaining warehouse discipline

Running a warehouse calls for superior management of people. A well-managed warehouse is also a well-disciplined warehouse, one in which people play by the rules because they know that to do otherwise will harm both the warehouse and their own jobs.

Because housekeeping, precise performance, and dependability are the hallmarks of a good warehouse, quality is closely related to discipline. When we see a warehouse that has products scattered throughout aisles and working areas, we quickly form the opinion that there is a lack of discipline.

A well-disciplined warehouse exhibits several features:

- ◆ Managers and workers cooperate in achieving housekeeping excellence.
- ◆ Errors and damage are minimized.
- ◆ When things are done wrong, workers receive feedback and encouragement to improve the quality.
- ◆ When new workers or outsiders drag down the operation, the rest of the warehouse crew pulls together to improve quality.

The best supervisors do not rely on punishment to control their workers. They know that positive reinforcement for *following* the rules is more effective than a negative response for *breaking* them. In a warehouse with good discipline, workers know what is expected of them. While rigid work standards may not be employed, there is a formal or informal understanding of what level of productivity is expected. Neither supervisors nor co-workers in a well-disciplined warehouse will tolerate an individual whose work is substandard. Procedures in a well-disciplined operation are clear, and everybody follows them. A warehouse procedure that is so complex that nobody can understand it is as bad as no procedure at all.

Warehouse discipline is not easy to define, yet experienced operators know it when they see it. When it is lacking, the signs are equally obvious.

Discipline by peer review

Traditional methods of disciplining employees sometimes foster an *us against them* mentality, which can create the perception that the company is not committed to resolving workplace disputes fairly.* Some employers deal with this by using a dispute resolution process known as *peer review.*

Peer review systems replace the traditional grievance arbitration process by allowing an employee to appeal disciplinary actions to a committee that includes co-workers. Normally, all disciplinary actions are subject to peer review, and the employee may challenge either the discipline itself or its severity. Some companies have narrowed the scope of their peer review system to cover only specified actions, such as involuntary terminations, overtime, or the proper application of a company's layoff procedure. Where peer review systems are limited in their coverage, companies usually maintain an *open door* for other review issues.

Generally, the peer review process begins when an employee lodges an appeal. Most companies require that employees initiate the process within five to seven days.

The employee's supervisor reviews the discipline and attempts to resolve the complaint. However, if the employee remains dissatisfied follow-

---

*   This subchapter is from an article by Theodore J. Tierney, *Warehousing Forum*, Volume 3, Number 4, ©Ackerman Company, Columbus, Ohio.

ing the supervisor's review, he or she may take the appeal to the peer review board.

Although the composition of the peer review board varies, a typical board is comprised of five members: the aggrieved employee selects two, the plant manager or personnel director selects two, and the four board members select the fifth.

The board convenes within a few days and the issue is presented in an informal, non-legal setting. The aggrieved employee and the supervisor present their side of the dispute to the board. The board may ask questions or call additional witnesses and, in addition, may review the employee's personnel records. Once the board has collected all the necessary information, the supervisor and the employee are asked to leave the room while the board deliberates.

In considering the employee's appeal, the board decides only whether there has been a violation of company policy. It is not empowered to change company policy. The board may uphold the discipline, reduce or increase its severity, or overturn the discipline entirely.

Majority rules and the board's decision is final in most companies, but some require a unanimous decision. If such a decision cannot be reached, a majority and minority report is given to the plant manager or personnel director, who then renders a final decision.

Upon arriving at a decision, the board immediately informs the supervisor and the employee. All aspects of the decision-making process remain confidential.

In companies that use some form of peer review, both employees and management comment upon it favorably. Employees are satisfied with peer review systems largely because such systems allow employees to participate in management decisions that have a direct effect on them.

Employers have found that board members take their responsibility seriously and do not abuse or undermine the process. In addition, employers recognize that peer review reduces employee discontent. Generally speaking, where discipline is imposed properly in the first place, employees hesitate to invoke their appeal rights under the peer review system. In fact, peers on the board are often harder on rule violators than management would be.

Summing up, peer review programs:
   ◆ Raise employee morale by providing employees with a voice
      in disciplinary matters directly affecting them, thus build-

ing a bridge between management and employees.

◆ Thwart attempts at unionization by removing a common source of employee discontent, the absence of employee participation in discipline.

◆ Reduce expensive litigation and arbitration.

◆ Support the company's position in any subsequent, related litigation, such as EEOC charges.

◆ Maintain company control over employee relations by keeping workplace disputes in-house.

Continuous improvement

No field of activity is more likely to change than the business of warehousing. A warehouse is a place that handles and stores products, and the products themselves are constantly changing. A high percentage of the articles we find in retail stores today did not exist twenty years ago, and those that will be sold twenty years from now are likely to change even more radically.

As products change, the packaging changes, and the storage and handling procedures must be altered.

Corporate and product growth is another stimulus for change. A distributor of fax machines needed a tiny warehouse in 1985, but a much larger facility in 1995. Product development and corporate development cause growth, and the growth requires bigger warehouses.

Sometimes this is accomplished by adding to existing buildings, and other times it requires a move to a new facility. Growth and movement are another form of change, and the change represents an opportunity for further improvement.

Today's intense commitment to quality is another stimulus for continuous improvement. No matter how good the quality is in your warehouse operation today, there are areas where it could be improved. Awareness of these improvement opportunities must be communicated throughout the organization.

Some hope to achieve continuous improvement by empowering the people who work in the warehouse. Empowerment means that everyone has a feeling of control over his work. This sense of control is a motivating factor and it includes these items: responsibility, trust, being listened to, working on a team, praise, recognition for ideas, direction, knowledge, support, resource availability, and communication both up and down.

Questions that solve problems

Test the willingness of the people who work in your warehouse to improve their commitment to the success of the company by asking questions as you tour the facility:

Q How frequently do our managers appraise the performance of their people?

C Answers should be carefully checked to be sure that the appraisals are really taking place and not just being planned.

Q How could we improve the warehouse layout?

Q How could we reduce the number of times each item is handled?

Q How could we improve scheduling?

Q How could we change or improve the way we measure performance in this warehouse?

Q How could we increase inventory turnover?

Q How could we reduce shipping errors?

Q How could we improve housekeeping?

Q How could we reduce damage?

We offer no comments on most of the questions. A wrong answer is certainly better than no answer, and creativity is as important as accuracy. Carefully noting the answers will tell you three things. First, it will give you some indication of how well motivated your people are and the degree to which they have an interest in improvement. Second, the answers will suggest ways in which your warehouse operation could be changed to improve its effectiveness. Third, they will demonstrate the creativity and leadership potential of your people. ❖

PART

4

Security

Chapter 18

Counting and reconciling

Why even take physical inventories? An obvious answer lies in the impact that inventory has on the corporate financial statement. Finance people are concerned about accountability, and public accountants are retained to verify the accountants' work. The fact that physical inventories are needed results from our failure to receive, store, ship, and record inventory correctly.*

Annual physical inventories are similar to annual medical examinations because they provide an early warning about problems and may provide an opportunity to correct past errors. Considering the impact that physical inventories have on operations, they deserve more attention and emphasis than they sometimes receive. Inaccurate inventories can impair a company's ability to plan materials requirements and cause uncertainty in financial planning. Inaccurate inventories lead to lost sales, lower fill rates, and lost productivity.

How often should you take a physical inventory? Your auditors may influence this decision, but bear in mind that loss of assets is not the only loss suffered by the company when the physical inventory and the book inventory do not balance.**

---

* Part of this chapter is based on an article by W. G. Sheehan, in *Warehousing and Physical Distribution Productivity Report*, Volume 16, Number 11, ©Alexander Research and Communications, Inc., New York.

** From *Distribution Warehouse Cost Digest*, Volume 12, Number 18, ©Alexander Research and Communications, Inc., New York.

How can a *physical* be improved?

Have you measured the investment in resources you make each year to perform physical inventories? How much time is spent in planning, counting, re-counting, and reconciling? What would be the potential savings for a 10 percent to 20 percent reduction in the hours required for physical inventories? In many cases the savings can be substantial.

Neglect may be the biggest problem. Communications deteriorate among warehouse and office people. This is often compounded by inaccurate counting on the part of those who record the physical inventory. Too much is taken for granted, too many potential problems are overlooked, and too much time is spent 'fighting fires.' Counts are not accurate, and hence have to be redone. Counts are impossible to trace, including who did what, where, when, and how.

Each department or function in your company needs the inventory results but each has a different reason. Finance needs the numbers for accountability. Marketing needs them to be sure what is available to sell and ship. Everybody should be concerned about accuracy.

The primary purpose of the physical inventory is to determine the correct quantity and location of material in storage. Accuracy in the storage location system alone will provide tangible improvement in warehouse productivity.

Fiscal responsibility for stored goods is an inherent responsibility of the warehouse manager. In addition to confirming the accuracy of inbound and outbound shipments, completing a reliable physical inventory is a measure of management's success in protecting stored merchandise.

For reliable results, conduct two separate and independent counts. Reconciliation of these two counts is paramount in proving the reliability of the physical inventory. Schedule the count when you will have time to verify it. When the warehouse manager can be completely sure a physical count is reliable, subsequent reconciliations with the book inventory are more credible. To be sure the counts are truly independent, no employee should count the same goods in both inventories.

Efficiency in inventories is achieved by minimizing resources required. Not only do we want an accurate count, but we also want the inventory completed in the minimum time.

Incentives

How can efficiency and effectiveness be combined? One way is to use an incentive system. Achieving a balance between effectiveness and efficiency is essential. There is little to be gained by rushing through a physical count, only to find so many errors that re-counts are excessive. Nor is it sensible for the counters to take so much care ensuring a precise count that the process becomes extremely time-consuming.

To achieve the proper balance, establish a goal for the maximum percentage re-counts or third counts. While this goal will fluctuate, 98 percent accuracy between the first two counts is realistic — Meaning two percent or fewer re-counts. Considering number of working hours invested in a physical inventory, rewards or incentive pay are reasonable for those who meet quantity and quality goals.

One warehouse incentive program provided money prizes to each member of the team that counted the most items or turned in the greatest number of inventory tickets. Another prize went to team members who achieved the most accurate count. One criterion, however, was that the winners in each category had to rank in the upper third in the other category. The team that counted the most tickets also had to have a reasonable level of accuracy, with the most accurate team also having to achieve a high level of productivity.

Achieving efficiency and effectiveness through motivation assures the reliability necessary for the reconciliation process. Reducing the number of third counts can materially reduce the hours devoted to the inventory-taking process.

Planning for physical inventories

An efficient physical inventory starts weeks before the actual inventory date. The first step is to assign an inventory coordinator for each of the physical inventories to be conducted. This appointment pinpoints responsibility and establishes a sole source for information flow. An annual wall calendar marked with inventory dates is helpful.

Get rid of obsolete items, waste, or excess material before the physical inventory. About two weeks before the inventory date, bring key personnel together to discuss responsibilities, availability of workers, equipment requirements, and supplies required.

Decide whether the inventory should be pre-tagged or tagged during the first count. Some computer systems can produce inventory tags pre-printed by location. Consider filling out inventory tickets in advance, omitting only the quantity. Damaged goods and items in the repack area should be counted in advance. Employees must be taught or reminded how to fill out tags and whom to contact regarding problems with the tags.

The importance of a cutoff date

A cutoff date for receipts and shipments must be established for an accurate reconciliation after the physical count has been completed. Certain areas should not included in the actual physical inventory: Material received after the cutoff date, or shown on the inventory records as shipped, even though it has not left the shipping dock, for example. Documents for this merchandise should be specially marked so they will be omitted.

Establish inventory zones

A useful technique zones the warehouse into sections that require similar amounts of time to count. The coordinator than assigns teams to each section. Once the planning is complete, the coordinator should conduct a briefing to highlight difficult-to-count items, potentially confusing product codes, or other unique identification problems. Have examples of such items available for everyone to see before starting a count. The briefing should cover special requirements, team assignments, designated zones, pallet patterns, the time schedule and how the tickets are to be filled out.

Arithmetic aids

If bar code readers cannot be used, encourage your warehouse personnel to use hand-held calculators. Issue guidelines on how and when counters should make calculations. Don't allow them to write numbers on the carton or, worse yet, on the inventory ticket. If they do, it becomes impossible to ensure the independence of later physical counts. Provide inventory teams with scratch paper and have them make calculations on the back of the ticket that is turned in. Keeping these calculations assists in providing an audit trail when reconciling discrepancies.

Controlling the count

Having a supervisor present during the count helps ensure an effective and efficient inventory. This individual should constantly spot-check procedures, read inventory tickets to see they have been properly filled out, and sample some counts for accuracy.

Proper control of inventory tickets is an absolute necessity. This control begins with each inventory ticket having a unique serial number. The tickets should be handed out in sequence, according to zones, and should be placed on the product, also in sequence, so that an audit trail is maintained.

This expedites third counts, since the counter will know precisely where to find the inventory ticket in question. The coordinator must ensure that inventory teams turn in all tickets, then verify that every ticket is accounted for at the conclusion of the inventory.

Reconciliation

The end of the count is not the end of the inventory because inventory is not complete until all counts have been reconciled and inventory records updated.

An important last step of inventory-taking is a review among team leaders, including representatives from the warehouse and office, that allows participants to cover problem areas and to solicit suggestions for improving future inventories.

Notes should be kept concerning the number of hours required for the inventory, the number of workers needed, the equipment used, the items counted, and the quantities of merchandise involved. This information is useful in planning for the next inventory. You can also use this review to recognize effective performance.

Cycle counting eliminates inventory errors

The goal of every warehouse and distribution center manager is inventory accuracy.* The best way to achieve this is to count a small percentage of the inventory on a regular basis. This sample of the total inventory can be compared easily to the inventory records. Since you are continually counting, when errors are identified you can define the cause of the error and take corrective action. This process of regular cycle counts, reconciling with the inventory records, identifying and correcting these errors, is called cycle counting.

It is important to realize that the immediate objective of cycle counting is not accurate inventory, but the identification and elimination of errors. A by-product of identifying and eliminating errors will be an accurate inventory.

To respond to the question, 'What to count?' one must realize that this question is really two questions in one. The first question is, 'How often should an item be counted?' and the second is, 'When should each specific item be counted?'

The answer to the first question lies in Pareto's Law (the 80/20 rule), or the A-B-C Concept:

- ◆ Approximately 80 percent of a warehouse's dollar through-put is typically attributed to 20 percent of the stockkeeping units (A items).
- ◆ Approximately 15 percent of a warehouse's dollar through-put is typically attributed to 40 percent of the stockkeeping units (B items).
- ◆ Approximately 5 percent of a warehouse's dollar throughput is typically attributed to 40 percent of the stockkeeping units (C items).

The obvious cycle counting application of this rule is that the A items should be counted more frequently than the B items, and the B items more frequently than the C items. A typical scenario would involve counting six percent of the A items, four percent of the B items, and two percent of the C

---

*   This subchapter is by James A. Tompkins, Ph.D., Tompkins Associates, Inc., Raleigh, North Carolina.

items each week.

The second question, 'When should each specific item be counted?' is relatively straightforward. An item should be counted when it is easiest and cheapest to get the most accurate count. When is this?

- When an item is reordered.
- When an inventory balance is zero or a negative quantity.
- When an order is received.
- When the inventory balance is low.

Thus, the answer to the question, 'What to count?' is that you should count on an A-B-C basis and count when counting is easy.

The number of people who should do cycle counts depends upon the quantity of items in inventory, the desired count frequency, the number of storage locations for each item, the number of count irregularities (such as number of recounts), accessibility of items, and physical characteristics of the items.

A realistic standard is that a cycle counter can count forty items per day. The cycle counters should be familiar with the stock location system, the warehouse layout, and the items being counted.

Cycle counters should be assigned to the job on a permanent basis, but this does not mean cycle counting is necessarily a full-time job. It does mean that the workers assigned to cycle counting should be part of a permanent team.

Cycle counters must recognize the probability of crossovers. When a count reveals an overage in one item, the counters should be able to identify and check those items that would normally be confused with the one that is not in balance.

Some auditors who are concerned with 'checks and balances' within a warehouse, believe that only people from outside the warehouse should be assigned full-time to cycle counting. In fact, true inventory management begins when management realizes that the job of maintaining accurate inventory is not that of auditors, but that of warehouse and distribution managers.

Having determined what to count and who should do the counting, management must answer the remaining question: 'What are the procedures for cycle counting?' Valid cutoff controls are critical because cycle counting should take place without affecting normal operations. This calls for careful coordination of counting and transaction processing. Any transaction that takes place after the inventory balance is reported and the actual count is made must be isolated so that an accurate inventory reconciliation takes place. This can be done in many ways:

- Record all inventory transactions and cycle counts in *real time.*
- Record the time when each location is counted and report transaction times.
- Coordinate transactions with the count process so counts are taken when transactions do not occur.
- Don't process any transaction for items scheduled to be counted until after the items are counted.

Once the cutoff controls have been set up, the next procedure is count documentation. The information that should initially be recorded on the cycle count document is:

- Part number.
- Part location.

The cycle counter should then record:

- Count quantity.
- Counter's name.
- Date and time of count.

The cycle counting document should then be forwarded to a reconciler, not be reconciled by the counter. Reconcilers should compare the cycle count to the inventory record and determine whether the count is valid. Validity is determined by compliance with a cycle count tolerance. Cycle count tolerance limits should be based on the value of the items being counted. For example, if a $1,500 item is counted, a cycle count of 490 is made, and this is reconciled against an inventory record of 500, it is clear that this is a bad count. But if a two-cent item is counted, a cycle count of 490 is made, and this is reconciled against an inventory record of 500, it is clear that this is a satisfactory count.

A typical count tolerance limit would be $50. That is, if the cycle count is within $50 of the inventory record, the count is acceptable. When a bad count occurs, the item should be re-counted. The re-count will determine whether the original count was bad and the item count is actually within the tolerance limit.

Whether the re-count variance is within the count tolerance limit or not, the reconciler should adjust the inventory record to agree with the verified re-count. If the variance of the re-count is outside the tolerance limits, further investigation is necessary.

The further investigation of a bad count is required to determine why the inventory record is incorrect. If the counted quantity is verified as less than the inventory record, there are two easily checked possibilities:

- An outstanding allocation of this item may have been filled without recording the transaction.
- A recently completed sales or production order may have been incorrectly subtracted from inventory.

If the variance shows that the count quantity is higher than the inventory record, replenishment orders should be checked to see if any product was received and not properly recorded, and recently completed sales or production orders should be checked for erroneous subtractions from the inventory records. It is important to recall that the objective of cycle counting is the *identification and elimination of errors*. Thus, the error investigation process is critical in cycle counting.

At the end of each month, prepare a cycle counting accuracy rating.

- Cycle Counting Accuracy = Good Counts / Total Counts

Some have questioned whether public accountants will accept a cycle count. The fact is that cycle counting was developed because of frequent and severe problems in the accuracy of traditional physical inventories. As cycle counting has matured, auditors have recognized that the procedure is far superior to the traditional physical inventory.

What does the future hold?

Considering where we stand now with computer technology and automated systems, it is feasible to project where today's technology is leading. By using bar codes or optical character readers, management can make the job of taking physical inventories less difficult and less time-consuming, as well as more accurate.

If inventory changes can be recorded and records updated as goods are received, sold, or shipped, then it is natural to anticipate an automated physical inventory system.

Product codes or item identifications can be input to computers through the 'wand' or readers now being used with several distribution systems. With portable keyboard/wand equipment, it is possible to input an accurate count either manually or on the basis of a standard unit-load program.

Questions that solve problems

If you aren't sure about the security of your warehouse inventories, here are some questions you might ask of your warehouse manager, your public accountants, or both.

Q What procedure have we followed in the past three years to verify the accuracy of the book inventories in our warehouse? How have we counted, how often, and what have the results shown?

Q To what extent could we use a cycle count to replace full physical inventories?

Q Is our inventory accuracy better or worse than it was five years ago? How and why did this happen?

The answers could highlight grave problems. Failure to control warehouse inventories is virtually equal to losing control of the warehouse. A warehouse management team that consistently loses control of the inventory is probably a team that should be replaced. Because of the critical nature of inventory control, management must ask questions such as these on a regular basis. ❖

Chapter 19

Theft and mysterious disappearance

Any product that moves through warehouses could be stolen, but those products most likely to attract thieves are either valuable, easily marketable, or both. A less common target is merchandise that is of great value but not easily sold, or readily sold but of low value. Thieves consider marketability more important than value.

Some commodities have changed in their attractiveness to thieves. Once computers were valuable but difficult to sell. Today the cost per-cubic-foot of computer product has gone down, but the marketability increased dramatically. Law enforcement officials or your insurance company can tell you which products are frequently stolen.

Some warehouse operators apply selective security standards, using the highest security measures for those products most attractive to thieves.

Responsibilities of the warehouse operator

The manager of a private warehouse is ultimately responsible for the security of everything stored in the building. For the third-party warehouse operator, responsibility is limited by the Uniform Commercial Code. By law, a third-party bailee is responsible only for the degree of care that a prudent owner would exercise. If you own goods stored in a public warehouse, your own insurance coverage should provide primary protection because the third-party operator is liable only when security measures are proven to be lax.

Two kinds of losses and two deterrents

Thefts from warehouses can be broadly categorized into two types. The first is a mass theft that could involve either a truck hijacking or a warehouse break-in. The second is pilferage, or *mysterious disappearance.*

Mysterious disappearance may involve collusion between truck drivers and warehouse employees to overload when shipping or to receive less than the full quantity of merchandise on an in-bound vehicle. Other pilferage involves the clandestine removal of small amounts of merchandise over an extended period of time. Small products of high value may be taken out in lunch boxes, handbags, or pockets — or they may be put into a trash barrel or other outdoor location for removal at a later time.

There are two ways to defend against theft and pilferage. The first is to develop physical deterrents in the warehouse that make it difficult for thieves to breach the security of the building and remove products. The second defense requires that you confirm the honesty of all employees.

Hiring honest people

Since the most elaborate physical protective devices can be defeated by dishonest workers, the only way to control pilferage is to hire only honest workers. In the United States a Federal law now prohibits most businesses from using polygraphs as a pre-employment screening tool. Popularly known as the *lie detector*, the polygraph is a device that measures changes in bodily functions to help determine if a person is lying. To replace the polygraph, some companies sell honesty tests for employee screening purposes.

The best honesty tests have two categories of questions: The first looks primarily at the applicant's *attitudes* toward honesty by asking direct questions about possible illegal activities. The second is a broader test of *personality.* These look at a wide range of work behaviors.

The evaluation of the multiple-choice responses is designed to detect whether a respondent has answered questions truthfully. The tests try to detect potential thieves and other dishonest people with a combination of subtle and not-so-subtle questions. The most direct questions simply ask the respondent if he or she has stolen from an employer in the past. Surprisingly, many people describe stealing not as a confession but as a description of behavior that they believe to be perfectly acceptable.

Other questions are designed to discover attitudes that are found in a person who is likely to steal. For example, a dishonest person often believes the whole world is dishonest. While the tests vary in length, they normally take no longer than one hour to complete.

The critical features of any employment test are validity, legality, implementation, and cost.

Is it valid?

On a written test, each question is thoroughly studied for its predictive ability by both in-house and third-party groups. The in-house studies, those performed by the test companies themselves, report excellent validity figures, but some academics have expressed concern that the tests may give false indications on any given individual. Others point out that the polygraph isn't perfect either.

Honesty tests may reject a few employees who are honest, and they may fail to screen out a few dishonest employees. However, the number of times that this happens is small. The testing companies' literature suggests that the tests cannot *with certainty* predict the behavior of every applicant, but that over a range of applicants the validity is extremely high.

Studies have also been conducted to determine whether applicants could fake their way through the test. The results show that even when test groups deliberately give fake responses, the high validity of the tests is still maintained.

Clearly the tests are not foolproof as an employee screening method. They should not be used as an absolute or stand-alone screening tool, but rather in conjunction with other screening methods. Personal interviews, drug screening, reference checks, and background investigations all have a place. Used in this manner, employers can benefit from the information the tests provide while using other means to discover the errors that may exist in a specific test.

Electronic security

Electronic alarm systems are more reliable than a watchman, but it is important to remember that any system designed by one human can be overcome by another — especially if the theft ring includes a former employee of an alarm company. Furthermore, some alarm companies use outside electricians as sub-contractors to install equipment. While the alarm company may have honest employees, the subcontractor may not. One dishonest electrician can defeat most systems.

However, it's harder to defeat the increasing sophistication of newer electronic monitors. Closed-circuit television cameras, when combined with videotape recorders, give a reviewable record of any occurrence seen by the camera.

Television is sometimes used primarily as a psychological deterrent. However, it also can aid in both detecting theft and convicting those involved. The TV system may be activated by the opening of a dock door, or by motion sensors, so the recorder operates only when people are present. Such systems can be set to monitor the facility evenings or weekends when the warehouse is closed, and security personnel can review the tape at high-speed later. False alarms are one drawback of any electronic burglar alarm. An overly sensitive system reporting directly to police can send so many false alarms that it quickly becomes a nuisance. While law enforcement officials encourage electronic alarms, they naturally want to minimize false alarms and some cities fine alarm users whose systems transmit more than a few false alarms per year.

The most sensitive electronic systems are likely to send the most false alarms. Heading the list are ultrasonic systems designed to detect movement and those sensors that are triggered by sound. For warehouses located in or near railroad yards, the normal switching of freight cars may be sufficient to trip a sonic alarm, and the vibration can set off a motion sensor. Some warehouses have an interior rail dock that is accessible to railroad crews who switch cars at night. Under these conditions, use of ultrasonic alarms is difficult, if not impossible.

The cheapest electronic alarms protect only windows and doors. This system will not stop a thief who is willing to cut through a warehouse wall. The walls of modern warehouses are usually not load bearing, and whether they are constructed of masonry, concrete, or metal, a thief will need little time to cut a hole in the wall sufficient to allow a mass theft.

In one such case, thieves backed a rental truck up to a wall of the warehouse. Working from inside the van, they removed concrete blocks from the exterior wall to gain entry, and then removed the highest-value product in the building.

Because of the vulnerability of warehouse walls, the best electronic alarms include a *wall of light* surrounding the storage areas. The thief who successfully penetrates an exterior wall will still sound an alarm when entering the storage areas.

Skylights and roofs are also easily entered, primarily because of the light-weight materials used in modern construction. Protecting an entire roof with electronic beams is not practical, but thieves know it is equally impractical to take out any significant volume of products through the roof.

One compromise involves installing sectional alarms that provide one standard of security for inventory of normal value, and a higher standard of security for areas where high-value items are stored. Ultrasonic systems may be practical in an isolated room designed for a small portion of the inventory.

Fire codes in most communities require many pedestrian safety exits along the walls of the warehouse. Since such doors can also make it easier to pilfer merchandise, there should be alarms on each emergency door.

Undercover investigation

Certain kinds of criminal activity cannot be detected by electronics. While most warehouses have extensive electronic security that will effectively prevent burglary, the efficiency of these alarms tends to mask the fact that the most serious warehouse thefts may occur through collusion, embezzlement, or fraud. Using an investigator is a proven way to detect such activity. This topic is covered in the next chapter.

Cargo seals

A seal is a thin serial-numbered metal strip that must be broken to gain access to stored goods. On well designed seals, the break is obvious and cannot be repaired. Properly used, the seal is a physical deterrent to cargo theft. Because theft from interstate commerce may be investigated by the FBI, the mere presence of a seal on a boxcar was for years sufficient to discourage unauthorized entry. More recently, however, bolder thieves have attacked the boxcars themselves.

If a boxcar is broken into while at the shipper's or receiver's plant, the railroad has a legal right to disclaim responsibility because the car was not under its control. For this reason, the use of an inside rail dock may be the only means of protecting against theft from a railroad car. A parked truck-trailer presents similar problems, and electronic alarm systems that extend coverage to trailers parked on your property are available.

While seals are not as effective as they once were as a deterrent, they at least provide a visible means to identify tampering. To use seals effectively, you must have control procedures as well as good communication between shipper and receiver. Never allow seals either to be applied or removed by unauthorized personnel, or in any manner that varies from the established procedure.

Restricted access

Only warehouse employees should have access to storage areas. Bank customers aren't offended by barriers that prohibit them from walking behind the counters where the money is stored and warehouse users should not be offended if their movement is restricted in the same manner. Even warehouse employees should be authorized to enter only those areas involved in their own work.

Despite this common-sense approach, many warehouses have no physical restriction to prevent people from wandering at will. Some warehouses don't prevent visiting truck drivers from walking or loitering in storage areas. Posting signs or painting stripes may not be good enough — fencing, cages, or counters can be used to prevent unauthorized persons from entering storage areas.

One way to reduce losses of highly vulnerable products is to place them on the upper levels of storage racks where they can be removed only by a trained lift-truck operator. Denying access to the unauthorized improves security as well as storage productivity.

Procedures to promote security

Personnel policies should be structured to encourage honesty. Establishing a strict policy on the acceptance of gifts is one example. If truckers obtain a convenient unloading appointment by making a 'gift' to your receiving clerk, the moral atmosphere that encourages pilferage is also likely to be present.

Honest workers and good security systems can be overcome by creative outside thieves, so strict adherence to security procedures must be carefully enforced. For example, if only foremen are to break and apply seals, you must have a system that shows which foreman performed the task.

Every empty container is a potential repository for stolen merchandise. An empty trailer left at a dock could be the staging area for a theft. The same is true of empty boxcars, and even trash hoppers. One approach is to restrict access to such containers. Empty freight vehicles should either be kept under seal, or inspected as they leave the warehouse. Furthermore, this inspection should be covered by a written record that it took place.

Control of documents is as important as control of freight. Fraudulent parcel labels or bills of lading can be used to divert shipments. Supervise the issuing of labels and shipping documents.

Many warehouse crews break for lunch or coffee at the same time, with no one available to inspect exposed docks or entrance doors. It's a good idea to stagger rest breaks, with a few individuals always on duty to protect against unauthorized entry.

Customer pick-ups and returns

Customer pick-ups create an unusual theft risk. One way to control this risk is to have merchandise for pick-up pulled from stock by one individual, with delivery to the customer made by a different worker. This procedure is based on the fact that usually only two people are involved in collusion thefts.

Customer returns present a different security problem — particularly if the merchandise is returned in high volume or in non-standard cartons. Be sure all customer returns are checked thoroughly and promptly. If your re-turned-goods processing is not current, you're inviting pilferage.

Perimeter security

Warehouse security starts with the outside perimeter fencing, lighting, park-ing, and grounds; then it works inward to the office, platform, paperwork, and the products you store in the warehouse.*

No one should park personal vehicles near the buildings or loading doors. As managers walk from their cars to the office, they should inspect

---

*   Adapted from an article by Dick Atlas, E.J. Brooks Company, *Warehousing Forum*, Volume 5, Number 3, ©The Ackerman Company, Columbus, Ohio.

the perimeters of the operation. The exercise will do you and your people good, and will reveal areas of theft potential.

Never permit vehicles to back into any slot unannounced. If the incoming vehicle is sealed, have the designated supervisor witness the breaking and examination of the seal in the yard prior to assigning a receiving bay. Retain all seals until the unloading is verified, and then make sure they are disposed of and mutilated so that they cannot be re-used. Never allow broken seals to be discarded in your yard.

Receiving

Receiving procedures should differ from shipping procedures. Make sure your company provides coin telephone access for drivers. Never allow drivers to walk onto the platform past other vehicles being loaded or unloaded. All unused docks should have their doors pulled down when not in use, including summer months.

The receiving area is as vulnerable to theft as the shipping area. Keep all incoming truck doors closed and sealed until proper personnel are assigned and available to receive the load. No other employees or outside drivers should be allowed on the receiving platform during lunch or break periods.

Security audits

Management must actively combat theft, focusing on the three aspects of defense: physical, personnel, and procedural. No one of the three will be effective without the other two, and a 'Maginot Line' complex can be as fatal in warehouse security as it was in military history. The greatest enemy of security is complacency. An outside security audit is a good way to guard against such complacency.

A periodic spot check of outbound truck shipments may be the best way to impress both warehouse employees and truck drivers with your vigilance. Under this audit procedure, perhaps one truckload per month leaving the warehouse is stopped, returned to the dock and thoroughly recounted to check loading accuracy. Common carrier management will cooperate with such a procedure when its purpose is understood, and you demonstrate to employees that you are serious about discovering any 'errors' that could cause mysterious disappearance.

Questions that solve problems

Few managers care to admit that there is a theft or pilferage problem, even when there is evidence that it exists. Therefore, your questioning of warehouse managers in this area must be particularly incisive to maintain management interest in security. Here are some questions you should ask:

Q Do we have any problem with theft or security? What evidence do you have to support your answer?

C Be sure the answer is supported with facts to support inventory accuracy.

Q How do we know that the most recent employees brought into the warehouse are honest?

C The answer will tell about the state of current security checks.

Q When did we last take any steps to audit our security system, either through investigators or some other kind of audit procedure?

C If nothing has been done lately, consider ordering a security audit.

Q Have we investigated new sources for security audits and investigation of prospective employees?

C The answer will tell about management interest in loss prevention.

Q When did we last run a test on our alarm system to be sure that the police are responding properly?

C This answer is also a measure of management interest.

Whether or not your line management is creative in looking for theft and disappearance problems, it is important for you to search constantly for new ways to protect the inventory in your care, either through better alarm systems, improved perimeter security, or procedures to hire honest people and discover those who are not honest. ❖

Chapter 20

Protecting the people

Although some think warehousing involves the management of *things*, those who know the field recognize that management of things is secondary to the management of *people*. A warehouse is only as good as its worst employee, so a good warehouse must be more than a building and equipment. It must be a *greenhouse* that grows the highest quality people. Workers cultivated in the best warehouses are healthy as well as honest. They have a high sense of ethics, which comes from examples set at the top. They not only *are* good, but they also *look* good.

Personal appearance – the key to housekeeping

Housekeeping is one of the top indicators used by people who judge quality of warehouses. Most discussions of housekeeping refer to neat stacks, clean floors, and clear aisles, but they overlook the importance of the personal appearance of workers. Do your people have the appearance of professionals?

One way to control appearance is to issue uniforms to everybody working in the warehouse. Uniforms may be less acceptable in our culture than in other parts of the world. Because Americans are individualists, some feel stifled by a requirement to wear a uniform. Others feel uniforms are a divider, since the hourly people wear uniforms and the managers wear civilian clothes.

One way to solve this problem is to issue uniforms to everyone in the company. In a some firms, everybody on the production floor wears a white shop coat. Members of management may have a business suit, but it is replaced by the uniform when they go to the factory floor.

Companies that use uniforms usually find that the economic value of the fringe benefit makes it desirable. The cost of company-provided industrial clothing is not high, and the supplier assumes responsibility for cleaning, alteration, repair and replacement. Some companies pay the entire cost of this service, while others have a cost sharing arrangement that passes some of the expense back to the employees.

Whether you have a uniform program or not, be sure to praise those workers who exhibit a professional appearance. Others who notice well-dressed workers garnering praise will get the message.

Safety

Injuries and accidents are expensive, whether they happen on or off the job. Because warehousing involves lifting, pushing, pulling and human interaction with power equipment, the potential for accidents in warehouses is high.

Most injured warehouse workers are not newcomers. A federal study shows that workers with five or more years' experience are more likely to be injured than those with less experience.* Those with one to five years' experience are second, and those with less than one month's experience have the least likelihood of injury. Apparently experience causes carelessness, which leads to injuries.

The same study shows that extreme fatigue may *not* be a factor in most accidents. Twenty-nine percent of accidents occur after only two to four hours on the job, and another twenty-three percent occur during the first two hours on the job. Only eight percent occur after eight or more hours in the workplace.

The most dangerous work in a warehouse is loading and unloading freight vehicles. Warehouses reporting the most accidents are wholesalers and retailers. Sixty-eight percent of all warehouse injuries are in these warehouses, as contrasted with only eight percent in warehouses devoted to transportation and public utilities. Presumably public warehousing is in this smaller category.

◆ Injuries are more frequent in larger warehouses. Those with eleven or more employees suffered 82 percent of injuries.

---

*   From *Injuries to Warehouse Workers*, by U.S. Bureau of Labor Statistics.

- Older workers are safer. 74 percent of injured workers were age 34 or younger.
- Though personal protective equipment will prevent injuries, the majority of warehouse workers do not wear such equipment. The most commonly used protectors are gloves and steel-toed safety shoes. Hard hats and goggles are less frequently used.
- While safety training is common, many workers never receive it. Training in proper manual lifting is the most popular, but only 28 percent of injured workers had received such training. Only 23 percent had received a forklift operator training course.

When workers were asked why accidents happen, 54 percent said factors other than workplace conditions were at fault. However, 22 percent felt that lack of space in the workplace was a factor. Some felt that working too fast or working in an awkward position was a contributing cause.

A common problem in warehouse safety is the stacking of corrugated boxes. Humidity in a warehouse can break down corrugated boxes and, if not well stabilized, they can collapse. Therefore, it is important to inspect high-piled merchandise for any sign of carton failure and to take down stacks before they fall.

Metal or plastic banding used to seal many types of containers is a common source of injuries. When this banding is cut it can fly back, causing serious lacerations or eye injuries that could be prevented by goggles and gloves. In addition, workers should stand to the side of the container, away from the banding, so they will not be hit if the banding flies. After the banding is cut, it should be disposed of so it doesn't trip someone or get tangled in a forklift.

More than nine percent of the industrial injury claims filed per year involve warehouse workers. The yearly workers compensation cost to insurance companies for lower back injuries alone is more than eleven billion dollars. This figure includes injuries in all work environments not just warehouses. The total yearly industrial injury cost in the United States is much higher. About 25 percent of all injuries, including non-warehouse environments, are related to manual handling.

If safety in the warehouse is not a top concern today, another look at these statistics should convince you that the warehouse environment is one in which injuries are likely to occur, and when they do, they will be expensive.

There are three ways to reduce the risk of manual handling tasks. These approaches involve the job itself, training workers, and employee selection.

The first option is to redesign the job so that the physical and mental demands can be safely met by the average worker.

The second approach to reducing job risk is to train workers in techniques that minimize task hazards. Training can be used to make the employee aware of the dangers associated with various tasks performed in a warehouse. At the very least, the idea that injury risk 'goes with the job' should be discarded. Show employees how to take the time and the precautions to perform a job safely. The effectiveness of the training can be measured by comparing injury rates after the program with those that existed before training started.

The third approach involves employee selection. Screen potential employees to exclude those individuals who cannot perform safely. Screening can involve physical fitness evaluations, strength and endurance tests, mobility tests, vision tests, and lower-back x-rays.

Reducing the injury risk of manual handling tasks should be viewed by the warehouse operator as an investment in worker safety, employee morale, reduced workers compensation costs, and increased productivity. Instead of protecting workers from hazards, put the emphasis on removing hazards from the workplace.

Preventing substance abuse

Over ten percent of the people in the workplace have some kind of substance abuse problem. Probably the most common illegal substance is marijuana, estimated at being used by over nine percent of workers. Certainly a higher number use alcohol, a legal substance that is sometimes abused. Abuse of prescription drugs is not uncommon, and use of cocaine and other hard drugs is a perennial problem.

Substance abuse problems are exacerbated when an employee steals to raise money to buy the abused substances. Some of these — alcohol, for example — are cheap and easy to obtain. Narcotics are quite expensive. The abuser who steals is likely to be addicted to one of the more expensive substances.

Warehouse workers operate motor vehicles from lift trucks to tractor-trailers. A mood-altering substance will create a hazard both for the operator and for fellow workers.

Effective customer service depends on maintaining a reasonably even disposition. Substance abuse, which often causes a mood swing, will affect job performance in dealing with the public.

Warehouse receiving and order picking depend upon accuracy in reading and recording information. This accuracy is severely impeded by some substances, particularly hallucinogenic drugs. Other substance abuse may encourage horseplay on the job, and this can be both disruptive and dangerous.

Certain physical symptoms and actions create reasonable suspicion of abuse. These include bloodshot or watery eyes, as well as pupils that are abnormally large or small. A runny nose or sores around the nose are sometimes signs of abuse, as well as bloodstains on shirt-sleeves. Watch for the individual who wears sunglasses in places where they should not be needed. Excessive perspiration or sudden worsening of complexion can be symptoms of abuse, as well as sudden weight loss. Abusers who are taking injections will wear long-sleeve shirts in hot weather. Slurred speech, unsteady movement, or tremors are other signs. In some cases, mood swings will cause unpredictable responses to ordinary requests.

The practice of testing or screening has generated considerable controversy. Screening is portrayed as denial of traditional personal freedom, yet warehouse workers can cause death or injury if they do their jobs in a reckless manner. If you fail to screen people whose habits may cause them to work recklessly, you then fail to protect the healthy people who work in your warehouse, as well as the goods placed in your custody. Therefore, consider whether failing to screen for substance abuse can cause more problems than a drug testing program.

Some companies deny or avoid the issue of substance abuse by failing to publish a company policy on this matter. Your policy should relate substance abuse to health, safety, property protection, and quality control. Set standards of conduct that are expected of *every* employee. If you have a rehabilitation program, the policy should recognize it. Finally, you must state the penalties you are willing to invoke for violating the policy.

Devloping your policy statement

Here is a sample policy statement, you should consider if you do not already have one:

This company is committed to providing its employees with a safe workplace and an atmosphere that allows its people to protect merchandise placed in their care. Our employees are expected to be in suitable mental and physical condition while at work to perform their jobs effectively and safely. Whenever use or abuse of any mood-altering substance interferes with a safe warehouse, appropriate action must be taken. The company has no desire to intrude into its employees' personal lives. However, both on-the-job and off-the-job involvement with any mood-altering substance (alcohol and drugs) can have an impact on the workplace and on our company's ability to achieve its objective of safety and security. Therefore, employees are expected to report to the workplace with no mood-altering substances in their bodies. While employees may make their own lifestyle choices, the company cannot accept the risk in the workplace that substance abuse may create. The possession, sale, or use of mood-altering substances at the workplace, or coming to work under the influence of such substances, shall be a violation of safe work practices. This violation may result in termination of employment.

Some managers prefer to ignore the issue of substance abuse. However, ignoring this problem does not make it go away, but contributes to its growth.

Some suggest that these matters should be left to the personnel department. Consider whether substance abuse is a matter that should be delegated to others, or one which you must handle yourself.

Undercover investigations

Americans dislike spying. The CIA has never been a popular agency and the idea of doing something in a covert manner seems to go against our preference for an open door and total candor.* The right to privacy is an American heritage, and certainly spying in the warehouse could be called an invasion of privacy. The prying boss is compared to 'Big Brother' of the

---

*   Most of this subchapter is from an article by Barry Brandman, Danbee Investigation, Warehousing Forum, Volume 6, Number 10, ©The Ackerman Company.

George Orwell novel *1984.*

In spite of this dislike, a time-tested method of uncovering unlawful activity within a warehouse is the undercover operative. Collusion theft or drug dealing can become almost insolvable puzzles in a large distribution center. With many people working in a wide area and spread over two or three shifts, it is difficult to discover who is responsible for thievery or drug transactions.

Undercover operative services are provided by major detective agencies as well as some specialist consultants. The undercover operative is hired as an ordinary employee, and that person does everything possible to become a typical employee and blend into the workforce. By befriending various members of the workforce, the operative gradually discovers the causes of problems. This is a delicate and dangerous occupation. Total confidentiality is essential, both to secure success of the project and to insure the safety of the agent.

Using an undercover investigator involves six steps:
- ◆ Selecting the operative.
- ◆ Preparing the 'cover.'
- ◆ Bringing the undercover agent into the warehouse.
- ◆ Establishing rapport.
- ◆ Collecting information from the investigation.
- ◆ Concluding the operation.

The first step in selecting the operative is to find an agency that can be trusted. Like any other service business, providers of such services include good and bad operators, and it is not easy to measure qualifications. The selection process is complicated by the fact that many agencies refuse to list recent clients as references, for obvious reasons. Secondly, the undercover agent must be evaluated as an individual. Does that person have the intelligence, maturity, and common sense to get the job done? Does he or she have the physical appearance and skills necessary to blend in with the other workers and perform the assigned task? Selecting the agency and the individual is critical if the project is to succeed.

When the operative has been selected, a carefully prepared *cover story* must be developed. This must include job references that will hide the agent's true background and add credibility to the assumed role.

Placing the undercover person in the warehouse follows the same interview and selection process used for other employees. The operative is also paid in the customary manner. A criminal already in the organization will be highly suspicious of any new people introduced to the workplace.

The process of establishing rapport will take some time, perhaps four to six weeks. The agent must win the confidence of fellow workers without appearing to be overly inquisitive or aggressive. This could involve participation in company athletic leagues or sharing a few drinks in the tavern frequented by fellow workers.

Most undercover service firms provide written reports of the investigation. These are prepared daily and mailed to the home address of the executive who hired the undercover operator. The reports are written so that if they fell into the wrong hands they still might not identify the author. However, they are designed to provide maximum information about criminal activity.

Concluding the operation can be as delicate as starting it. In one case involving drug dealing, the operation ended with confrontation and dismissal of nearly one-third of the workforce. The undercover operator was fired along with the drug dealers in order to preserve the cover.

Users of undercover services must recognize that the agent is in a dangerous job. Breaking the cover could risk the safety of the undercover operative. For this reason, a minimum number of people within the organization should know of the existence of the undercover investigation, and the cover should be preserved even after the investigation is over.

Ethics in warehousing

American businesses generally adhere to high standards of conduct by prohibiting bribery, kickbacks, conflicts of interest, or insider trading. The system does not always work, but its worst violators risk the punishment of the public as well as the law.

In warehousing, there are substantial temptations which confront people daily.

In some communities, it is common for a truck driver to offer a warehouse worker cash in return for either leaving a pallet on an inbound truck or loading an extra pallet on an outbound truck.

Other forms of dishonesty are more subtle. One worker may ask another to punch out his or her time card. The motive may be innocent, just saving a long walk to the time clock. Other times the motive is less innocent: Time *is* money, and stealing one is stealing the other.

One wholesale grocery company condemned a practice they call *grazing*, or the sampling of stored merchandise to provide an extra snack at lunchtime or break time. This wholesaler pointed out that grazing is simply stealing on a smaller scale, and the stored merchandise is not put there for that purpose.

Users of warehouses expect the operators to provide good care for the merchandise stored there. This requires healthy, caring workers who treat the goods they handle as if they owned them. In the broadest sense, they should be honest people.

Warehouse operators face peculiar ethical challenges. The third-party warehouse operator is a guardian of property belonging to others. Some shippers have been known to test the honesty of the public warehouse by deliberately shipping excess quantities on inbound loads. If the overages are not reported, the ethical standards of the warehouse operator are called into question. On the other hand, a few users of third-party services try to charge the warehouse company for all shortages without providing any credit for overages.

A shipping error will typically cause a *cross-over*, a shortage in one SKU with a corresponding overage in another. Failure to balance the overages with the shortages represents a 'heads I win — tails you lose' approach to dealing with the third-party warehouse.

Competent warehouse operators, both public and private, recognize their duty to provide the highest standards of care for goods moving through their facility. They also have a duty to provide the best available service without bias to one customer or department. Warehouse managers and warehouse workers have an ethical responsibility to provide the same level of care and diligence in handling merchandise belonging to others that they would provide for property they own.

Protect your people by demanding the highest standards of ethics and honesty in warehouse management. In return, the majority of your workers who are honest people will help you find and eliminate dishonesty. The best way to protect your people is to set an example for ethics and honesty that demands that they respect each other and the company that employs them.

Questions that solve problems

When it comes to protecting the people, it may be well to ask questions of your hourly employees to find out how they feel about the security of their workplace. Here are a few you can use:

Q Do you enjoy working here, and is there anything we could do to make your job more enjoyable?

C This non-directive question should bring out any concerns people might have about things in the workplace that make them nervous, including dishonesty and substance abuse. While some people may not wish to say exactly what is troubling them, if you sense that there is trouble in the workplace, it is well to look at potential causes.

Q Have you seen any hazards in your job that good management or better work practices might prevent?

C Many warehouses have safety committees and safety meetings, and these might seem to make this kind of question unnecessary. However, everyone appreciates management's concern about safe work and conditions, and such questioning may be both popular and informative.

Q Can you suggest any change in methods that would make your job easier?

C Workers are usually the best source of ergonomic changes that can lessen the risk of manual handling injuries. If your people demonstrate a way to make the job easier and safer, be sure to reward them for their good ideas.

Q Does our company convey an image of honesty and upright conduct?

C Listen carefully to these answers — not all workers will tell you just what they think you want to hear. ❖

Chapter 21

Protecting the property

There are three kinds of major losses that could affect your property:

- ◆ A business interruption interferes with the ability of the warehouse to function normally. This includes any occurrence that makes it impossible to ship, receive, or move materials.
- ◆ Some casualty losses affect both the building and its contents.
- ◆ Other losses may affect just the warehouse structure.

Casualty losses

The most catastrophic loss is fire. A warehouse fire, once out of control, is likely to destroy both the building and its contents.

Windstorm is a common threat to warehouse buildings. The modern warehouse is particularly vulnerable to windstorm damage because its wide expanses of flat roof are readily damaged by high winds. When such roofs are constructed with asphalt, insurance carriers limit the amount used to reduce risk of fire. Asphalt is an adhesive. When you reduce it to cut fire risk, you increase the risk of damage by windstorm.

The risk of water damage includes both floods and sprinkler system malfunction. Sometimes ill-trained emergency fire brigades may set off the sprinkler systems, and the leakage can cause as much damage as a fire.

Overloading the building, structural failure, or earthquake may all cause a building to collapse. The risk of explosion is influenced by the products stored in or near the building.

Vandalism and malicious mischief clauses cover losses caused by sabotage or other acts of malicious destruction. A more general risk is that of *consequential loss* — the losses that may come as the result of an earlier event. One example is a power failure that disables the refrigeration system in a freezer, with spoilage of stored products as a consequential damage.

Fire

One of the best ways to control fire risk is to purchase both insurance and *loss-prevention advice* from a carrier who emphasizes loss prevention. The more progressive insurance companies have continuing research and development on loss prevention. These companies control losses by making every employee aware of how to prevent fires.

Sprinkler systems

Means of controlling the risk of fire vary in different countries, but in the United States today the most widely accepted method of fire risk reduction is the automatic sprinkler system. The automatic sprinkler is a series of pipes installed just under the ceiling of a warehouse building, carrying sufficient water to extinguish or prevent the spread of fire. There are two widely used types of sprinkler systems — dry-pipe and wet-pipe systems.

Dry-pipe systems

The dry-pipe system uses heated valve houses, each with a valve containing compressed air that keeps water out of the sprinkler pipes. When the air is released, water is permitted to flow. Dry-pipe systems function in unheated warehouses or in outdoor canopies where temperatures fall below freezing.

Sprinkler heads are installed on the pipes at regular intervals. Each of these heads has a deflector to aim the flow of water and a trigger made of wax or a metallic compound that will melt at a given temperature. When heat reaches that temperature, the trigger snaps and allows water to flow through the system and onto the fire.

Most systems include a water-flow alarm that will ring a bell and send an electronic signal to summon the fire department. The electronic signal is particularly important for controlling a false alarm or an accidental discharge.

Wet-pipe systems

In the wet-pipe system, water fills all pipes up to the sprinkler heads, which means the entire warehouse must be kept above freezing. The wet-pipe system works faster since compressed air does not have to be released first. This speed makes it a better system for fire control. Furthermore, the wet-pipe sprinkler is less susceptible to false alarms than the more complex dry-pipe system.

All sprinkler systems are equipped with master control valves, which present two risks: accidental closure and deliberate shut-off by a vandal. Nearly a third of dollar losses from fires occur because the control valves were closed.

Other protection against fire

Fire extinguishers are an important first response for fires. A portable extinguisher often prevents a small blaze from becoming a major fire. The best way to be sure that fire extinguishers will be used effectively is to have periodic training and drills.

Most fire protection systems also include fire hose stations to be used before the fire trucks arrive. When fire drills are held, these hoses should be included. Many major fires are prevented by teams trained to act effectively the instant a fire is discovered, and well before the fire department can arrive.

The warehouse operator's proficiency in loss-prevention is usually reflected in the rate insurance underwriters assign to the facility. Some public warehouse operators will advertise their fire insurance rate, knowing that it reflects their success in loss prevention. Fire underwriters measure both management interest and employee attitudes toward fire protection. They recognize that loss risks can be increased by careless smoking, poor housekeeping, or even troubled labor relations.

A new type of sprinkler system

Approval of the Early Suppression Fast Response (ESFR) sprinkler system is one of the most significant advances in the long history of sprinkler systems. In most of the world, sprinkler systems are regarded as an American invention and are often considered unacceptable because of the danger of water damage. In the United States, such systems are required by building codes in all warehouses but the smallest.

Two developments of the past few decades have made sprinkler system protection more complicated: the increased use of storage racks, and storage of more products that contain volatile or poisonous chemicals.

Protection experts consider rack storage to be hazardous because a typical rack arrangement leaves vertical spaces that act as a flue in the event of a fire. The insurance underwriters' solution to the problem was to specify installation of intermediate sprinkler heads within the rack.

This brought cries of dismay from warehouse owners because intermediate sprinklers are expensive and they destroy layout flexibility. Racks equipped with intermediate sprinklers are expensive to be adjust or move. Furthermore, it is relatively easy to strike the in-rack sprinkler heads by accident while handling freight. For these reasons, many warehouse operators have stubbornly resisted underwriters requests for in-rack sprinkler systems.

Eliminating the need for in-rack sprinkler systems is the primary virtue of the ESFR sprinkler system. ESFR has two unique features: a quicker response time and a heavier sprinkler discharge. When a sufficient quantity of water is dropped onto a fire at an early stage, the fire will be suppressed before it presents a severe challenge to the building itself. Furthermore, the ESFR system typically opens fewer sprinkler heads than a conventional system and therefore reduces water damage. Reducing the size and duration of the fire will also reduce smoke damage.

There are two ways to deal with fire — suppression and control. Standard sprinkler systems operate on the control principle. The sprinkler system allows a fire to develop, but retards its spread by opening 20 to 30 sprinkler heads. This widespread discharge soaks surrounding storage piles so they will not ignite. The water discharge protects the building by cooling the steelwork and preventing structural failure and collapse. Suppression is left to firefighters.

The ESFR system is designed for suppression rather than control. The goal is to apply enough cooling water to a heat source before a fire plume has any chance to develop.

Wind storm losses

Certain parts of the country are recognized as having a higher hazard from storms. Gulf Coast areas are notable for hurricanes and parts of the midwest have repetitive problems with tornadoes.

Probably no economical warehouse design could withstand a direct hit from a tornado or the full force of a hurricane. However, certain kinds of construction have proven more resistant to such perils.

A pre-engineered metal roof, for example, has greater wind-resistance than a built-up composition roof, simply because the metal roof does not rely on asphalt or any other chemical adhesive. Overhanging truck canopies should be avoided in high-wind areas, since they are particularly susceptible to wind damage.

Flood and leakage

One way to control the risk of loss from either flood or leakage is to be sure that no merchandise is stored directly on the warehouse floor. The use of storage pallets or lumber dunnage to keep all merchandise a few inches above the floor can provide a measure of protection in the event of leakage.

Mass theft

Warehouse managers should never assume that a protection system will always prevent mass theft.

Periodically, you should deliberately breach the security system just to learn how fast the police will respond. Holding this kind of burglary drill is potentially dangerous, and managers who do it must be sure that they to not become victims of a police accident. One way to reduce this risk is to inform the police chief, but not the alarm company, that a drill is taking place.

Since the technology for electronic protection is constantly being improved, the alert warehouse operator should always look for new equipment better than that currently installed. But all such equipment should be *fail-safe* — meaning that it will ring an alarm if wires are cut or power is interrupted.

Outside lighting is an important deterrent to mass theft. Intense outside light will make a thief feel conspicuous. Rather than run the risk of being seen, the thief probably will select a less well-lit building.

Vandalism

Vandalism, sabotage, or other deliberate destruction is difficult to control. The most serious vandalism risk is the intentional closure of sprinkler valves. There are electronic devices to counter this. Also, it is possible to apply a seal that shows at a glance if a valve has been turned by an unauthorized person. The risk of vandalism increases during a period of labor strife, and management should be especially alert at those times.

Surviving an insurance inspection

The insurance inspector is far more concerned about the materials in your warehouse than the building itself. With few exceptions, warehouse buildings are fire-resistant. If you are fortunate enough to be warehousing non-combustibles, and if those materials are in bulk with no combustible packaging, then you have a very safe warehouse. However, almost every warehouse is filled with products that contain some paper or corrugated packaging, plastics, wood, and combustible chemicals.

The insurance industry rates combustibles in five classes:

♦ A **special-hazard product** is one in which the plastics content of packaging and product is more than 15 percent by weight or more than 25 percent by volume. Expanded plastic packaging, such as that used to protect computers and television sets, is particularly hazardous.

♦ A **Class IV commodity** can be any product, even a metal product, that is packaged in a cardboard box if non-expanded plastic is more than 15 percent of the product weight, or if expanded plastic is more than 25 percent of the product's volume. An example of such an item is a metal typewriter with plastic parts that is protected by a foam plastic container.

♦ A **Class III item** is one in which both product and packaging are combustible. An example is facial tissue in cartons.

♦ A **Class II product** is a non-combustible item that is stored in wood, corrugated cardboard, or other combustible packaging. While the contents will not burn, the package will. Examples include refrigerators, washers, and dryers.

◆ A **Class I item** is the least-hazardous commodity — non-combustible products stored in non-combustible packaging on pallets. The pallets themselves will burn, but if everything on the pallet is non-combustible, it is rated as Class I.

The fire inspector will consider the quantity of material in your warehouse that falls into each of the five classes and the manner in which you store materials. From a protection standpoint, solid-pile storage — free-standing stacks that are snugly against each other — provide the least-hazardous storage arrangement. The exception would be a commodity that is in itself quite dangerous, such as a flammable chemical.

The fire inspector will also look at the number and width of your aisles, and the height at which goods are stored. Nearly all underwriters request that goods be at least 18 inches below sprinkler heads; but with more hazardous materials, an even greater space between product and sprinklers will increase the possibility that the sprinkler system can control a fire.

The problem with high-piled storage is a chimney or flue effect. If you have a 30-foot pile of combustible boxes with a six-inch space between rows, a fire will move up the 30-foot flue like a blowtorch. The flame at the top will be extremely hot and violent, and this heat can expand the steel framework of the building and cause a collapse.

You can make storage racks safer from the underwriter's point-of-view. Allow a vertical space between rack structures, to permit sprinkler water to run down into the racks. Pallet racks or installations that use metal grates are considered safer than solid-steel shelving, simply because the openings allow water to run down through the levels.

Fire safety for the most dangerous materials is improved with ample aisle separation. If the hazardous products are separated from the rest of the merchandise by wide aisles, the chance of controlling a fire is increased. In some cases, extremely hazardous materials are put in a special-hazard building separated from the rest of the facility. A fire in that building will then not threaten the larger warehouse.

Plant emergency organizations

An emergency plan can greatly reduce the risk of major loss. For this reason, casualty underwriters strongly encourage well trained plant emergency teams.

The emergency team functions after an emergency is discovered and before the fire department or other professionals arrive.

The emergency organization should always include representatives of plant *maintenance* or *engineering* departments, since these people are the most familiar with the protection systems, control panels, and circuit breakers. The plant emergency team should know how to operate all protective equipment and be trained to react with confidence and accuracy.

The most important aspect of training is practice drills. Such drills should include sounding the alarm; moving to a prescribed emergency station; and handling fire hoses, extinguishers, and sprinkler system controls. The last of these is the most complex, since a large sprinkler system usually has many valves as well as a booster fire-pump. A good emergency organization also is schooled in first aid, since the first priority is to save lives.

Emergency teams need regular drills and preparation. When emergency plans are made and then forgotten, the team rapidly becomes disorganized and useless.

Questions that solve problems

Insurance people are particularly curious about whether senior management is actively involved in loss prevention. Therefore, you should never be too busy to ask questions about your company's protection systems. Here are some points of inquiry that will demonstrate your active involvement in protecting the property:

Q **Have there been recent inspections by fire underwriters or other protection authorities? If so, have copies of their reports been sent to me?**
C No matter how busy you are or how critical your position you should receive these reports if warehousing is your responsibility.

Q **Has the company suffered any casualty losses during the past year? If so, is there anything we might have done to have prevented them?**
C If you had to ask the first question, you may be too far removed from operations. However, asking the second is a legitimate exploration of ways to improve protective procedures and systems.

Q **Have we considered installation or retrofit of the new ESFR sprinkler systems?**
C Even though this new technology was introduced several years ago, it is surprising how many people are not aware of its existence.

Q **Are there any unusual hazards associated with any of the materials stored in our warehouse?**
C You can't ask this one too often, since the introduction of any new product into your warehouse could represent a new and possibly unrecognized risk.

Q **What drills are rehearsed to teach our people how to be safe in case of windstorm, flood, or fire?**
C The answer will provide some indication of the quality of your emergency planning. ❖

PART 5

5

Handling of Cargo

Chapter 22

Receiving, putaway, and storage

Nothing can be distributed until it has been received. Therefore any consideration of cargo handling must logically begin with the act of receiving.

Receiving is the process of accepting material into the warehouse.* It transfers possession from shipper to receiver and, while this may or may not involve the transfer of title, normally it does. Because the acceptance of responsibility for the material makes receiving a financial risk, the process requires an audit trail. Receiving requires more care than many operators give it.

Physical activities of receiving

Receiving starts with acceptance at your dock of a vehicle with material consigned to you. You unload the material, count and confirm the quantity with shipping documents, and inspect for quality assurance. Inspection ends with a decision to accept or reject the load. If it is accepted, then your employees move the load to storage.

There are three ways to receive material, and they are listed in order of efficiency:

1. Unload from a carrier, and move across the dock for outbound. This is the simplest warehousing method because it requires no storage.

---

* The first two subchapters are adapted from an article by William J. Ransom, Ransom and Associates, *Warehousing Forum*, Volume 7, Number 7, ©The Ackerman Company, Columbus, Ohio.

2. Unload from the carrier and move material directly to storage. This is the second-best receiving method, because it does not require rehandling.

3. Unload the material from the carrier to temporary storage near the dock. This step is taken if:
   ◆ The material requires additional checking, inspection, or price marking.
   ◆ Storage space is not available or assigned.
   ◆ Material handlers are not available.

Number three is the least-preferred receiving method because it requires rehandling the material. Storage space is required on the dock to hold unloaded material until it is moved to storage. If space is scarce, use pallet racks in or near the receiving dock.

If the physical activities of receiving are not closely supervised, you may be charged with damage for which you are not responsible. Furthermore, whether through accident or deliberate dishonesty, you could sign for material that never was actually received. Training of the receivers and material handlers is often a neglected function. As you examine your receiving operation, consider how you could change your system so that most materials go directly from truck to truck, or truck to storage.

Receiving as a process

Receiving consists of seven sequential steps. Your operation may not require every step, but omit steps only with good reasons.

1. The carrier calls and your employees establish a delivery time.
2. Before the truck arrives, the receiver verifies that a manifest is available and that it applies to this load. If not, the shipper is contacted by phone to provide the manifest or packing list.
3. A receiving dock door is assigned to the trucker when he arrives.
4. The vehicle is safely secured before unloading, with confirmation by a supervisor that all security steps have been taken.
5. The truck driver is present when the seal is broken and initial inspection is completed.
6. If accepted, the load is removed from the truck with three variations:
   ◆ Unitized or palletized material is unloaded by lift truck.

- ◆ Loose or floor loaded material is properly stacked on pallets for movement to storage.
- ◆ Material is removed by conveyor to a shipping dock or staging area.

7. As materials are unloaded, you should count and inspect constantly to be sure that quality and quantity conform to specification.

As you review the process in your warehouse, ask yourself if it is possible to convert all receipts to unitized loads to eliminate palletizing by hand.

Check-in requires absolute accuracy. The methods used to achieve accuracy may be one or more of the following. Listed in order of potential error-free receiving, they are:

1. Bar-code wanding. Scan each package with a bar code scanning wand. The scanner feeds the information into a computer to register receipt.

2. Blind receiving. The checker writes down the received quantity and items without reference to the manifest or packing list that shows the expected quantity.

3. Where the receiver knows the quantity and item, there are two variations:
   - ◆ The receiver has a listing of the items but records the quantity received.
   - ◆ The receiver has a listing of quantity and item. The receipt is simply checked.

The design of the receiving tally, the first document prepared at the warehouse, should contain necessary receiving information. The figure shown below offers a format to use in designing your own form.

RECEIVING TALLY

DATE: LOT NUMBER:

Account	Car No. or Freight Bill No.
	Route
Shipper	Seals
Origin	Total Weight

Qty Rec'd	Description	Units per Pallet	Tally Record				Location

DAMAGE INFORMATION

				Reconditioning		
Qty	Product Description	Damage Description	Cause of Damage	Good Stock	Rejects	Hrs.

Unloader	Lift Operator	Checker

The receiving tally is the start of the audit trail. Therefore, this document must be accurate and complete — noting in detail any exceptions, including overages, shortages, and damage. The rule is, *Always count twice before signing once.*

Checking is the most critical step in the receiving operation, and receiving is not complete until:

◆ Receiving documents match the manifest or packing list.

◆ You note any discrepancies and document them fully.

The final step in receiving is to assign a storage location to the material, or move it to the next area for processing. Move damaged material to a reco-

operage area or immediately refuse it and return it to the truck driver. In the recooperage area, you dispose of damaged material by:
- ◆ Shipping it to the vendor
- ◆ Salvaging what is repairable by repacking good items and removing damaged ones
- ◆ Scrapping

Putaway

In altogether too many warehouses, the inbound putaway decision is left to the forklift operator. Since that worker is motivated to be fast and productive, it is natural that the operator's decision will be one that saves time without saving space.

Your warehouse should have at least one person designated as a storage planner. That planner should know where empty storage locations are, where additional space can be created by re-warehousing, and what inbound loads are expected.

The planner scans the identity of items on the inbound loads to budget space for each item that is in transit to the warehouse. With this information, the planner should develop specific storage instructions for each item on every arriving load of freight.

Stock locator systems

A key element in space planning is an effective warehouse locator system. The locator system is primarily designed to reduce lost time during order picking when the picker must search for misplaced merchandise.

Many warehouses have formal computer- or paper- based stock locator systems. Such systems are not new, and yet some warehouse operators question their value.

The need for locator systems is governed both by layout and complexity of the inventory. A warehouse that contains only one SKU, such as a bulk silo full of grain, obviously needs no system to tell where the grain is located. A warehouse with only two or three SKUs may not need the locator system, either.

But warehouses with more SKUs gain at least seven advantages from the use of stock locators:

1. A locator system saves space. Where an item is stored in more than one location, a system can be programmed to consolidate locations and open up a new slot that can hold an additional item.

2. A locator system saves time. Warehouse workers do not have to search for a spot to put the new merchandise — an empty location has already been assigned before the stock is unloaded. Outbound goods see a similar time saving because the order picker does not have to search the warehouse.

3. The locator system provides an extra control. Some order pick lists require the operator to go to a specific location, and then to find a given item. If location and item do not match, there must be an error. If every item and location discrepancy are double checked, there will be fewer shipping errors.

4. Order picking is expedited with a locator system. Choosing strategic picking locations can provide a shorter path for picking outbound orders.

5. A locator system provides control of individual lots for product recall. In manufacture of some materials, each batch is considered to be a separate lot. Therefore, a single SKU may consist of several lots. When each lot is recorded in a separate location, the control of these lots is greatly improved.

6. A locator system improves *first in first out* (FIFO) control. By listing the location that holds the oldest stock, you can program the locator system to control FIFO.

7. Locator systems are used for product quarantine. Some products are quarantined pending a quality control check, and a locator system can enforce the quarantine.

Installing a locator system

When you decide to install a stock locator system, you will have several options. One is whether or not to have quantity controls by location. Such a system would show that item 4321 can be found at four locations. but not how many pieces will be at each location.

The order picker moves to the first location and may take all of the stock found in that spot. If stock in the location is exhausted, the order picker puts a zero next to that location so the system can be updated. If additional stock is needed to fill the order, the picker moves to subsequent locations until sufficient stock has been found to fill the order.

A locator system that traces quantity by location allows more precise picking. If 100 pieces are needed to fill an order, the picker can select a location that has sufficient stock to handle the entire order. The primary disadvantage is that maintaining accuracy in a quantity locator system is more difficult, and the more detailed the location control, the more numbers and characters needed to control the system.

The question you must answer is: How detailed do you want your system to be? The most precise system could isolate each item to a given flow-rack slot, to a specific position on warehouse shelves, or to a single storage bin.

A less precise system might show one pallet position, even though more than one item is stored on that pallet.

An even less precise system may isolate items to a single bay of the warehouse, requiring the worker to search within that bay for the specific item.

One control issue in locator systems is the intelligent use of bin, gravity-flow rack, or shelf systems. Small-quantity order picking can be expedited by using any of the three to place a minimal quantity of product in a position where it can be selected quickly and easily by the order picker. However, some warehouses have two kinds of orders: Customer orders are for small quantities that are picked from the shelf or rack stock but other orders are bulk stock transfers to alternate storage locations. The typical customer order may be less than one case or a few cases, while the bulk order might be hundreds of cases. Clearly the bulk order should not be pulled from the pick line, which means that certain items on orders will by-pass the pick line and be pulled from overflow stock areas. The locator system must recognize when to use the pick line and when to use the bulk areas.

In designing your system, keep it as simple as possible. Where you can, relate locations to directions (east, west, north, and south) so the system makes sense to newcomers.

Maintaining a locator system

Effectively using a locator system starts with planning for in-bound merchandise. The system identifies empty locations available for storage. Empty locations may be created by consolidating partial pallets or partial rows and when new merchandise is received, the space planner assigns each inbound SKU to an empty location. The person who unloads the truck is able to move the merchandise directly from receiving dock to designated location.

When goods are shipped, the order pick list shows the location first, then the SKU. Order pickers who find another item in the location report the discrepancy so the error can be corrected. The space planner should make frequent location checks throughout the warehouse to discover opportunities to save space through re-warehousing, and to make more efficient use of the available space.

An effective locator system requires good communication, discipline, and immediate correction of errors. When a physical inventory is taken, the locator system provides a time saving control over the counting process.

Though a few warehouses operate without a formal locator, nearly all function better when one is in place.

Your warehouse layout

Most decisions on warehouse layout are influenced by two major activities: storage and handling.

Five layout features can improve storage to allow more productive use of available space. The five are: housekeeping, security, inventory level variations, physical characteristics, and packaging strength.

Housekeeping is considered the most important barometer of good warehouse management. An excellent storage layout makes it easier to maintain good housekeeping and sometimes the most important reason to change a warehouse layout is to improve the appearance of the facility.

Security includes the risk of fire as well as theft. An effective layout from a protection standpoint has these features:

- ◆ Theft-prone merchandise is stored where it cannot easily be stolen.
- ◆ Extra-hazard sprinkler systems or explosion-proof rooms are reserved for storage of hazardous materials.
- ◆ Dangerous products are identified and isolated.

Inventory level variations occur when certain items are popular in one season and inactive during the rest of the year, or other items surge through the distribution center when they are on a promotion or sale. These variations must be considered as the layout is planned.

Physical characteristics of each item in the warehouse should be analyzed in planning a layout so similarly sized and shaped items can be stored in the same area. For example, tubing, piping and other extra-length items may be stored in a cantilever rack or a *lean-to* storage area along one wall. Since these items cannot be stored effectively in block stacks, pallet racks, or other conventional storage arrangements, it makes good sense to keep them together. Similar considerations should be given to other items of unusual package size or shape.

Packaging strength must be considered by the storage planner who seeks to maximize use of available cubic space. High-block stacks with no racks are the best arrangement for merchandise that is packaged well enough to support this kind of storage.

Packaging, rather than clearance, is usually the limiting factor in high stacking. Where packaging is weak, storage racks are the most common means of achieving efficient space use. Therefore, a knowledge of the stacking capability of each package is essential in layout planning.

Handling considerations

Layout decisions can improve or impede materials handling productivity. These include measurement of order size, order picking requirements, ergonomics, minimizing travel time, compatibility of handling equipment, and special operations.

Order size

In considering order size, you should know the typical inbound quantity for each item as well as outbound quantities. In a warehouse that usually receives one truckload inbound for each of the most popular items in storage, storage slots are arranged with a size that holds just one truckload.

The same kind of analysis is applicable to outbound shipments, too. If the most common outbound order is three cases, but a few stock transfer orders call for 300 cases, the layout must adapt to both low-volume and high-volume shipments.

Order picking

Order picking requirements are closely related to outbound order sizes. If orders call for frequent shipping of broken-case quantities, the pick line must facilitate the opening of cases and the use of tote bins or shipping cases to consolidate partial-case quantities.

When 20 percent of the items in the line account for 80 percent of the activity (Pareto's Law), it is sensible to locate those popular items in spots where they can be most easily handled.

Velocity of turn is another important consideration in order selection. If some items move so rapidly that they come in one door and go out the other, it may be desirable to keep this fast-turn merchandise in a staging area and never put it into storage slots.

The ideal storage layout places popular and high-velocity items in locations that minimize handling labor. The slowest-moving items are put in those locations that are most difficult to reach.

Ergonomics

Ergonomics and warehouse productivity are important considerations in a layout. Ergonomics is the science of minimizing physical strain in performing a job. Just as office furniture manufacturers have designed ergonomic chairs that make sitting easier, a warehouse planner designs an ergonomic layout that eases handling of merchandise. For example, boxes that must be handled manually are most easily lifted and put down when they are at a height ranging from waist high to eye level. Increased recognition of ergonomics will make warehouse labor both easier and safer, since extra effort can result in back injuries or strained muscles.

Minimizing travel time

Minimizing travel time improves picking productivity. A layout that is coordinated with the order pick list makes it easy for the order picker to move down the list without having to criss-cross the warehouse several times.

Compatible handling equipment

Limitations of the available handling equipment may cause you to adjust the layout to fit the capabilities of your lift trucks. Consider the equipment you now use as you calculate stack height, aisle width, and dimensions of storage slots.

Special operations

Some warehouses include special operations. These might include repackaging or refurbishing damaged or returned goods, final assembly, kitting, or packaging. The layout provides space to support these special operations and the locations must be considered in relationship to the flow of material between receiving docks and the shipping and storage areas.

Simulating to plan for contingencies

and the future

One way to understand how a new warehouse layout will function is to create visual aids or models to illustrate the appearance of the future warehouse.

Several methods will accomplish these simulations, but one of the oldest and most dependable is a flow chart. Flow charting helps the planner learn more about the job by describing that job, step by step. Flow charting imposes a discipline, makes you plan ahead, and may generate new ideas for layout and product flow.

A newer option is computer aided design (CAD), which uses a plotting machine to develop a detailed picture of the warehouse layout. This technique enables the planner to see how the warehouse will look when layout recommendations are implemented.

Any layout must be adaptable to change. What if inventory grows to twice the size it is today? What if inventory is cut in half? If the handling operation includes use of specialized lift trucks such as a turret truck, what will you do when that truck breaks down? What provisions have you made for disasters such as fire, windstorm damage, or earthquake — or breakdowns such as power failure, equipment failure or computer breakdown? Keep future options and contingencies in mind as you design a warehouse.

The prime objective of warehouse layout is to use effectively the available space, but also to handle materials at minimum cost. The layout planner must allow maximum flexibility to deal with changes, some of which cannot be anticipated. Developing an effective warehouse layout is really a process rather than a formula. Once you understand the process, you can develop a layout that will work well in your own operation.

Questions that solve problems

As you appraise the effectiveness of receiving and storage, you should ask your managers a few questions about how they get the job done.

Q Can you describe in detail our existing receiving procedure?
C If there is a written procedure, perhaps an evaluation of it is the best answer to the question. However, the procedure is not effective unless it is always followed. Therefore, you might want to follow the question with an inspection to learn how receiving *actually* takes place.

Q What steps have we taken to improve receiving accuracy?
C If your warehouse managers aren't considering bar coding, find out why not.

Q Who makes the decision on where inbound products should be stored?
C If you don't hear a storage planner described by name or function, you are missing an opportunity to improve warehousing operations. If you have a storage planner, find out how that individual works.

Q Can you describe to me how our stock locator system works?
C If there is no system, you have identified an opportunity for improvement. If there is one and responsible people don't know how it works, it's possible that the system exists only on paper and does not function effectively.

Q How many storage locations do we have for item XYZ?
C Choose one of your most popular items. If it is stored in many locations, this may be a symptom of a poor locator system or none at all.

Q Are you satisfied with our warehouse layout? How could it be made better?
C Don't ask this until you have time for a long answer and considerable discussion. A manager who is satisfied, or has no ideas for improvement, may be either out of touch or complacent. ❖

Chapter 23

Order picking and shipping

Order picking and shipping comprise the largest expense category in most warehouses. Picking and shipping are also the most critical functions performed in most distribution operations and, if your warehouse doesn't get this job done right, nothing else can make up for it. Therefore, when we consider order picking and shipping, we are considering both the costliest and the most critical functions in your warehouse.

Adapting to growing velocity

Since the mid-1970s, logistics professionals have seen a continuing increase in the velocity of inventory turns. Two conditions have driven this change: First, the cost of money rose and the presumption of constant inflation disappeared. Second, improved communications and computing capabilities allowed a degree of inventory control that was not cost-effective before. Logistic managers have both the *incentive* and the *ability* to turn inventories faster than ever before.

The ultimate in high velocity is when merchandise moves in through one door and almost immediately moves out through another. The term for this movement is cross-dock operations.

Cross-dock operations

Cross-docking is a distribution system in which freight moves in and out of a distribution center without ever being stored there. Cross-docking includes the receipt, sorting, routing, and shipment of products in a minimum amount of time. On occasion, value-added services such as repackaging or kitting may be included in a cross-dock operation.

The movement of freight from one vehicle to another is nothing new. For years shippers have assembled pool cars and sent them to distributors. Pool-car or pool-truck distribution is the unloading and reshipping of segregated loads consigned to smaller customers. This operation is economically feasible because the difference in freight costs between full truckloads and small shipments exceeds the cost of pool distribution.

Cross-docking adds one operation: The facility receives bulk shipments and assembles the smaller orders on the warehouse floor. Compare costs of cross-docking to conventional warehousing operations (receiving, stowing, order picking, and shipping).

Cross-docking works best when it is limited to the most popular items, those sold on the basis of fast and precise delivery.

Information is the key to cross-docking. To function effectively, the cross-dock operator should receive information on both the incoming shipment schedule and the outgoing customer orders. Until such information is received, the sorting operation cannot be started.

New technology provides breakthroughs in information and in controls. One cross-docking operator monitors the flow through the facility by using bar coding and real-time information systems. Forklift operators carry radio-frequency terminals, and dispatching instructions are provided for each unit load. Using this system, the cross-dock warehouse runs with virtually no paperwork.

Manual methods can be used to control a cross dock operation. By recording all of the numbers for both inbound shipments and outbound bills of lading, and keeping those numbers in the same place, employees using a tracking system can trace movement of product through the facility. Because each outbound bill of lading also makes reference to the inbound shipment numbers, there is an audit trail to track the physical inventory.

Examples of successful cross-docking

By its nature, cross-docking is primarily horizontal rather than vertical product movement. Ideal materials handling vehicles are low-lift pallet movers or stand-up lift trucks that allow the operator to mount and dismount with ease. Conveyors and automatic guided vehicle systems (AGVS) are sometimes used in a cross-dock operation. Integration of information handling and materials handling equipment is critical. When RF terminals are used, they may be mounted on the lift trucks.

While most cross-dock operations are the result of a careful planning process, others are unplanned and motivated only by a certain series of events. When urgently needed goods are received, the best warehouse procedures call for immediate cross-docking of the hot items to expedite their handling.

One manufacturer found that five SKUs represent 25 percent of dollar value shipped, and these hot items are now in a 'warehouse on wheels' program. To reduce warehousing costs, these items are moved from factories or central distribution centers direct to break bulk points, where they merge with slower moving SKUs. These five popular items are not stored in the regional warehouses, but instead moved across docks just in time to serve each customer.

One grocery distributor uses cross-docking primarily for promotional buys. The cross-dock merchandise sits a maximum of three days in the distribution center, and it is never placed in storage racks.

One wholesale distributor uses cross-dock procedures as a support for private trucking, moving sufficient additional tonnage in a cross-dock situation to create economical truckloads for the private fleet.

Cross-docking for consolidators

Cross-docking can also be used to facilitate the consolidation of inbound materials. To eliminate the handling of many small shipments arriving at a receiving dock, some buyers arrange for supplier delivery to a remote consolidation terminal.

For example, all vendors in the Chicago area would ship their products to a consolidation terminal so goods arrive shortly before they are needed. The consolidator converts these small shipments into a single truckload.

If a company truck is used, the consolidation provides a needed backhaul that reduces the cost of private trucking. Otherwise, a common carrier may be used. In either case, the cost of inbound transportation is reduced.

Cross docking in your warehouse

Will cross docking work for you? Consider three primary advantages:

◆ Cross-docking may replace field warehouse operations. By substituting a cross-dock for a regional warehouse, you eliminate the expenses of that warehouse operation.

♦ You eliminate field inventories stored in regional warehouses.

♦ You reduce administration costs.

But cross-docking has pitfalls as well as benefits. Handling activity
must be *precisely timed* to coordinate the arrival of inbound loads with the
availability of outbound orders. Therefore substantial peaks and valleys in
volume are common. This can create a significant challenge in labor utilization, because hiring enough people to handle the peaks wastes labor when
no merchandise is flowing through the terminal. Facilities and equipment
are also used unevenly. The number of pallets must meet peak requirements, and those will be idle during periods of lower activity. Dock doors
and floor space may also be idle for part of the time.

Though cross-docking will never eliminate warehousing, it will cause
some warehouses to be relocated, others to be closed. The consumer products distributor who once used 30 regional warehouses to support a national market may achieve the same results today with three — but those
three will be more critical than ever before.

Reverse order picking

Reverse order picking, a variant of cross docking, is a simple system that
combines the function of receiving with the make-up of outbound customer orders.* The system works only if completed orders are available before the inbound shipment arrives. The unloading crew makes up all
available outbound orders as the product is received, thus saving a second
order picking operation and re-staging.

In many warehouses, receiving and shipping are segregated — frequently on opposite sides of the building. The receiving function is designed to minimize time, the goal being to unload each vehicle as quickly as
possible.

For reverse order picking, a computerized recap sheet (Figure 1) contains a vertical column representing each item on the inbound load. The
horizontal lines list each outbound order by order number and customer

---

*   Adapted from an article by Jesse Westburgh, *Warehousing Forum*, Volume 1, Number 4
        ©The Ackerman Company, Columbus, Ohio.

name. Using the sheet shown in Figure 1, an office worker creates warehouse pick tickets that identify customers, load number, and number of cases ordered.

Figure 1

	15045	16116	17315	17354	18518
434718 Grocer 1		10	200		25
434732 Grocer 2	30			50	10
434744 Grocer 3		25			
434740 Grocer 4	40	30	400		
434745 Grocer 5		15	200	25	
434729 Grocer 6	40			20	10
434741 Grocer 7	15	20	10		
434728 Grocer 8	200	50		25	15
434728 Grocer 9	10	10		100	200
434731 Grocer 10		15	30	15	50

A ticket is made for each stock item. For example, product code 17315 (see Figure 2) has shipments destined for five different consignees. Using the pick ticket, the receivers segregate the merchandise for each of the five outbound orders as they unload and check the freight from the truck. Once these five orders are segregated on separate pallets, each pallet is labeled with the name of the customer and load number.

Some claim that reverse order picking slows the receiving process. Admittedly it complicates receiving, but the total effort in receiving *and* shipping is reduced. The system works best when strict time schedules for inbound and outbound truckers are followed. The staging area limits the quantity of product you can receive, so the best way to implement this system is to allow a maximum number of hours per day to be devoted to receiving by expanding the appointment schedule for inbound merchandise. In addition, the dock area must be designed with an ample amount of staging space — possibly including pallet racks to hold staged orders.

How much time does this process save? With a conventional receiving and shipping system four people are needed: receiver, putaway, selector, and shipper/loader. Under the new system, two people accomplish the same work: receiver/selector and loader.

Figure 2

Product code		17315
Order	Load	Case Quantity
Grocer #1	5	200
Grocer #4	9	400
Grocer #5	1	200
Grocer #7	3	10
Grocer #10	13	30
		840

The greatest virtue of the system is its simplicity. Warehouse workers deal with easy-to-read pick tickets. Assembling outbound orders at the time of receipt greatly simplifies the picking, staging, and shipping process. This approach can improve operations and once the employees learn the system, picking errors are reduced.

Four kinds of order picking

The job of selecting orders can be divided into at least four categories: discreet picking, batch picking, zone picking, and wave picking.

Discreet picking is the most common means of selecting an order. One order picker takes a single order and fills it from start to finish.

With **batch picking** the order picker takes a group of orders, perhaps a dozen. A batch list is prepared that contains the total quantity of each SKU found in the whole group. The order picker then collects the batch and takes it to a staging area, where it is separated into single orders.

Zone picking assigns each order selector to a given zone of the warehouse. Under a zone picking plan, one order picker selects all parts of the order that are found in a given aisle and then passes the order to another picker who selects all of the items in another aisle, and so on. Under this system, the order is almost always handled by more than one individual.

Wave picking groups shipments by a given characteristic, such as common carrier. For example, all of the orders for UPS might be picked in a single wave. A second wave would pull all of the orders destined for parcel post, and still other waves would select shipments routed by other carriers.

Order picking in your warehouse

It is possible for warehouse operators to design a system that is nearly error free, to implement a dedication to quality through training, and then to insist upon standards of order picking that are flawless. Those who believe in zero defects and plan for it will come close to achieving this goal. One warehouse operation has an error rate of less than .01 percent.*

The order-pick line consists of pick slots (locations) where the product is available for selection in the quantity called for on the picking document. The location of the pick slots depends on the system, but they must always provide the necessary picking identification and be physically conducive to low fatigue and error-free picking. One way to achieve this is to put the fastest-moving items between waist and eye level.

Variances in package size and configuration, picking quantities, stocking quantity, and inventory requirements often necessitate more than one picking system. There are three basic picking methods:

♦ A full-pallet load is the minimum amount selected. (unit-load picking).

♦ Nothing less than a full case is selected, (case picking).

♦ Individual containers are removed from cases, (broken-case picking).

Order picking can be manual, power-assisted, automatic, or a combination of these. A manual system uses two- or four-wheel hand trucks or carts pushed through the pick line and hand loaded. A powered system uses unguided or guided vehicles to transport and elevate the warehouse worker through the pick line. The worker manually loads pallets, carts, or other containers. An automatic system uses computer information and controls to guide pickers to the pick locations, elevate them to the proper height, and indicate the proper pick quantity. Automated picking provides additional controls that replace the order picker.

Discrete (single order) picking requires the picker to assemble each order before moving to another one.

---

*   This subchapter is based on writing by William J. Ransom, Ransom & Associates.

Discrete picking has these advantages:
- ◆ Maintains single-order integrity.
- ◆ Simplifies the picker's job.
- ◆ Avoids rehandling or repacking.
- ◆ Provides fast customer-order service.
- ◆ Allows for direct error checking and establishes direct error responsibility.
- ◆ Is highly efficient when the number of stock keeping units (SKUs) per order is small.

Discrete picking has these disadvantages:
- ◆ Requires full order-picking route travel for all orders.
- ◆ Doesn't allow for speed-picking of large quantities of an individual item.
- ◆ Requires the highest number of picking personnel for a given number of orders.

Batch picking is the retrieval of the total quantity of each item for a group of orders.

Batch picking has these advantages:
- ◆ Reduces travel time up to 50 percent.
- ◆ Permits volume picking from bulk storage, thus reducing the need for restocking pick lines.
- ◆ Provides a second count of the quantity picked by comparing the batch picked against the individual quantities in each order.
- ◆ Improves supervision by concentrating final order-assembly in a smaller area.

Batch picking has these disadvantages:
- ◆ A second pick, or a distribution of the picked quantity, is required to fill individual order requirements.
- ◆ Space is required for the order-assembly operation.
- ◆ Individual orders cannot be shipped until the entire batch of orders is complete.
- ◆ Counting is done twice and differences in count may require reconciliation time.

In designing an order-pick line, consider how restocking will be accomplished. A minimum of one day's picking requirements is usually kept in the pick area. When restocking volume is equal to picking volume, it may be better to pick those items from the bulk supply area rather than from the pick area.

Order picking efficiency is dependent on accessibility of material to be picked. Labor content for order picking is usually the highest of all the jobs in the warehouse, so picking offers the greatest opportunity for cost reduction through improved layout, better methods, and faster equipment.

Equipment for picking and shipping

Equipment used on shipping docks receives the hardest use of any equipment in the warehouse.* Lift trucks used on the dock, make short runs, are started frequently, stop often, and are maneuvered. This activity accelerates wear and requires more maintenance.

Special factors you need to consider in choosing lift trucks for dock work include:

- ◆ Install the biggest, widest tires possible. Wider tires reduce damage to both warehouse and trailer floors.
- ◆ Lowered height for lift truck masts should not exceed 83 inches. This height allows entry into even the oldest of trailers. Specify a free-lift upright for both unloading and loading of trailers. The free-lift upright elevates the load without increasing the overall lowered height of the fork-lift mast, which allows workers to remove double stack loads inside a trailer.

Stationary equipment is subject to impact from trucks and lift trucks. Equipment needs to be rugged and well-maintained to stand receiving dock use. Choose the heavy-duty options on equipment for shipping. Increased uptime will more than cover the increased cost.

Stationary dock equipment is as important as the mobile equipment at your shipping dock. Specifications for dock equipment should include:

---

*   Ibid.

- Automatic dock levelers to provide full height adjustment for variances in truck heights. Levelers should include a hook to secure the leveler to the trailer and prevent premature movement. Be sure the leveler includes bumpers to protect the dock from the impact of the truck.
- Dock seals or shelters will shield the inside dock area from outside weather, reduce heat loss, and prevent unauthorized entry into the warehouse.
- Lighting should illuminate the inside of the trailer to help avoid accidents.

Questions that solve problems

As you appraise the effectiveness of order picking and shipping in your operation, here are some questions for your warehouse supervisors:

Q Do we pick each order independently (discrete picking) or do we use batch picking?

C Whichever answer you receive, you should then ask whether anybody has considered the alternate method.

Q Have we isolated the cost of order picking and shipping so we know what percent of total warehouse costs are represented by this function?

C Failure to do this may indicate a lack of awareness of how important this function is. On the other hand, you may find that it is a smaller percentage than you previously thought.

Q Have we eliminated any regional warehousing through cross-dock operations?

C If cross-dock operations have never been considered, you should initiate a feasibility study to test the potential advantages of this system.

Q Are you fully satisfied with our parts numbering system and our order picking forms?

C This is a good question for your warehouse workers as well as for supervisors.

Q Have we tried reverse order picking?

C If your people don't understand the term, you may be missing an opportunity. ❖

Chapter 24

Unitizing

While attempts to unitize marine freight go back to ancient history, unitized handling as we know it today started with the military during World War II. The industrial truck was in its earliest development and those in charge recognized a wood platform or pallet as the best way for a fork-lift truck to transport a number of small pieces of freight.

Unitized handling's origin

The first such platforms were skids, consisting of a deck of wide boards nailed across two or more runner boards. This raised the platform enough to allow the forks to slide underneath and pick it up. Because of the need for stacking stability, additional boards were nailed across the bottom and the skid became a pallet. Pallets were and are made of wood because wood is the cheapest construction material available.

At first, skids and pallets came in a wide variety of sizes — some measuring as little as three by three for low-volume grocery products, others as large as four by eight feet (stevedore pallets) used in marine transportation. Because each warehouse had a different storage rack system, pallet standardization seemed impossible.

The standard pallet

Pallet standardization was fostered by the U.S. military, which used a standard pallet to move war-time supplies. Huge quantities of these became surplus in 1945 as World War II ended.

The Australian government had a particularly large supply of materials handling equipment left over after the war. The Australian government formed a Commonwealth Handling and Equipment Pool, later abbreviated as CHEP. Because the Pool had a standard size military pallet, Australia achieved standardization, as a legacy of its war surplus.

Standardization came to the United States during the 1960s. General Foods deserves prime credit for the introduction of a standard grocery pallet. This standard (see Figure 1) specified the size and spacing of the boards on the top and bottom deck, as well as the size of the runner boards or stringers. Notches on the stringer boards allowed the forklift to lift the pallet from all four sides, though it is handled most easily from the 40-inch face because of its larger openings.

Figure 1

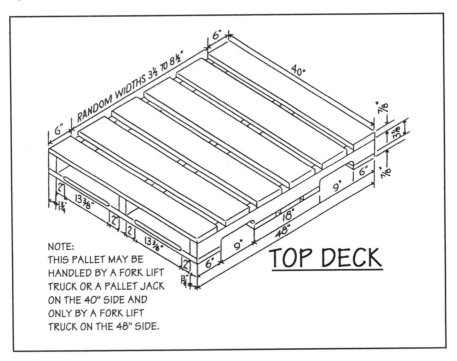

Because of its influence on both suppliers and customers, General Foods introduced and enforced a standard size for grocery pallets. The Grocery Manufacturers of America (GMA) endorsed the concept and finished the job of establishing the General Foods specification as an industry standard.

Wholesalers and chains adapted their materials handling and storage rack systems to use the new standard pallet.

A Grocery Pallet Council was established, but eventually efforts to maintain pallet standards disintegrated. As the hardwoods in the General Foods design became scarce and expensive, many pallet users switched to cheaper woods. Others changed thickness and spacing of deckboards, making a less durable pallet. Eventually the Grocery Pallet Council disbanded, and today the only remaining standard specification is the size: The 48 inch by 40 inch (1 by 1.2m) pallet remains the predominant size used in the grocery products industry, and most storage rack systems are designed to accommodate this size unitized load.

Alternatives to wood pallets

While the wood pallet is the oldest and easiest method of handling unitized loads, it is not the only method available. The first developments of substitutes for pallets began as early as the 1940s, when materials handling manufacturers cooperated with paper companies in developing a disposable shipping platform known as a slipsheet.

Figure 2
Photo courtesy of
Cascade Corporation

Constructed of high tensile laminated paper, the slipsheet is much thinner than a wood pallet and cannot be handled safely with conventional forks. Equipment manufacturers developed a special device known as a 'push/pull' attachment. The device is designed to grip a protruding tab of the slipsheet and pull the sheet with its load onto flat metal plates that support the load while it is being transported. At the destination, a pusher moves the loaded slipsheet onto the floor of a trailer or warehouse. Figure 2 shows the slipsheet and push/pull attachment in use.

Another special device that has been in use since the 1960s is the carton clamp or grab truck. Figure 3 shows a clamp truck with a load. This truck's paddles allow it to be lifted by squeezing the sides of the load. Originally designed for cotton bales and rolls of paper, some clamp trucks have been designed to rotate the load so that it can be inverted or placed on its side.

Figure 3
Photo courtesy of
Cascade
Corporation

The clamp truck works best with relatively large and sturdy packages. Because it requires side pressure to lift the unit, improper pressure adjustment or weak packaging will cause product damage. In the early days of clamp truck use, extensive damage to home appliances occurred when a warehouse operator using a grab truck with improperly adjusted clamps dented each unit it lifted.

The clamp device must be carefully maintained to control damage by operator abuse. Some warehouse operators use clamp attachments to pick up everything from bicycles to bailing wire, causing damage to both the clamp attachment and the merchandise handled.

Because of the way it functions, the clamp truck does not require any loading platform. It can pick up a load and transfer it from one loading platform to another. One disadvantage is that it causes some space loss in warehouses and trailers because a few inches of side void are left for clearance of clamp arms.

Comparing options

The wood pallet is the fastest and simplest way to store and transfer unitized loads. It is easier to operate an industrial truck equipped with forks than with any other kind of loading attachment.

The generous-sized openings in standard pallets allow them to be safely stowed and retrieved even when they are in a high stack and the lift driver is maneuvering a load 20 feet off the ground.

To be most economical, the pallet should be transported with the load from origin to destination. If the material is hand stacked from a warehouse pallet to the floor of the truck, or if the process is reversed, the loading or unloading process will take more than six times as long as unitized loading. One time study of the process showed that manual loading of 22-pound cases will be done at a rate of eight pallets, (480 cases) per man hour. The loading of full pallets can be accomplished at the rate of 50 pallets (3,000 cases) per hour.

If full pallets are loaded, the shipper has the option of donating them or taking other pallets in exchange. Pallets are costly, and most users are reluctant to donate a platform that costs between six and ten dollars. On the other hand, exchanging pallets with the trucker, vendor, or supplier runs the risk of trading a costly pallet for a cheap pallet.

Few warehouse people can quickly recognize the difference between expensive species of wood and cheap ones. Few operators have time to check the thickness and spacing of deck boards and bottom boards. As a result, there is no practical way to enforce the design standard at shipping and receiving docks. Industry frustration with the junk pallets increased after efforts to police a standard system collapsed.

Fire protection is another significant problem. Underwriters consider high stacks of wood pallets to be one of the worst hazards in a warehouse. The spaces between boards allow combustion to create a *flue effect*, which causes a very dangerous fire. Therefore, preferred risk underwriters typically restrict the stack height of empty pallets in a warehouse.

To avoid wasting valuable storage space, warehouse operators often store empty pallets outdoors where they are subject to deterioration and contamination by birds and rodents. They are exposed to the elements and are further deteriorated by sun, rain, snow, or ice. Finally, wood does not lend itself to steam cleaning or other cleaning methods.

Slipsheets are more compact and less costly than wood pallets. Their compactness allows them to be stored in a much smaller space, and because of their construction they do not present the fire hazard of a wood pallet.

However there are no standard specifications for slipsheets either. They can be made of everything from paper to plastic. One brewing company uses plastic slipsheets just once before they are ground and remanufactured. Slipsheets require special equipment and handling because the conventional low-lift pallet truck is designed specifically for wood pallets. When slipsheet loads are received at a company using forklifts, the loads are usually transferred to a wooden pallet.

The clamp truck is used to accomplish this transfer, since it can lift a load and place it onto a platform. Procter and Gamble developed its *trucker owned pallet system* (TOPS). Each transportation company wishing to enjoy the labor savings of a unitized load brings pallets to the company's dock, and clamp trucks are used to drop unitized loads onto the trucker's pallets. However, clamps don't work well on every kind of load. Unitized loads of very small boxes are not practical for clamp loading since smaller cartons are likely to drop out of the center of the unit load.

The search for a new pallet

In 1989 and 1990, frustration with the damage caused by *junk* pallets caused an intensive search for alternatives. Cleveland Consulting Associates developed two studies for the Joint Industry Shipping Container Committee, a new group sponsored by Food Marketing Institute, Grocery Manufacturers of America (GMA), and National American Wholesale Grocers Association (NAWGA). The study concluded that pallet cost to the grocery industry alone is $1.9 billion per year, which translates to sixteen cents per case of groceries, or ten dollars for each unit load. These costs include product damage caused by poor pallets, replacement and repair of damaged pallets, extra cost to motor carriers in transporting pallets, productivity loss as pallets are sorted and selected, workers compensation costs from pallet-caused injuries, and administration of pallets. One wholesaler esti-mates that seven out of ten injuries in his warehouse are caused by pallets.

The joint industry committee announced a competition to develop a one-way disposable shipping platform.

At least four alternative expendable pallets have been designed.

- ◆ Pressed-wood-fiber pallets have about the same durability as wood, and they save space because they are designed to be nested. They are nail free, which avoids product damage.
- ◆ Corrugated fiberboard pallets are less durable than wood and are not repairable, but they could be suitable for single-use shipping applications.
- ◆ Plastic pallets are more durable than wood. While they are not repairable, they can be made of a recyclable material and are often used in a closed-loop system where the pallet is always recovered for re-use.
- ◆ Metal pallets have similar characteristics and have the same uses.

Both plastic and metal can be sanitized to meet FDA requirements for food processing. The U.S. Postal Service has experimented with both a nes-table wood fiber pallet and a nestable plastic pallet.

Perhaps the most significant design change for permanent pallets is a full four-way entry rather than the notched support board used in the ear-lier standard pallet. Figure 4 shows a full four-way entry block pallet.

Figure 4

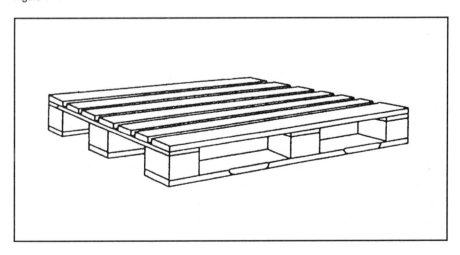

Some warehouse operations require that the stringer dimension face the aisle, and in high stacking it becomes nearly impossible for a lift driver to insert forks in the notches without damaging the pallet. Some truck loading patterns also require rotation of the pallets, and an attempt to handle them through the notches creates similar damage opportunities.

Because of the need for full four-way entry, there is strong pressure to develop a practical block pallet that offers equal ease of entry from any side.

In 1992, the chairman of the joint industry committee made a preliminary recommendation for a new pallet — a full four-way block pallet. The chairman pointed out that this new design offered handling from all four sides by either lift truck or pallet jack, something not available before. He also indicated that a leasing program was necessary because the cost of the four-way block pallet was relatively high.

While the report was labeled as 'preliminary', it was a clear sign of progress. Because unitized handling remains one of the biggest challenges for warehouse operators, everyone hopes for continuing progress in providing more attractive options.

For both the one-way and the permanent pallet, there is also new emphasis on environmental features. Some 63 million pallets are destroyed each year. Some are burned as boiler fuel, but others must be hauled to landfills at great expense. Environmentalists want a pallet that can be recycled or compressed and placed in conventional trash containers.

Pallet leasing

In 1958, CHEP was purchased from the Australian government by Brambles Industries Limited. This privatized pallet pool offered pallets on a lease basis to users in a variety of industries. After proving the concept in Australia, Brambles expanded into New Zealand.

To launch the European campaign, Brambles merged with a British firm, GKN. A pallet leasing pool started in the United Kingdom in 1974, and it spread throughout Europe. GKN Brambles launched its leasing program in the United States in 1990.

The CHEP pallet follows the original General Foods specification, with one exception. The wood specified is southern pine or Douglas fir, not the 'hardwood' of the original standard pallet because the wood is lighter. The CHEP pallet has a weight of 65 pounds compared to 80 pounds in the General Foods specification. The loading deck covers 81 percent of the 40 inch by 48 inch surface, and the bottom deck covers 57percent of the surface. CHEP pallets have a bright blue paint on the side surfaces, which allows the pallets to be easily identified and separated.

The truly distinctive feature of the CHEP system is that the pallets are not sold, only leased. The pallet owner, not the user, is responsible for maintenance of the pallets. When a pallet has been emptied, it either must be returned to the lessor or re-leased from CHEP.

CHEP collects a fee if the pallet is lost, but presumably there is no fee for damage unless it can be proven that the pallet was abused. Of course competitive alternatives to CHEP have also been established.

Consider the relative advantages of pallet leasing or disposable shipping platforms:

Empty wood pallets, whether leased or owned, are still a fire risk when stacked indoors. If outdoor storage is used, the contamination and deterioration problems remain. CHEP assumes this burden by keeping idle pallets at its own depots, but a two-day supply of pallets must be kept by each grocery manufacturer using the system.

In contrast, the one-way shipping platform is designed for material handling rather than for storage. A low-cost shipping platform is not strong enough to use for high-piled storage stacks. Therefore each unit load must be transferred from the shipping platform to a durable warehouse pallet. Such transfer is clearly feasible, but it represents an additional expense.

A leased pallet made of some material other than wood could be an attractive alternative, particularly if the material could be stored indoors or steam cleaned.

Understanding pallet costs

While pallets are recognized as a major challenge for most warehouse operators, few have attempted to analyze the cost of maintaining a pallet supply. Once the pallet is purchased, it must be stored, repaired, sorted, and eventually sold or destroyed. Continuing costs are usually lost as they are combined with other cost categories. If repairs are done internally, the cost of labor and materials must be isolated. Now that the option of leasing pallets from a third party exists, operators need to develop their true total pallet costs in order to compare these costs with pallet leasing programs.

The search for a better permanent warehouse pallet continues. One of the goals for both the one-way and the permanent pallet is to have a weight of less than 50 pounds each. No permanent pallet design has achieved the desired weight, but a few have come as low as 55 pounds.

Figure 5	**Alternatives to Present Pallet System** **Total System Financial Recap**				
	Cost per Pallet Trip			Millions	
System Alternative	**M'facturer**	**Distributor**	**Total**	**Industry Savings**	**Investment Required**
Present System	$7.06	$3.03	$10.99	Base	Base
Industry Co-op Pallet Pool *	2.02	1.12	3.14	$1,333	$1,100
Private Pallet Pool Rental	4.58	0.86	5.44	892	0
Private Per-trip Pallet Rental	8.21	(2.22)	5.99	787	0
One-way Disposable Shipping Platform					
At $3 each	3.21	0.06	3.27	1,303	48
At $4 each	4.21	0.06	4.27	1,117	48

* Committee rejected this alternative because of the size of investment

Courtesy of Cleveland Consulting Associates

Designs have been submitted by trade associations representing the plywood and pallet manufacturing industries.

Suppliers are testing materials other than wood, particularly plastic. Some designs use a mixture of hard woods and soft woods. The non-wood pallets continue to be quite expensive, but the cost is moving down.

Questions that solve problems

Here are some topics to discuss with your people as you investigate unitizing in your warehouse operation:

Q Aside from conventional wooden pallets, have we ever considered any of the available materials handling options?

C If the answers reflect a *we've always done it that way* outlook, ask why some experiments could not be undertaken with slipsheets, clamp trucks, or both. Warehousing can be a traditional business — be sure your people are not dedicated to the old ways of doing things when better ways are available.

Q Do we exchange pallets with any of our major customers?

C If the answer is affirmative, get some details about exactly how the exchange works and whether you are trading expensive pallets for cheap ones.

Q Have we calculated exactly what it costs to maintain pallets in our warehouse, and have we reduced this to a cost per pallet?

C The answer may indicate that further exploration of alternatives is not profitable, or it may show the opposite. A high pallet maintenance cost should stimulate the exploration of an internal repair operation to salvage and recondition broken pallets. ❖

Chapter 25

Specialized storage

While most warehouses are designed to handle packaged products at ambient temperatures, some are equipped for specialized storage. These specialists may offer temperature-controlled warehousing, hazardous materials storage, order fulfillment or handling of household goods.

Temperature-controlled warehousing has expanded with the growing popularity of frozen foods and fresh produce. Temperature-controlled warehousing for non-food products is needed for distribution of chemicals that require refrigeration.

Warehousing for hazardous products may not have grown in popularity, but it has certainly grown in complexity. As environmentalists increase our awareness of chemical hazards, those warehouse operators who store such products have experienced growing regulation and risk-management problems.

A growth area in specialized warehousing is fulfillment, the handling of mail order and express shipments that move directly to the consumer.

While there is nothing new about household goods warehousing, many logistics managers have adapted these techniques for office equipment and other commercial products.

Temperature-controlled warehousing

There are four kinds of cold storage warehouses. The standard food freezer operates at 0 degrees to -10 degrees Fahrenheit; ice cream freezers operate at -20 degrees to -25 degrees Fahrenheit; blast freezers combine extreme cold with rapid air circulation to freeze freshly packed products quickly; and chilled warehouses hold product at 35 degrees to 45 degrees Fahrenheit. When you are designing a cold storage building, consider potential future uses and the cost of conversion. For example, if you are building a chilled warehouse, you may design the building to allow for future conversion to a freezer warehouse. The lower the temperature one wants to maintain, the higher the cost of the building.*

In the early decades of the twentieth century, most temperature-controlled products were chilled rather than frozen. Consumer-sized packages of frozen foods were introduced in 1929 but did not become popular until the 1940s. By 1970, freezer space was over 75 percent of the total public refrigerated warehouse space in the United States. *Cooler* space is used primarily for fresh fruits and vegetables, dairy products, and eggs. There is increasing use of chilled storage for non-food products such as plastics, film, seeds, and adhesives.**

One significant difference between temperature-controlled and dry warehousing is the cost of the facility. A freezer warehouse usually costs two to three times as much as a dry storage warehouse of similar size. The cost difference in utilities is even more extreme, so the successful cold storage operator depends on excellent conservation and building maintenance to control energy costs.

Temperature gauges should be placed throughout the freezer room, one at eye level near the entrance and others in the corners of the room. In addition, a temperature recorder with a weekly disk should be used for a permanent record. A continuous monitoring system that warns of temperature fluctuations of three degrees or more should be installed. These reduce exposure to liability for temperature fluctuations and fire. Plastic curtains together with hydraulic doors help control energy costs.***

In a dry warehouse, walls may be thin steel panel with a modest amount of insulation. In contrast, the walls of a freezer are an important part of the insulation system and a freezer may have six inch foam insulation panels, clad by sheet steel, both inside and out. The floor is an important insulator in a frozen warehouse. A typical specification would be six

---

*   From *Temperature-Controlled Warehousing: The Essential Differences*, by Tom Ryan and Joel Weber, United Refrigeration Services, Inc. This article appeared in *Warehousing Forum*, Volume 3, Number 11, ©The Ackerman Company, Columbus, Ohio.

**   From *Operational Training Guide*, ©International Association of Refrigerated Warehouses, Bethesda, Maryland.

*** From Jesse Westburgh, Wales Industries, Inc., Columbus, Ohio.

inches of concrete poured on top of six inches of foam insulation. To protect against heaving of the earth beneath the floor, heat is provided by piping warm ethylene glycol through a layer of sand beneath the insulation. The insulation layer thus serves a dual purpose: Keeping the cold in and the heat below out.

While the roof of a dry warehouse may consist of nothing more than a thin steel deck with a small amount of insulation, most temperature-controlled warehouse roofs start with a steel deck strong enough to hold refrigeration equipment mounted on the roof. Above the deck is a layer of three-quarter inch fiberboard. Above that is an additional 10 to 12 inch layer of foam insulation and another layer of fiberboard. The weather seal is single-ply rubber roofing protected by a layer of stone ballast.

Lift trucks are affected by cold, especially the sub-zero temperature of a frozen-products warehouse. Tight insulation and recirculated air prevent use of internal combustion engines. Electric trucks need heaters for the electric contact points, as well as heavier-duty batteries. Because the harsh conditions produce additional wear and tear, preventive maintenance is even more critical than in dry storage warehousing.

The batteries on electric equipment used in a cold environment will last longer if they are charged every four to six hours rather than the eight hours recommended in normal temperatures. The warehouse that has both dry and cold space should rotate fork trucks so that each truck spends only part of the time in the freezer. Some trucks are specifically designed for this environment, with an enclosed cab to allow relief from the cold.

Workers should have a break room where they can relax with coffee or soft drinks. A ten-minute break each hour will improve productivity for people working in the freezer. Rotate employees from all areas of the warehouse so that each worker spends only part time in the freezer.*

Most warehouse operators provide protective clothing for employees, including insulated boots, gloves, and freezer suits. Working in a freezer results in greater fatigue since a significant portion of body energy is spent in keeping warm. In an ambient-temperature warehouse, a work crew is capable of handling an overtime or emergency assignment of well over 12 hours

---

*   Ibid.

without significant loss of productivity or accuracy. Fatigue takes its toll in a much shorter time in a frozen warehouse. Most operators experience a greater amount of sick leave among workers in a frozen environment.

The task of supervision is more difficult in this environment. A supervisor in a dry warehouse can watch the loading dock and gain a good idea of what is going on throughout the warehouse. In a temperature-controlled warehouse, the dock is separated from storage areas by walls and doors and a supervisor on the dock cannot see what is happening in the storage rooms. Effective supervision in the cold storage area requires additional foremen in the cold rooms. Supervisors have even greater risk of health problems, because they may move in and out of cold rooms more often than workers and are less physically active.

The nature of cold storage changes the way work is scheduled. Because the cost of space is very high, operators tend to select outbound orders as close as possible to the time of shipment in order to minimize space committed to staging. The need to preserve cold product may prevent staging outside the freezer area. Performance of motor carriers is particularly critical, so the cold storage operator must run a scheduled truck-dock.

Housekeeping is another function that is affected by the harsh environment in a frozen warehouse. Spills that are not cleaned up will freeze, causing accidents and floor stains. Scrubbing a freezer floor is far more expensive than in dry warehouses, because it requires the use of a non-freezing solution. Some cleaning solutions are banned by Food and Drug Administration (FDA) rules and sometimes the only way to clean a floor in a frozen environment is to scrape it.

Because the consequences of operations failure are so serious, the cold storage warehouse requires an extra measure of management precision. Failure to maintain temperature control of the product can have very costly consequences for the owner of the merchandise. Therefore the warehouse operator must not only protect the product, but provide ample proof that such protection was continuous.

As the use of chilled and frozen products seems to be growing faster than the economy as a whole, it is likely that temperature-controlled warehousing will enjoy similar growth.

Hazardous materials warehousing

Attitude is the key to successful storage and handling of hazardous materials. There can be no shortcuts, and there is a significant commitment required in terms of capital and management involvement.*

It is our responsibility to protect our habitat. Those choosing to warehouse hazardous materials must assume the responsibility to follow the appropriate rules and regulations. While recent laws have created new responsibilities, the moral responsibility is the same as it was: We must not pollute or adulterate our environment.

What is a hazardous chemical?

Hazardous materials are grouped into the following categories: flammables, explosives, corrosives, poisons, radioactive materials, and oxidizers. In addition, as the EPA's classification of materials continues to be expanded, the number of materials considered hazardous is likely to increase.**

Since many agencies have responded to different regulatory needs, each has its own definition of hazardous commodities. OSHA excludes products packaged for retail sale. For example, swimming pool chlorinators are excluded from the hazardous commodity list, but similar chemicals may also be included. At times, the local fire marshall may reach decisions that are in conflict with OSHA.

Before you permit any unfamiliar material in your warehouse, you need to know its hazards. Unfortunately, no single reputable source of information is available. Despite the difficulty of making a determination, you are responsible for any mistakes you might make once you have made the decision to store hazardous materials.

The problem is particularly difficult for third-party warehouse operators. The U.S. Department of Transportation has held that warehouse operators are *offerers* of material for transportation. In the past, third-party warehouse operators were considered by D.O.T. to be *agents* of the owners,

---

*   Part of this section is based on an article by Mark Campbell of Southland Bonded
     Warehouses in Atlanta, Georgia.
**   From *Hazardous Materials Storage: The Essential Differences* by Lake Polan III of Allied
     Warehousing Services, Inc., *Warehousing Forum*, Volume 4, Number 4, ©The Ackerman
     Company, Columbus, Ohio.

and could be held responsible only for failure to carry out the owner's instruction. In the eyes of hazardous chemical regulators, the warehouser has a responsibility to the community, the customers, and the customer's customers to act in a way that does not harm any part of the environment.

Regulations and training

The regulation of hazardous materials storage and handling comes from several sources, three of them federal. The U.S. Department of Transportation publishes hazardous material regulations that apply to anyone who ships such material in interstate commerce. A typical D.O.T. regulation requires that every shipper provide training for all the people who handle the product.

OSHA has regulated warehousing activities for many years, and the agency is particularly concerned with hazardous chemicals. One OSHA regulation requires that every employee working with hazardous chemicals be trained to use a respirator, which must be available for emergencies.

A third federal regulator is the Environmental Protection Agency (EPA). Part of EPA's concern is storm water regulations, that restrict the handling of storm water discharges from warehouses with hazardous materials.

In addition to federal regulations, most of the states in the United States have their own regulations. Below the state level, there are usually city or county rules affecting warehousing of hazardous commodities. With so many regulators, it is a complex job to verify that warehouses in various jurisdictions remain in compliance with all of the local, state, and national regulations that could be applied.

The best hazardous chemical warehousers view every warehouse worker as a skilled craftsman. To comply with current regulations, one warehouse organization prepared a two-day weekend course on the handling of hazardous materials. It is not only necessary to provide such training, but also to document the fact that everyone handling such materials has successfully received and absorbed the training materials.*

---

* This section is based on material provided by Robert T. Walther of Brook Warehousing System.

Reliable hazardous materials information

It is not unusual for the warehouse operator to find that the person responsible for regulation knows less about the product than the operator does. In
such situations, it is wise to influence selection of the authority having juris-
diction, since this can have a dramatic effect on cost. Sometimes the
warehouse operator becomes the authority by default, simply because no
other authority is willing to make a decision.

Unfortunately, it is not practical to provide a simple how-to that encom-
passes all the product variables and provides the storer with instructions on
safe procedures. So where does the operator go to learn the best way?

Third-party warehouse operators might seek information from other
companies that handle similar products. Private warehouses might share
information with third-party warehouse operators and with other operators of private warehouses. Even storers of competitive products are willing
to share information about safe warehousing practices, simply because
everyone is anxious to learn from others in this field.

Consultants who specialize in environmental safety assist both produc-
ers and storers of hazardous chemicals. The names of reputable consultants in the field can be obtained from your local or state fire marshall or
emergency planning office. *Hazmat World*, published by Tower Bornes Pub-
lishing Company, carries advertisements for experts in this field.

Finally, National Fire Protection Agency (NFPA) is the leading authority
on fire safety, and the cost of membership in this association is nominal.

Because regulation in the field is changing rapidly, there is a danger
that the information you have is now out of date. To be sure that your warehouse is in compliance with current standards, it is wise to use the services
of an agency specializing in interpretation of the federal register.

Of all the information sources available, the best is the manufacturer of
the product. The producer is required to prepare information about the
safe keeping of that product.

Becoming a competent warehouser of hazardous materials requires a
serious commitment in organization, manpower, and capital resources.
The warehouse operator is exposed to increased risks, uncertain requirements, greater costs, and a potential regulatory nightmare. Successful hazardous materials warehousing requires tight discipline throughout the
organization, since the consequences of failure can be most severe.

Storers of hazardous materials must first be concerned with safety, then
with service, and finally with cost. As the requirements become more strin-

gent, only the most competent warehouse operators will remain in this line of business.*

Fulfillment warehousing

Six special features make product fulfillment warehousing different from most public and private warehousing.** These are the following:
1. The warehouse operator has direct contact with consumers.
2. Information requirements are instantaneous.
3. Order sizes are much smaller than typical warehouse orders.
4. The order-taking function at warehouse level is much more precise, particularly because it involves contact with the consumer.
5. Customer service requirements are different and typically more demanding.
6. The transportation function is more complex.

Storage and materials handling functions are quite different because fulfillment warehousing involves more than simple storage. Fast turns and low volumes mean gravity-flow racks and high-security areas are almost always needed.

The handling function will also differ from that of the more conventional warehouse. While there may be some less-than-truck load shipments, there will be a much higher concentration of parcel service, and handling operations will include the metering of parcel shipments. Thus the materials handling equipment investment will have more emphasis on scales and meters to control outbound movements.

Paper flow for a fulfillment warehouse is more complex than for most other warehouses. Many orders are received by telephone and a significant amount of time is spent in handling customer returns. Because a fulfillment operator deals directly with individual consumers, the customer service function is particularly critical.

*   Polan, Op. Cit.
**   From presentations by Jeffrey A. Coopersmith, Columbus, Ohio, and by James E. Dockter of Professional Book Distributors, Atlanta, Georgia. From *Warehousing Forum*, Volume 2, Number 2 ©The Ackerman Company, Columbus, Ohio.

Some users want the fulfillment center to create invoices, or even dunning notices. Accounts-receivable aging reports are another service that can be a by-product of invoice handling.

Nearly every fulfillment center must handle the major credit cards easily, through either a local bank or an outside service agency. Many fulfillment centers handle banking for their customers, thus a superior banking relationship is necessary.

The best of fulfillment centers offer a 24-hour turnaround on orders. While a few take two or three days to process and ship, fast turnaround is becoming a standard.

This fast turnaround requirement makes labor flexibility imperative to deal with seasonality and variance in work load. Superior fulfillment centers maintain a pool of part-time workers who are available if a second shift must be added or if extra people are needed quickly.

A fulfillment center has serious exposure to claims and theft. Because product shipped can be misdirected by a dishonest person who is running a postal machine, care should be taken in selecting the individual for this job. Many fulfillment centers negotiate the inventory variance to be allowed in advance, based on the customer's own experience with errors. Some users will allow a predetermined formula for shrinkage, that is in line with their internal experience.

A fulfillment center must absorb the financial consequences of its mistakes — the public warehouseman's usual limitations do not apply in this service. The fulfillment center normally needs more equipment for communications than for shipping, including the ability to handle credit cards and toll-free phone lines. Compared to the conventional warehouse, order volume is extremely high. The ability to automate many tasks with a computer is far more critical in the fulfillment center than in the conventional warehouse. Such an operation will also usually be responsible for a high number of stockkeeping units.

As companies constantly seek new ways to promote their products, fulfillment is a warehousing service that is destined to increase in popularity.

Household goods storage

Although there are many similarities between the warehousing of household goods (HHG) and other merchandise, there are three essential differences that define the activities and the way they are managed.

First, merchandise warehousing typically deals with *new* products. In contrast, the warehousing of household goods is usually *used* furniture. Second, HHG storage is almost always a part of the transportation contract, rather than a separately defined distribution activity. Third, the ownership of the goods handled has passed to the end consumer, which personalizes the activity to a degree that does not exist in other warehousing.*

In spite of these differences, warehousing of household goods has a great deal in common with merchandise warehousing. Both have accommodated the same changes in technology, from unit loads to computerization. Both require a high degree of cost control and information availability in order to meet the demands of their customers. Both are engaged in the growth of value-added services to ensure customer satisfaction and to produce increased revenues.

Third-party warehouse operators in both industries began much the same way: They were entrepreneurial businesses providing a localized service.

Because the HHG warehouse operator is required to provide transportation, trucking capability is mandatory but this is not always the case in merchandise warehousing. The transportation contract often calls for movement over a long distance, so the furniture warehouseman needs state and federal authority.

In order to make a profit on a long distance run, the HHG warehouseman also needs to find backhaul loads. To solve the backhaul problem, HHG warehouse operators banded together in agency relationships, and many of these evolved into national van lines. These associations provide the means of controlling equipment, and they also offer a division of revenue for services performed. HHG van lines have established a closer bond and a more formalized sharing of information than any of the voluntary merchandise warehouse groups.

Mechanization and unitization have changed household goods storage much as they have changed merchandise warehousing. With general merchandise, materials handling evolved from case handling to the movement of palletized unit loads. With household goods, containers called vaults are

---

*   This section is adapted from an article by J. Thomas Foley and Frederick S. Schorr, *Warehousing Forum*, Volume 7, Number 11. ©The Ackerman Company, Columbus, Ohio.

used to eliminate the piece-by-piece handling of furniture and personal effects.

Because of the specialized storage requirements of household goods, the multi-story buildings have retained their economic viability. Some operators developed creative programs to produce revenue, including customer self-storage and records storage. There is a significant liability problem in handling used furniture, so self-storage is particularly attractive to the HHG firm.

Preparation of HHG for storage is labor intensive. Because weight and configuration of many items requires more than one person to perform the service, handling costs are a larger part of the total expense than they are for merchandise storage.

Household goods are more vulnerable to damage than general merchandise. Furthermore, because the products are not new, the question of where the damage occurred is a potential problem. Frequency and cost of claims is greater for HHG than for general merchandise. HHG warehouse operators usually offer a supplemental cargo insurance and they provide a claim service to provide expeditious repair or adjustment for damage.

The diversification of services offered by HHG operators has been driven by two forces: Seasonality (most moves take place during the summer months) and diversification.

Seasonality forces HHG companies to seek low season sources of revenue. Diversification requires a search for products other than used household goods. These additional commodities fall into two categories:

- **High-value products:** Items such as computers, office products, medical diagnostic equipment, and exhibits for trade shows.
- **New products:** Furniture, fixtures, and appliances.

One of the fastest growing HHG segments is the temporary warehousing, consolidation, delivery, and installation of inbound shipments of furniture and furnishings for hotels, offices, and hospitals. Major hotel chains contract directly with moving companies to receive and store their products, including everything from furnishings and carpeting to wall hangings, drapes, kitchen equipment, silverware, and china. This requires coordination among builders, decorators, and warehouse operators. The period between the completion and the grand opening is usually *just in time.*

Van line service has long been recognized as an important third-party supplier for makers of computers and other large office machines. Van lines offer a service different from that of a common carrier in that they can store and transport an office machine in an unpackaged state. The padded-van approach to distribution can eliminate the cost of packaging.

A reverse logistics service is performed as office machines are returned for refurbishing, leasing, or resale. In this case, the machines move from the office to a consolidation center. They may be refurbished or redistributed from there, or returned to the manufacturer.

Trade shows have become increasingly popular as a marketing tool, and the crating and/or handling of materials into exhibit halls is a major growth area. Serving this market takes considerable mechanical skill as well as JIT capability.

Another growth area is the handling of oversized items, such as telephone switching equipment, which requires the use of a rigger to move it into buildings. Some HHG operators have created specialized divisions to provide these services.

HHG operations place a special demand on management. You are dealing with consumers rather than managers. Although the arrangements may be made by a corporate manager, the goods are usually moved under the watchful eye of the owner. Both the beginning and end of the transaction take place away from the premises of the HHG company. Add to that the usual stressful nature of a family being uprooted and it is easy to visualize the communications problems that can complicate the moving of household goods. In each HHG transaction, managing the exception seems to be the rule.

Questions that solve problems

The questions you ask regarding specialized storage will vary depending on whether you are a user or provider.

Q Are we absolutely certain that we can identify each and every hazardous material now stored in our warehouse and that we can verify that there are no hazards which have escaped our attention?

C Consider an independent audit if you have any doubt. Companies that specialize in training and auditing of hazardous materials operations are an emerging industry.

Q Are one or more of the specialized types of storage described here found in our organization but controlled by a different management group?

C While we do not advocate empire building, you may wish to question why specialized storage is managed separately from the primary warehousing activity in your company. You should look at the potential management advantages if you consolidate the specialized functions with the general warehousing now performed.

Q Do we know as much as we should about specialized types of storage?

C Discuss whether you should do these jobs yourself or subcontract them. Consider whether some specialties represent a neglected opportunity. ❖

Chapter 26

Storage and handling equipment

A warehouse is more than a storage building; it is a system designed for maximum effectiveness in moving and storing materials. The system includes equipment as well as facilities. The equipment can be broadly divided into two categories — equipment to improve storage efficiency and machines dedicated to the movement of materials.

Equipment choice is usually governed by these six factors:
- Degree of flexibility desired.
- Nature of the warehouse building.
- Nature of the handling job — bulk, unit load, individual package, or broken-package distribution.
- Volume to be handled.
- Reliability.
- Total system cost.

Understanding space economies

The lowest cost space in any warehouse is that area closest to the roof. This is true because the incremental cost of adding interior overhead space is relatively small compared to the cost of floors and roofs. Failure to use existing overhead space could cause the need to acquire or construct additional warehousing at a far higher cost. Calculate the highest practical stack height in the building, then determine whether or not the available cubic space is being used.

Saving space also saves time, since storage in a more compact area reduces horizontal travel. The justification for purchasing storage equipment is to increase cube utilization by allowing product to occupy a maximum of available space. Live storage equipment not only increases the use of cube but also moves material. For example, a gravity flow rack provides storage for merchandise and allows product to move from the rear of the rack to the picking face.

Improving storage with racks

Because the storage rack is relatively simple, it is easy to overlook ways to increase capacity. The most common storage rack found in warehouses — the three-high rack system — when installed throughout a warehouse of 100,800 square feet will allow up to 6,930 pallet positions as shown in Figure 1. Some warehouses have sufficient cube to permit the installation of rack extensions or the replacement of the system with a higher one.

Figure 1

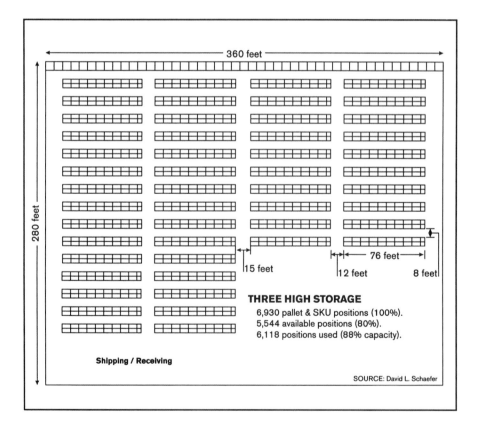

THREE HIGH STORAGE
6,930 pallet & SKU positions (100%).
5,544 available positions (80%).
6,118 positions used (88% capacity).

Shipping / Receiving

SOURCE: David L. Schaefer

Once the rack is extended, it also is possible to bridge it over cross aisles to further increase storage capacity. If this is done, the storage capacity shown in Figure 1 is increased 39 percent, from 6,930 pallet positions to 9,600.

Figure 2

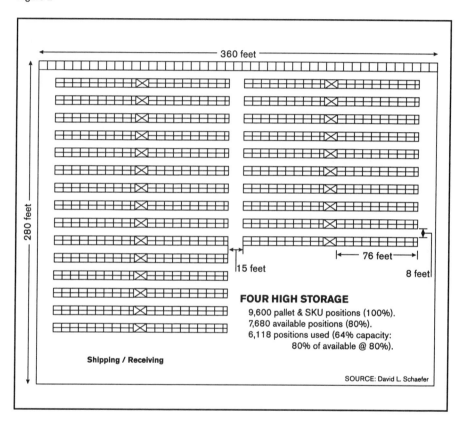

360 feet

280 feet

76 feet

15 feet

8 feet

FOUR HIGH STORAGE
9,600 pallet & SKU positions (100%).
7,680 available positions (80%).
6,118 positions used (64% capacity:
80% of available @ 80%).

Shipping / Receiving

SOURCE: David L. Schaefer

Reducing number of aisles

One way to reduce the number of aisles is a rack system designed for two-deep storage. As shown in Figure 3, this increases the total pallet positions to 12,560, nearly double the amount shown in Figure 1. However, because the double-deep rack denies access to the inside pallets, the total number of SKU facings available is fewer than the storage plan shown in Figure 2.

Therefore, the double-deep system would be used only when storage capacities can be increased without needing to increase the number of SKU facings.*

Figure 3

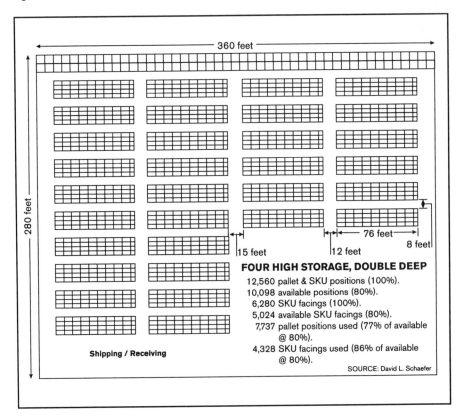

360 feet

280 feet

76 feet

15 feet

12 feet

8 feet

FOUR HIGH STORAGE, DOUBLE DEEP

12,560 pallet & SKU positions (100%).
10,098 available positions (80%).
6,280 SKU facings (100%).
5,024 available SKU facings (80%).
7,737 pallet positions used (77% of available @ 80%).
4,328 SKU facings used (86% of available @ 80%).

SOURCE: David L. Schaefer

Shipping / Receiving

Other varieties of pallet rack

Warehouse managers sometimes ignore or overlook portable rack, frequently referred to by a trade name such as Tier-rack.™ Portable rack is one of the oldest and best available methods for achieving high stacking of cer-

---

* From *Improving Existing Warehouse Space Utilization*, by David L. Schaefer. Published by W.E.R.C., 1981.

tain type of products such as tires, which are stored without packaging and lack structural strength.

While portable racks can be dismantled and economically stored when not in use, some users prefer to store them outdoors and not dismantle them. In either case, space within the warehouse is freed for storage of other materials. In contrast, conventional pallet rack, when empty, cannot be economically stored or removed from the building.

The double-deep rack described earlier increases density by allowing deeper rack storage. Still greater storage density is achieved by using either drive-in or drive-through racks. Each load is supported by a flange that grips the edge of the pallet. The drive-through rack is open at each end, and the drive-in rack can be approached only from one side. While this deeper rack improves density, handling efficiency is sacrificed because an operator must drive the lift truck carefully through a narrow alley between the uprights.

Rack-supported buildings

Some buildings use the storage rack as the structural support for the walls and roof of the warehouse. Under earlier tax codes, there was a significant advantage to the use of a rack-supported building, since rack is considered to be mechanical equipment with a depreciation life of ten years (versus a thirty-five year write-off for buildings). Professional tax advice should be sought to evaluate your situation with respect to the tax advantages of rack supported warehouses.

Typically the rack-supported building is used with an automated storage and retrieval system (ASRS) to move pallet loads on a unit/in-unit/out basis.*

A rack-supported building provides all the storage racks for the interior of the warehouse. In a conventional building, the storage racks can be relocated at will; but when the rack is part of the structure, it obviously cannot be moved.

---

* Adapted from an article by Lee P. Thomas, *Warehousing Forum*, Volume 2, Number 10, ©The Ackerman Company, Columbus, Ohio.

Live storage

Some storage equipment is designed to allow stored goods to move by gravity from the back of the row to the face of the rack. One type of live storage is full-pallet gravity-flow rack, which allows pallet loads to roll to the front of the rack as each facing pallet is removed.

Gravity-flow racks, unlike conventional static shelving, slope from the back (feed-in side) toward the front (picking side). The flow rack will vary in depth (front-to-back) from as little as four feet to as much as 20 feet.*

Two factors allow gravity-flow racks to improve order-filling rates:

1. If the back-up or reserve cases are located behind the pick location instead of to the side or on top of it, then the actual pick surface can be reduced.

2. Because of reduced pick surface, flow rack allows an order picker to reach a greater number of items within a limited space. An order picker standing in front of the rack can select a greater number of items, minimizing travel between picks.

Properly designed, with intelligent item placement and careful item selection, flow racks should increase order-picking speed considerably.

Since order-picking speed depends not only on the number of lines ('picks' or 'hits'), but also the space between lines, the speed of order filling is improved by reducing the facing of each line. Thus, all facings should be made with the short side of the carton forward rather than the wide side. It is important to use the left-to-right span of each rack shelf to the utmost, and this requires careful initial arrangement of cartons.

Vertical space between shelves also is important. To waste as little space as possible, cartons of similar height should occupy the same shelf. For ease of picking, it's best to put tall cartons on the lower shelves, and shorter packages on the upper shelves.

Order size also is a primary factor that contributes to efficiency. Small orders that require a long walk between lines can reduce the effectiveness of a gravity-flow rack. A badly designed flow-rack installation does nothing

*   From Vol. 17, No. 8, of *Warehousing and Physical Distribution Productivity Report,* by W.B. Semco, former president of Semco, Sweet & Mayers, Los Angeles, CA, ©Alexander Communications, Inc., New York, NY.

to increase order-filling speed.

What's the difference between an effective flow-rack installation and one that wastes money and space? Flow racks will provide little benefit unless the orders to be picked have enough lines in them to make the flow-rack technique work. For example, flow racks containing slow-moving items are often ineffective. Generally, items picked less than 20 times per month should not be in flow racks.

Flow-rack with one hit every four or five feet — three or four hits for the whole flow-rack system — will be picked at about the same speed as merchandise in static shelving. While flow-rack can enhance order-picking speed, the benefits depend on minimizing space between hits and having enough lines to establish a fast pick rate.

You must also consider the cost of loading time. Flow-racks take more time to load than shelves.

Any operator who installs a system to hold 100 percent of the items in the warehouse will have a cosmetically beautiful system with marginal utility. The best order-picking system is a hybrid, using flow racks for those items having high activity, and shelving or bins for those items with less activity or uncommon sizes.

Pick to light systems

The term *pick-to-light* describes a computer-assisted picking system. The system is a combination of gravity-flow racks, and computer controls. By using computer information systems, a paper pick list is replaced with a series of LED (light emitting diode) displays at the face of each picking position. These lights are illuminated in sequence as the order is picked. When an order filler enters the area, a light indicates a quantity to be picked. After the operator selects the indicated quantity, he or she confirms completion of the task by pressing a button which activates another light-emitting diode for the next item. This system frees the order picker from paper, and allows both hands to be available for picking without the need to read, search, and write. With this freedom, order pickers reach high productivity with minimal training and achieve pick rates that typically exceed those with conventional systems. Furthermore, error rates are reduced because the opportunities to make a mistake in misreading are eliminated.

Carousel storage systems

The carousel saves money in the warehouse by eliminating human travel and aisles. Instead of a person moving to the item, the merchandise is brought directly to a picking station.* The carousel is usually in the shape of an elongated O, and several can be placed side by side with a minimal amount of clearance.

Carousel equipment is most efficient when there are many SKUs, and the boxes to be picked are small. Items such as small parts, catalog pages and pharmaceuticals are well suited for this kind of equipment. The carousel is particularly effective for picking of less-than-case quantities, and items too small or too large for gravity-flow racks.

Once the decision is made to use carousels, how should merchandise be arranged? The most common stock arrangement uses a pre-determined pick list sequence to minimize the rotation of the carousel. However, one of the virtues of such equipment is a control that automatically moves the next required bin to the front by the shortest distance — clockwise or counterclockwise.

Most installations have multiple carousels with computer controls so one operator can pick from one while the second is rotating for the next pick. One manufacturer offers a computer control system capable of controlling and monitoring an inventory of up to 100,000 stockkeeping units.

Justifying the carousel

Investment in carousel systems is paid back primarily in reducing travel time for picking, but a second cost reduction is in storage space. In many cases, picking labor may be reduced by 30 percent to 40 percent. In one installation, storage space was reduced from 12,000 square feet to 4,000 square feet. The picking effort, which had required 24 people on two shifts, was accomplished with only nine people on one shift.

The carousel allows the user to integrate the picking system with a computer more easily than with flow racks. Expanding the system is accommo-

---

*   From T.A. Ewers first published in Volume 19, Number 11, *Warehousing and Physical Distribution Productivity Report*, ©Alexander Communications, Inc., New York, New York.

dated by changeable shelves and the ability to increase the number of bins.

On the other hand, cost per-SKU in a carousel is higher than in a flow rack, and the carousel picking method is slower than a flow rack. If you may have to move the equipment to another building in the near future, consider the costs of disassembly and reinstallation, which will be higher with carousel than with flow rack.

While some believe flow rack and carousels are competitive, the experienced user will recognize that they are not. You should be aware of the advantages of both systems, recognizing that there are relatively few times when one system is not clearly better than the other for a given application.

Conveyor systems

Conveyors are one of the oldest and least flexible of the live storage systems. They are commonly employed in manufacturing, but their use in warehouses is declining. Seven factors should be considered if you are thinking about a conveyor system:

1. Product or material to be handled.
2. Measurements and characteristics of package.
3. Number of items and flow rates.
4. Specific goals for the conveyor.
5. How large an expenditure would be justified?
6. How fragile the product is.
7. Other restrictive factors such as space available or allowable noise.

Five kinds of conveyors

The *monorail* consists of an overhead rail on which a trolley runs. The load is carried on one or more trolleys.

The *dragline conveyor*, or *tow conveyor*, is a power chain under the floor that is engaged by dropping pins mounted on the front of four-wheeled carts through the chain slot. Track switches allow alternate routes or destination spurs for each cart.

Skate-wheel conveyors are gravity conveyors on which skate wheels are mounted. Skate-wheel conveyors can be set up on portable stands with power boosters (*belt conveyors*) at intervals to move the product.

Belt conveyors are widely used in order-assembly operations. They are more suitable for order assembly when small or odd-shaped packages are to be handled because they provide a continuous, moving, flat surface.

The *slat conveyor* has steel or wooden slats fixed between the strands, generally at every pitch. These are used mainly to handle heavier loads, or in cases where the unit load could cause damage to a belt due to projections on the bottom of the load. By installing tilting slats on a chain conveyor, it is possible to sort at fast speeds. The tilting slats tilt on command, dumping the load into specific slides, chutes, run-out conveyors or bins.

Guided vehicles

The most common replacements for conveyors in today's warehouses are automatic guided vehicle systems (AGVS). As the technology has improved, the relative cost has come down. Sometimes the AGVS is justified by its ability to make an obsolescent building practical. The guidance system can be a wire or tape applied to the floor or a light beam. In either case, it is easy to change the path of the system to adapt to a new storage layout.

There are four main types of vehicles:

1. A towing vehicle designed to haul a string of pallet trucks or trailers.
2. A unit-load transporter designed to carry one individual load of up to 12,000 pounds. These vehicles are designed to accept loads delivered from a guided fork truck or from a powered or non-powered conveyor or load stand.
3. An automatic guided pallet truck, similar in appearance to the conventional jack used for order selection in grocery chains. These pallet trucks can handle up to four pallet loads or a total of 6,000 pounds.
4. A light-load transporter, a smaller vehicle designed to handle lighter loads such as parts or mail.

The heart of the AGVS is an onboard microcomputer that controls and monitors vehicle functions, giving each vehicle the ability to travel independently and automatically to a programmed destination. If layout changes occur in the warehouse, the paths can be altered.

In operating the system, a warehouse worker takes a load from the home area, places it on the guided vehicle, moves the vehicle onto the guide path, keys in the destination address, and pushes a start button. Once this is done, the computer takes over. The vehicle moves to the designated drop location, deposits the load at a specific address, and then returns to the home area for a new assignment.

In newer systems, the guided vehicles are controlled through a central queuing station in which they are programmed to make certain stops along their paths. The vehicle enters the queuing station and is programmed by the central computer for a whole day's jobs. When each job is finished, the AGV is programmed to return to the queuing station for its next duties.

The chief advantage of an AGVS is that the guidance system eliminates travel time by warehouse *workers*. A value can be established for this travel time through the use of generally accepted warehouse standards. A standard developed by the U.S. Department of Agriculture (USDA), states that a warehouse worker needs 7.7 minutes to travel 1,000 feet. If one assumes that the fully burdened cost of a warehouse worker is twenty-five dollars per hour (42 cents per minute), this sets the cost of each such trip at $3.23. The cost of a $35,000 microprocessor that eliminates 684 miles of travel per year will be paid back in three years. Larger warehouse operations will eliminate at least this amount of travel. For example, eliminating 27 round-trips of 300 feet per day will cut somewhat more than 684 miles of travel per year.

Another advantage of AGV systems is their flexibility. Older buildings that may be available at bargain prices could be made economical with an AGVS. In some cases, these are buildings with docks that are not convenient to storage areas. Others may be multi-story buildings that cannot be operated economically with conventional equipment. Automatic vehicles, in combination with vertical conveyors, can transport inbound loads to a storage address without intervention by people.

A benefit that is frequently overlooked is the ability of AGVS to save space. Because tracking of the vehicle is precise, lanes between loads can have small clearance between passing vehicles.

Choosing a lift truck

Consider the options of power source, operator location, lift attachments, vehicle characteristics, and competitive brands and you will discover thousands of choices. You can reach a decision by examining each category of the options. Approach the decision systematically to select the lift truck that works best in your warehouse.

Power source

The lowest-cost source of power is the human body, and some low-lift pallet trucks provide vertical lift from a hydraulic pump and horizontal travel from the operator's push or pull.

When external power is required, the two options are internal combustion engines and electric motors.

There are four power sources for internal combustion engines: propane, gasoline, diesel fuel and compressed natural gas (CNG). Propane has grown in popularity because it generates little exhaust and therefore is safer and cleaner than gasoline or diesel engines. CNG, the newest fuel, is cleaner and cheaper then propane. Though they emit significantly greater amounts of exhaust and odor, gas or diesel are sometimes preferred for outdoor operation. Fuel availability and cost will influence the choice among the four alternate internal combustion sources.

Operator location

There are three options in operator location: walkie (also referred to as operator-walking), rider, or man-up.

Walkie trucks are the most economical lift trucks to buy and operate. Often referred to as 'pallet jacks,' these vehicles are designed to facilitate horizontal travel of unitized loads of product. They are also used for order picking from floor locations. These trucks elevate the load a few inches. Fixed fork spacing requires that the pallet size be standardized. Electric walkie trucks reduce fatigue and are frequently used where loads are heavy or distances to be covered are long. One type of walkie truck offers higher lift, permitting the operator to raise the forks up to 13 feet for stacking or placement in storage racks. Some models have extended forks to handle two pallets instead of one. A few will handle four pallets, two deep and two high.

The rider truck is the most commonly used lift truck. While more costly than the walkie truck, it provides greater speed and comfort. Within the rider category, there is the option of having the operator sit or stand. Mounting and dismounting is easier in a stand-up vehicle but fatigue is greater.

The man-up truck has operating controls on a platform adjacent to the fork carriage, allowing the operator to ride next to the forks. Most man-up trucks have a guidance system so that the operator controls the up and down movement but not the steering. Because the operator can pull a few cases from a pallet without removing the entire pallet from a storage rack, the man-up vehicle will save time in selecting small orders. Furthermore, order pickers have significantly better visibility because they can move close to the freight being selected. Some models have two sets of controls that allow operation of the truck either from a platform or from the truck chassis.

Types of lift attachment

Lift attachments represent a wide range of choices. Forks are the fastest and simplest means of moving unitized products. Most of the options to forks are designed to eliminate the use of pallets. The attachment designed to handle slipsheets, is a *push-pull* attachment. It is designed to grasp the extended lip of a slipsheet and pull the load onto a set of wide platens or forks which support the slipsheet in transit. A push device then reverses the process to remove the slipsheet from the forks.

Palletless handling is also achieved with carton or roll clamps. These are vertical paddles to grasp the sides of cartons or paper rolls and lift them.

Some specialized attachments grab and lift cargo with a vacuum cup, a magnet, a top-lift device, a boom, or a revolving carriage. Each of these alternates is more costly and more difficult to use than the fork attachment, but for certain products it may be safer or more versatile.

In comparing the options, find out whether or not the attachment has been used successfully by other warehouse operators handling similar products. There have been cases where significant product damage occurred because of misuse of specialized attachments.

Conventional or narrow-aisle trucks

The common lift truck with a 3,000 pound capacity requires a 12-foot aisle. A few very-narrow-aisle trucks will operate in an aisle slightly wider than the truck itself. These trucks eliminate the need to turn the entire vehicle to place merchandise in stacks. Figures 4 and 5 outline the advantages and disadvantages of selecting narrow-aisle lift trucks.

Figure 4   **Operator Location**

	Advantages	Disadvantages
Operator Walkie	Facilitates horizontal travel. Good for order-picking tasks. May add power source to reduce operator fatigue. Reduces task time because operator need not mount and dismount frequently.	Not suited to long distance travel. Fixed fork width, thus pallet size must be standardized. Low lift capability. Slow travel speed.
Rider	Operator may sit or stand. Greater speed than walkie truck. Reduces operator fatigue. Good lift capacity.	More costly than walkie. Increases task time when operator must mount and dismount truck.
Man-Up	Operator may move up and down with platform. Task time saver for order pcking jobs. Better visibility in selecting loads.	Requires automated guidance system to steer. Most expensive. Less flexible for various tasks.

Figure 5   **Aisle Width Capacity**

	Advantages	Disadvantages
Conventional Aisle Truck	Industry standard truck. Easily transferrable to various tasks. Greater load stability. Greater load capability	Requires 12-foot aisle. Decreases available storage space.
Narrow Aisle Truck	Reduces need for counterbalance trucks. Decreases required aisle width. Increases available storage space.	Less flexible for various tasks. Lower load capabilities. Less load stability. May require "super flat" floor.

Brand selection

In selecting an equipment brand, consider five priorities:

Priority one is the quality of the local dealer. This quality is measured in both quantitative and subjective terms. On the quantitative side, consider the financial stability, parts inventory, and service record of the dealer being considered. Even the best of equipment will malfunction occasionally, and your dealer's ability to correct the malfunction quickly is of prime importance. Talk to the dealer's other customers to be sure that the service record is as good as advertised.

There is a qualitative measure involved in attitude. Are you convinced that key people in the dealership are truly dedicated to providing service? Attitude can be detected without making a customer survey. Visit the service department of the dealership and appraise the performance of the people who work there.

A second priority is standardization and the ability to substitute vehicles. When you mix brands in a warehouse, each truck has operating characteristics different from the others. An operator who is accustomed to one brand may be more accident prone when using a truck with different controls. Therefore, it usually makes sense to standardize on one brand.

Reliability is the third priority. In most operations, the cost of down time is far more significant than the price differences between competitive equipment. A cheaper lift truck that is unreliable is always a bad bargain. There are two measures of reliability: Your own past experience with a brand and the testimony of other companies using the same kind of truck.

The fourth priority is ease of training the operator as well as the operator's satisfaction. This does not mean that a warehouse manager should let the workers make the brand decision for fork-lift trucks. However, if every worker in the warehouse tries to avoid using one particular machine, there may be reasons that cannot be ignored.

Nearly all materials handling dealers offer training courses, but some are better than others, so training quality should also be examined when making a dealer decision.

The last priority is cost. The initial cost of the lift truck is far less than the labor and maintenance costs connected with the vehicle during its useful life. Choosing on the basis of initial price is probably the worst possible way to make the brand decision.

While lift truck technology has changed slowly, any article written five years ago about selecting equipment would have significant differences from one written today. Changes in technology and engineering will create new options and some new points of emphasis in the selection decision.

Fundamentally, the buyer is simply purchasing *a tool*, and the design and value of that tool must be related to the warehousing job to be done.

Questions that solve problems

When you ask your people about equipment choices, you want to learn whether they have been sufficiently thorough in investigating a potential purchase.

Q Are you sure you know the real reason why you need new equipment?

C Some warehouse operators are impulsive about equipment purchases. We have seen new lift trucks purchased when similar vehicles were kept and not fully used. Never permit your people to be impulsive or emotional about acquiring new equipment.

Q Have all the options been considered?

C The same impulsive buyer may fall in love with one equipment solution and remain blind to the potential of other options.

Q Have you isolated all of the potential pitfalls involved in using this equipment?

C Your search for the negatives will tell whether the investigation has included talks with other users and meticulous investigation of the disadvantages as well as the advantages of a given line of equipment.

Q How will the proposed equipment change our storage or handling efficiencies?

C Be sure the justification is related to the prime functions of warehousing: space and labor. ❖

PART

6

Information Systems

Chapter 27

Computers and customer service

Computers came to warehousing about as early as they did to other businesses. Early decisions about computer hardware and software were substantially different from today's and managers have found that it is not easy to cope with this change. We need to understand both the history of data processing and the present scene. History is important because the 'state-of-the-art' changes so quickly.*

Defining the terms

Hardware is the computer equipment itself: the central processing unit (CPU) and its peripheral devices.

Firmware describes software that is integrated with the hardware and is always present whenever the computer is used. Some firmware is implemented into the electronic circuitry of the computer. Other firmware is located in nonvolatile memory chips that can be changed to update the instructions. These chips, called ROMs (read-only memory) are non-volatile because they retain their instructions even when the power is off. Some ROMs may be erased and re-used. One example of firmware is the program that activates when a computer is first turned on — the 'bootstrap' program.

Software is the general term to describe instructions used to control the hardware. Several specific kinds of software must also be defined.

---

* This section was adapted from an article written by Bill McDade, of Terminal Corporation in Timonium, Maryland. Bill Blinn, of Proficient Computing Solutions Corporation in Columbus, Ohio, provided valuable assistance and editorial comment.

Operating system software is a set of programs to control the computer and allocate computer resources as required. The operating system accepts input from the user, manages data processing tasks, and routes output to a printer or screen. Every general purpose computer requires an operating system. Commonly used operating systems include MS-DOS, UNIX, OS/2, and RSX.

Application software is a set of programs that enable a computer to carry out a specific function for a user. Examples of application software are inventory systems, order processing systems, locator systems, and accounting systems.

Program development software is used by programmers as they create new programs or modify existing programs. This software translates the instructions written by programmers (sometimes called source code) into machine-readable binary language, or object code. BASIC, Pascal, Fortran, COBOL, and Progress are all development software. Instructions executed by computers are in binary code, a series of ones and zeros.

Changes in hardware and software

In the early days of the computer industry the few major vendors of hardware sold proprietary software systems along with their hardware. The operating systems and even the programming languages and development tools were unique to each manufacturer.

Application software written for one computer system would not run on another brand of computer without an expensive conversion. Incompatibilities existed even among computer models made by a single manufacturer. A programmer who had developed skills on a particular system could not transfer these skills to another system.

The cost of even a modest computer system was vastly greater than it is today. Hardware systems alone ran to a six-figure and frequently to a seven-figure purchase price. Indeed, *monthly* rental costs for most computers were higher than the *purchase* price of many business computers today. Most managers felt that a wrong decision in the choice of hardware could spell financial disaster.

Therefore the first two decades of computer use in business saw a primary emphasis on hardware. Many companies bought computers first and then had to find software that was compatible. This meant that choices were very limited: The amount of packaged software was infinitesimal and finding a software program specifically designed for warehousing was usually impossible.

Users who did not have application software and could not find a suitable package were forced to choose from what the hardware vendors offered. The choice frequently depended upon other software, operating systems, program development software, and data base management systems.

Micros, minis, and mainframes

In 1980, the distinction between micros, minis, and mainframes was clear. Micros were desktop units limited to a single user. Mainframes were large, expensive units capable of supporting dozens to hundreds of users. Minis were mid-range systems, capable of supporting from a few to a few dozen users.

Since the late 1980s, the micro has cut into the mini's market share. Most people are familiar with the single-user micro, the desktop 'personal computer,' an indispensable business tool. But today's high-end micros are capable of supporting dozens, or even a hundred users with the proper operating system. Most warehouses today do not need a mainframe or even a mini, but can satisfy their needs with a micro. The opportunity for cost savings and increased productivity is staggering.

The emergence of an industry-standard platform

Today hundreds of companies assemble micros, but they largely are selling an industry standard product. Of these, a few market leaders have about half the market. The heart of most of these products — the CPU — is an industry standard processor like the Intel 80X86 line for MS-DOS machines or the Motorola 68000 for the Macintosh. Only a few companies still sell proprietary CPUs, such as IBM with the RISC-6000 processor, but IBM's and Apple's RISC-based PowerPC and Power Mac could change the marketplace.

What unifies these products is that for the first time there is an emerging industry standard multi-user operating system. The UNIX operating system, and UNIX derivatives such as Xenix and AIX offer a standard, *open system* platform for application software, program development tools, and data base systems. Computer systems from many manufacturers can run this software with little, if any, conversion expense.

The industry standard platform protects a company's investment in application software by limiting conversion and retraining expenses when it is necessary to upgrade hardware. Data processing budgets can be directed toward improving existing applications and writing new ones, rather than simply maintaining the status quo.

Finally, the system capable of supporting a dozen users, which might have cost $100,000 in 1982, can now be acquired for under $15,000.

Which is first: hardware or software?

While hardware may have been emphasized in the early days of computers, the software comes first today. However, while ten years ago the focus was on application software, today the emphasis is on operating systems and program development software.

There are occasional exceptions. A company with a substantial investment in application software may upgrade its hardware by choosing a computer that is compatible with its existing software — but this is the exception, not the rule.

In absence of strong reasons to the contrary, today's user couples an industry standard operating system with compatible program development software. The hardware can be any brand that will function with the software system.

A case example

A food distributor with a large warehouse was using a small mainframe computer and faced the need to upgrade its system. There were no larger systems compatible with the current hardware, so the company faced a significant conversion expense. Instead, management chose to purchase a micro-based UNIX system.

The total conversion cost was about equal to the cost of a larger mainframe, but the conversion cost to UNIX was a one-time expense rather than a recurring expense.

The real saving was in hardware costs, which were approximately 20 percent of the cost of another mainframe: $50,000 rather than $250,000. These savings alone were a compelling reason to choose the micro platform using UNIX.

The value of benchmarking

Benchmarking is a methodology by which the processing requirements of a system are simulated and the performance is measured in comparison with other systems. Benchmarking is its own science (or black art), and finding a benchmark that truly simulates daily operation is very difficult.

The goal of benchmarking is to prove that the system you are considering has the features and processing power needed for a successful application.

Sometimes the results of an inexpensive benchmarking exercise are astonishing. When a warehouse company wanted to upgrade from an IBM System 34 mini computer, one member of the data processing staff suggested considering a micro. Most people were skeptical. How could a PC substitute for a mini computer? Benchmark tests showed that one type of PC was three to five times faster than the System 34. More extensive benchmarking tests confirmed the conclusion. Benchmarking, done correctly, will reduce the bewildering complexity of factors involved in computer system performance and format the decision in easily understood numbers.

There are two ways to run a computer benchmarking program. First, your people can actually run typical programs on each of the platforms being benchmarked. Second, you can observe a particular application software package in another warehouse and measure how the system runs in that environment.

Hardware and software do not run independently of each other. Because all must come together in a single integrated system to deliver what the user needs, benchmarking must test the integrated system.

Choosing warehousing software

If your warehouse does not have adequate software, and you do not wish to spend the time and money to develop a proprietary system, you have many choices of *off-the-shelf* systems — some of which can be highly customized — marketed by other companies. The problem is to find the applicable candidates and then to evaluate the alternatives.

Sadly, even today some managers rely on a hardware salesperson to tell them what application packages are available. That salesperson has a motive to sell a particular application package.

There are many other information resources available. Perhaps the most complete is a guide to logistics software published each year by Arthur Andersen and Company. There are other product guides, such as one put out by Uniforum, a UNIX industry association in Santa Clara, California.

The first step in evaluating application software is to define the functions you need performed. Once you have defined the functions, you should evaluate all available packages based on their ability to deliver the capabilities you need. This process should reduce the number of software packages you must consider.

When you have identified an application package that appears to be suitable, the next step is to check references. Contact current users, at least some of which should have an operation similar to yours. Include on-site visits to observe the package in a real world environment, meet the people who use it, and learn firsthand what experiences others have had in applying the system.

In checking references, a key point is the quality and availability of support. No matter how well the system works on the day it is installed, changing conditions in your warehouse will require modifications in the information system. How you will be able to adapt to those changes depends on how much help you can get from the software vendor.

Consider the effect on your company if the software supplier should go out of business. Do you have access to the source code to protect yourself in the event that the software supplier is not available at some future date? A number of otherwise successful software systems have met disaster because of lack of support after the system was installed.

Training and development

A key step in the successful implementation of a new information system is training people to use it. This training must be supported by software vendors, but the most successful installations keep dependence on outside trainers as short as possible. As the system matures, modifications will be made to adapt to changes within your warehouse, and therefore training should be a continuous process. The best training program is one that is eventually handled by your own people.

The warehouse information system is a dynamic product, one that is in a constant state of change and growth. Success depends on training your people to initiate the system and to gradually improve it to meet the changes in your warehouse.

Adapting clerical procedures to the computer

Just as information has become the most critical item in logistics management, it has also become the most important aspect of warehousing. A
number of executives believe that quality of information systems is the defining factor that differentiates third-party warehouse suppliers. Certainly
the same could be said for private warehouse operations.

Today's information system emphasizes the interface between the
warehouse and the warehouse user's computers. In a third-party situation,
there are times when the warehouse employees feed information directly
into a customer's computer. The potential for disruption because of clerical
error is greater today than ever before.

Furthermore, computer technology has moved from the office to the
warehouse where workers equipped with radio frequency terminals and
bar code scanners provide input for the information system. Carelessness
or malfeasance originating on the warehouse floor could affect the entire
system.

While warehouses have always had an office, today that function is an
information center that has a substantial role outside as well as within the
warehouse organization.

Locating the information center

The clerical function no longer needs to be located at the warehouse building. Modems, telefax machines, and other communications equipment permit information handlers to work nearly anywhere and to send output to
shipping and receiving docks via wire. Some information workers do some
or all of their jobs from machines located in their own homes. This process
is called telecommuting.

While telecommuting is technically practical, most managers want
clerical workers under one roof to exchange information or ideas. For the
same reason, managers want these people located in the same building as
the warehouse operation. When clericals are in the warehouse they can also
participate in inventory and quality checks, or other activities that involve
cooperation with materials handling people.

Clerical operations and customer service

Reduction of total cycle time is a goal for most warehousing operations. A key factor is shortening the time from sales order entry to the time when shipping documents are available. The clerical time lag is frequently greater than the materials handling time lag.

What is acceptable depends on who the customer is, and standards differ between private and third-party warehousers. Allowable time varies substantially from one industry to another as well as from customer to customer in the same industry.

For the private warehouse operation, the critical customer is the receiver of the merchandise shipped from the warehouse. In some private warehouses, other corporate managers are viewed as customers.

A third-party warehouse has three customers to serve:

 ◆ The client.
 ◆ The client's customer.
 ◆ The shipper of inbound materials.

The **client** is the party who hires and pays for third-party warehousing services. The **client's customers** are the consignees who take deliveries from the warehouse. The **inbound shipper** is usually the client, however that shipper may be another department of the client's company or a supplier to the client.

Consignees and shippers can be critical elements in the customer service package. Even though they did not hire the warehousing service, their satisfaction or lack of same can be very important to the success or failure of a warehousing program.

Speeding delivery

A standard order response time is essential, and in the third-party warehousing industry, an old standard was this two-part rule:

 ◆ All orders received by noon are shipped on the same day.
 ◆ All orders received after noon are shipped on the following day.

Today, the responsibility of the warehouse operator should not end with the act of shipping. Shipping does not solve a customer's problem, only delivery does that. Therefore, the shipper should be held responsible for selecting and controlling delivery services that adhere to a dependable standard that places the merchandise in the hands of the customer when the customer expects it. Your warehouse standard should trace time from the minute that you are aware of the need to make a shipment until the shipment has been accepted and signed for at the customer's dock.

Testing customer service

How can you test customer service in your warehouse operation? The *quantitative* side of customer service can be tested with record keeping. For example, success in maintaining error-free operations is measured by noting the ratio of errors to total transactions. This error rate can be compared from one month to the next. Since damage is part of customer service quality, the frequency and cost of warehouse damage can also be measured and compared.

The more *qualitative* aspects of customer service are harder to measure. If you want to check on courtesy and competence of telephone handling in your office, call the switchboard occasionally and ask for yourself. If the receptionist knows your voice, listen in while a friend makes the call. After several calls, you will know how well your employees handle calls. If you feel that you are getting a runaround, you may need to provide training in telephone handling techniques.

Retailers hire professional shoppers to test the quality of customer service. While we've not heard of this being done in warehousing, there is no reason why it could not be done. At least you can ask your customers to rate the quality of your service. Such questions should not be asked only of senior management, but of all of the people who deal with your warehouse. By performing your own tests and asking customers for their opinions, you can create a continuous flow of information about the quality of your customer service.

Organizing the information center

Traditional warehouse offices usually organize work either by clerical function or by customer account. In the functional system, certain individuals handle all the documentation for receipts, and others do nothing but prepare bills of lading and other shipping documents. Another group is engaged in the maintenance of inventory records. Thus when a customer needs some information, all of these people might be involved in supplying the answer. The functional system allows people with limited skills to be employed in repetitive work. Just as the manufacturing assembly-line worker may do nothing but install wheels, the receiving clerk will do nothing but prepare receiving reports.

The better alternate is a customer account organization set up so that each information worker has total responsibility for one (or a group) of customer companies. This account coordinator is responsible for at least having knowledge of all clerical functions affecting his or her customers.

When the customer calls, one person in the office has sufficient familiarity with all functions to be able to answer questions immediately or to obtain quickly an answer affecting the movement of that customer's merchandise.

The account-oriented system requires greater versatility and skill from each information worker. However, it also affords a more personalized approach for the customer.

Using information to improve the operation

A bonus benefit of computerized clerical operations in the warehouse is the development of a management information system that can control the operation. The operations manager can gain information on productivity and labor expended for each warehouse account. Payroll reports can be reviewed to control overtime and measure materials handling productivity. In a public warehouse, cash flow is controlled through reporting on aging of accounts receivable.

Regardless of the proliferation of equipment, ultimately the system depends on well-motivated personnel. Tabulation of errors and a search for the cost of these is another kind of management information that can be a by-product of a well-designed system.

Questions that solve problems

At a time when information systems may be the hallmark of warehousing excellence, you cannot be too careful in questioning your people about both quality and functionality of systems that are in place or proposed.

Q Are you fully satisfied with the information system we are using now? If not, what would you like to see changed?

C Be sure you ask these questions of every key person in your warehousing organization. The *last* people you should ask are those who work in data processing.

Q Are there any bottlenecks in our warehouse operation that are caused by information problems?

C Be sure you get a full description of these bottlenecks and steps that can be taken to correct them.

Q Have you ever felt at a competitive disadvantage because of our information systems?

C Obtain detail to support the answers.

Q What is the best single feature of our information system? What is the worst?

C Be sure that your answers are detailed, and compare the answers you receive from various people in the organization.

Q What changes have taken place in our information system within the past twelve months?

C Failure to change could mean that your information system is state-of-the-art and no changes are indicated, but it is more likely that you are falling behind and nobody is doing anything about it. Failure to change is usually equivalent to a failure to make progress.

Q How do we measure customer service?

C If you find that the *squeaking wheel* approach predominates, there is room for progress in your clerical procedures.

Q What changes have we made in our order cycle time in the past three years?

C The answers should include numerous changes in the information handling side of the business. If there has been no progress made in the information sector, you may need to question your clerical people about potential lost opportunities to improve the operation. If you find that the greatest gains in cutting cycle time have come in the information area, congratulate your people for meeting or exceeding the current state-of-the-art. ❖

Chapter 28

Electronic identification

Perhaps no technical development has shown greater potential for ware-housers than electronic identification. Several methods exist to 'machine-read' information from a package, but the most common is bar coding. The concept has existed for decades, but its full potential in ware-housing has been realized only since the late 1980s.

Bar coding improves warehouse operations in several ways. First, electronically reading and copying data from a bar code is both faster and more accurate than any manual process. A government study showed that the process is 75 percent faster than entering the information through typing, and 33 percent faster than entering the information on a ten-key data board. Keypunchers had an accuracy of 98.2 percent, but a study of over 1.25 million lines of bar code data produced an accuracy rate of 99.9997 percent.

Bar codes – what they are and how they work

Bar codes are groups of bars and spaces in a pattern that can be read by a machine that communicates with people or other machines. A sample is on the back cover of this book. The bar code itself can be applied when the car-ton or package is manufactured and printed. The cost of applying or print-ing the code at that stage is virtually nil, since package lettering has to be printed anyway. The code can also be produced by a small printing ma-chine and then applied on-site at the receiving dock of the warehouse.

Once applied, the code can later be read or 'captured' by one of several kinds of bar code scanners or readers. Used in the warehouse, this method of electronic identification offers many advantages, and new applications are constantly being developed. At the receiving dock, a code is read and the identification used to update the inventory. Since inventory errors occur because of mistakes in receiving, this application has great potential. As the product is identified, a determination can be made as to the best storage location, and instructions can be relayed to the receiver.

When a physical inventory or a location check is made, electronic identification verifies that items are correctly identified. When it is time to ship, automatic identification drastically reduces the possibility of shipping error through misidentification. Furthermore, if every item is scanned as it moves on a loading conveyor, count of items loaded can be verified.

In those operations where broken-case order picking is involved, bar code identification verifies that the right number and assortment of inner packages are included in each master carton. Additionally, electronic identification can be used as input for automated sorting equipment. As the identification of each package is determined, instructions are given to the sorter.

A user's view of bar coding

Bar coding, more than any other technology used in warehousing, is more often discussed than implemented; but a trip to your supermarket will demonstrate the effectiveness of bar coding. Information is held in the cash register until the last item is scanned, when the clerk presses a button to create a shipping document — your grocery bill. Occasionally the clerk must override the system to key an item that could not be scanned, but the process goes smoothly and you leave the market confident that your purchases have been calculated accurately.

You can achieve all of the following benefits of bar coding:
- ◆ Improved accuracy.
- ◆ Improved productivity.
- ◆ Increased space utilization.
- ◆ Quick return on investment.

Bar coding will not eliminate confusion in a poorly run warehouse. Purchasing bar code equipment to achieve discipline in that warehouse will likely achieve a new kind of chaos. Bar coding works best where systems are already documented, good warehouse discipline is present, and employees understand their responsibilities.

What will bar coding cost?

A basic data collection system costs about the same as a new forklift. Data collection allows warehouse employees to scan a series of codes and then plug in the scanner to a personal computer to download information.

Management often delays a decision to acquire bar coding by trying to justify an overly sophisticated system whose capabilities are beyond the needs of the warehouse. It's better to purchase a more modest system that fits your facility's needs and budget.

What will bar coding do for you?

Bar coding reduces the time required to process information in your warehouse. Consider the receiving process as an example. Without bar coding, the warehouse worker first writes a receiving report while unloading each inbound shipment; then she carries the report to the office for entry into the inventory system. A clerk compares the documents to resolve any discrepancies found, and then enters the information on the receiving report. Then the clerk obtains the appropriate storage locations for the merchandise and writes those locations on the receiving report. Finally the report goes back to the receiver for putaway.

With bar coding, the clerk's work is eliminated. The receiver scans a label on each item and then downloads the information to the computer system. The system resolves discrepancies by comparing what was scanned with the advance information transmitted by the client to the warehouse. A screen then displays the appropriate storage location for each unit scanned. This process takes just a few seconds.

In one case, bar coding and EDI (electronic data interchange) improved a warehouse's accounts receivable by two days and reduced the need for one clerk. Bar code equipment can send an electronic message containing current inventory levels within minutes after a shipment is made, while a traditional warehouse would need much more time.

Bar coding keeps track of each individual worker's productivity because transactions can be associated with an employee's clock number. Recording the time spent on each activity, the system generates a daily report that shows productivity levels by employee, by customer, by function, or any other measurement received during the scanning process. This productivity information is available in real time, enabling a supervisor to monitor individual productivity and spot potential bottlenecks as they are happening.

What are the pitfalls?

The worst pitfall is resistance from those workers who will be using the system. Many people feel threatened by change, and the introduction of a bar code system can be unsettling if not done tactfully.

The proper way to introduce bar coding is to involve hourly employees in the decision because what works on paper may not work in practice. Warehouse people know more about the workplace than the systems department and management. For this reason, they must be part of an evaluation team that plans bar code implementation. Workers should feel that their input is important as the company gradually builds a constituency in favor of the change.

Labels and cartons

Another pitfall is the bar code label. When label quality is inadequate, the warehouse worker must replace or reproduce the label at the receiving dock to avoid interrupting the receiving process.

It is unproductive to label or scan each carton of a pallet of identical SKUs. A popular alternative is to apply a pallet label that displays a part number and perhaps a unique lot or serial number; the warehouse worker then counts and enters the number of pieces on the pallet by using a keypad on the scanner.

You can design your own pallet label for carton handling operations. Warehouse workers begin the receipts process by obtaining a pallet label from a bar code printer on the receiving dock, attaching the label to the pallet, scanning the bar code, and then key entering the quantity of cartons on the pallet. In less than two seconds, the system tells if there is a discrepancy and specifies the location where the pallet should be taken.

One user manufactures a product in small cartons. Cartons are stored in full pallets and are shipped to customers after case picking. Orders average twenty line items and none of the product is bar coded. The user sends the warehouse a manifest containing SKU number, quantity and other information.

When picking, warehouse workers obtain a master picking label with header information displaying a *ship to* address. They scan the bar code and the system displays the first location to pick from and the number of cases of the first SKU to be picked. A worker travels to that location and scans the master pallet label. As the picking process continues, the computer follows five rules to improve efficiency:

- ◆ Minimize the worker's travel distance.
- ◆ Follow selection priorities (FIFO, LIFO, or lot number).
- ◆ Picks similar case configurations together for pallet stackability.
- ◆ Reduce inventory by the count of cases picked from each pallet.
- ◆ Compare the bar code label on each case with the bar code on the picking label and warn if they do not match.

This system allows bar coding to be used on products that arrive with ordinary labels. Through bar coded serial numbers you can trace every pallet or carton in the facility.

Too many standards

A third pitfall is frequently seen in public warehousing. Each customer, certainly each industry, uses different bar code methodologies and different characters in bar coded label fields. For example: Automotive, paper, chemical, forms, and grocery manufacturers all use different bar code systems, none compatible with another. Manufacturers will not change their systems for a single public warehouse, so the warehouse operator must ignore the client's label and affix his own pallet label.

Planning for growth

If your volume expands beyond the capabilities of the hardware or software, system response time falls off rapidly and the resulting delays frustrate users.* Planning for growth when purchasing a bar code system is time well spent, and over-specifying capacity of components is sometimes a good investment.

Proper training is critical. Vendors of hardware and software provide some orientation; however, few vendors provide sufficient training on an

---

*   Some of this chapter is based on an article by Russell A. Gilmore III, *Warehousing Forum*, Volume 6, Number 11, ©The Ackerman Company.

ongoing basis. You should designate an operations person to provide this training. The trainer may receive suggestions from warehouse workers as the system matures and should be able to communicate clearly with the hardware or software vendor.

Experienced workers are the best trainers. In start-up situations, assign experienced workers to work with new hires. A *buddy system* method of training should last about a week followed by refresher training and information or system updates as needed.

Implementing a bar coding system

Here is how the system will work in the warehouse cycle.* At the receiving dock, the bar codes for inbound materials are read and entered into the computer. The computer returns instructions on the locations to be used in storing inbound goods.

As the *put-away* function is completed, the warehouse operator enters both the stock location and the SKU identification. These are verified to ensure that the specified put-away instructions have been carried out accurately. Employees also read their personal bar code identifiers, so that a record is kept as to who put the merchandise away and how long the operation took. This allows identification of errors as well as tracking of individual productivity.

The order-picking function gains the greatest advantages from the use of automatic identification. In most warehouses, order picking is labor-intensive and error-prone. Through an automatic identification system, the computer guides picking by selecting the shortest feasible path to pick the items on the list. The picker scans both the SKU identification and the warehouse location identification. The computer verifies that both are as specified, which provides a double verification that the right item was selected.

Once goods are picked, they are typically repacked in larger shipping containers. Packing has always been a manual operation, but computer analysis will provide information to speed the process. By considering the cubic volume of each product, the computer will indicate the number and

---

*   This section is by Morton T. Yeomans. It first appeared in *Warehousing Forum*, Volume 2, Number 11, ©The Ackerman Company, Columbus, Ohio.

size of repackaging boxes that will be needed.

Automatic identification will be used to prepare the final packing list as items are placed in the reshipment box, speeding the process and improving accuracy.

At one company, the payoff was a 30 to 50 percent increase in warehouse productivity, which yielded a subsequent reduction in labor costs. Unquantifiable results included a reduction in errors, faster processing of each order, and a general improvement in customer service.

Alternatives to bar coding

Bar coding is not the only kind of electronic identification. For years, the banking industry has used machine-readable characters to identify and sort checks. Other types of readable coding are available, but bar code has been the most widely used form of labeling in warehouses.

Questions that solve problems

If your warehouse is not now using bar coding, your questions should determine why. These are not appropriate questions for hourly warehouse workers, but should be directed to systems people and line managers.

Q Is there anything in our existing information system that would impede the use of bar coding?

C Sometimes impediments will arise from unusual causes, such as lighting systems that confuse bar code scanning equipment. A more common impediment is mental attitude. You should be sensitive to complaints that really originate from resistance to change.

Q Has bar coding been investigated? If so, when, and what was the result of that investigation?

C If there is negative feedback here, be sure that it is based on fact rather than emotion. Consider the use of a benchmarking approach for exploration of bar coding.

Q Has electronic identification been implemented by any of our competitors, and have they gained any advantage over us by doing so?

C In most industries, you cannot interchange ideas with competitors. You may, however, be able to discover whether or not your company has lost competitive advantage by failure to implement bar coding, or by a system inferior to those used by others in your industry. ❖

Chapter 29

Warehouse automation

Making a profit from investment involves taking risks. Experience enables these risks to be evaluated and the benefits assessed. The main problem with investment in warehouse automation is that it is frequently a *once-in-a-lifetime experience* and it is easy to make a mistake. The secret of success is meticulous planning and the use of an appropriate level of technology, taking into account the difficulty of predicting what the various operations within the warehouse may be required to do.*

One mistake is not considering the possible changes in throughput and thus failing to justify the cost. High technology carries a greater initial cost and lower variable cost than low technology. This means that although the unit throughput cost may be favorable to advanced technology at the planned volume, that cost rises rapidly if the throughput is reduced. Confidence that planned volume levels will be maintained is a necessary prerequisite for the use of advanced technology.

Another frequent mistake is to compare the cost of a high-technology operation with one using existing methods, without considering ways the methods could be improved by simpler and more flexible techniques. A project advocate can play an important role in generating awareness and enthusiasm, but may over-zealously pursue automation without considering the alternatives.

To make radical changes in methods as a response to an immediate problem is a recipe for disaster. Technology changes should be included in

---

* This chapter was written (with the exception of the last sub-chapter) by John Williams, a materials handling consultant from Southampton, England.

the corporate strategy plan and play a part in achieving your objectives. Properly planned and implemented, and with methods chosen to match future strategy, technology will enhance modern warehouse operation. With an increasing tendency toward inventory consolidation in larger and higher throughput warehouses, there is increasing opportunity to use automated techniques.

The relevance of technology

Two basic warehouse operations are storage and sorting. When the storage operations are virtually nonexistent, we have a cross-dock warehouse in which sortation systems are almost mandatory, particularly for small packages.

For now, let's consider the operation in a more conventional warehouse that receives and stores goods on pallets, selects orders in carton or broken-carton quantities, and ships to multiple locations.

Receiving: Vehicle unloading is almost certainly by lift or pallet truck. The main uncertainties are fluctuating throughput volumes and the degree of control that can be achieved over inbound deliveries. The extent of standardization of pallet type, unit load size, extent of overhang, and degree of pallet damage will all be factors in determining whether unit loads can enter an automatic system without re-palletization.

Depending on the distance to be moved and throughput, it may be feasible to convey unit loads from the unloading dock to storage zones. The more flexible automated guided vehicle system (AGVS) is likely to be a better solution in many applications.

Common to all methods will be pallet identification by bar coded label. The greatest flexibility is achieved by using bar coded labels in conjunction with on-board radio frequency terminals and scanners that communicate with a warehouse management computer. This proven method is the benchmark against which the benefits and costs of more advanced technology should be measured.

Reserve storage is comparatively easy to automate with reliability because it is normally a pallet-in/pallet-out operation. The advantages are very narrow aisle (VNA) operation combined with the cheaper space obtained by use of height. Because 80 percent of a building's cost is in the floor slab and roof, higher buildings reduce the cost per cubic foot in general.

But beyond certain heights and depending on building codes and wind loads, costs increase. Rack-supported buildings are an attractive alternative to conventional structures, but rack-supported warehouses must be built with some care because the stress normally carried by the building structure must be carried by the racks. Rack distortion may be sufficient to make a stacker crane system inoperable.

A reduced number of storage locations is one of the benefits of computer-controlled reserve storage. For example, quarantine items may be secured and their removal barred to those who haven't the necessary password to operate the computer procedure. In a similar manner, reserved merchandise may be accumulated and held until released.

With complete automation (high racks and stacker cranes) allowing stacking heights up to 120 feet, there is a safety problem if order picking operators work at the same time in the same area. One solution is to handle manned order-picking on the day shift and allow crane operation only at night. High-stacking cranes have problems of aisle transfer. Below 40 feet the flexibility of the VNA lift truck and its complementary order-picking truck must be considered.

Order selection: For a long time to come human order pickers are unlikely to be replaced by more automated methods. However, the increased emphasis on preventing back injuries will stimulate re-design of some warehousing systems, leading to reduced-weight cartons or to cartons being presented to the operator in a manner that eliminates excessive bending, stretching, or body twisting. This may involve mechanized carton lifting devices or increased use of *goods-to-picker* systems rather than conventional selection from racks.

There are two basic types of order selection systems using the human operator. The first and most common is the *picker-to-goods* system. The operator on a *man-up* lift truck or crane can be automatically moved to the next picking location. In a *goods-to-picker* system, the operator remains at a workstation and pallets or cases are moved to and away from the workstation under computer control.

Completely automatic picking systems are used for very high throughput picking. In these systems, cartons are loaded into gravity lanes and fed on to a conveyor by computer-controlled gate mechanisms.

Staging for shipping: There are variations in the ways cartons are moved from the order picking area to be sorted into outbound loads. In the simplest systems, the order picker moves the accumulated order in a bin or on a pallet to be deposited at a staging area. At a higher level of technology, tow conveyors, automatic guided vehicles, or sorting conveyors can be used. In some applications, order pickers accumulate a group of orders by walking through one warehouse zone, which stores a portion of the SKUs in the warehouse. Simultaneously, pickers in zones are selecting merchandise from the same group of orders, all identified by bar code labels that specify the staging location. Some systems use a carton conveyor that is built into the order selection crane.

It is not difficult to see some of the problems that can arise in balancing workload between zone pickers and the effect that these imbalances can have on shipping operations. Matching the throughput volume with product mix, order size variations, and picking zones is the toughest part of the balancing act. You may require computer simulation to get the design right.

The benefits of automation

If you expect to justify warehouse automation solely by the reduction in the cost of handling and storage, you are likely to be disappointed. The justification for advanced technology often lies elsewhere.

One of the most frequent justifications for the use of automatic storage and retrieval systems (ASRS) in high-rise buildings is the reduced warehouse footprint, which permits higher storage volume on a restricted but strategically located site. It is not difficult to see the investment justification when the costs of site change or increased transport costs are taken into account.

Another benefit of automation can be better resource use. The machines work at their own tempo, without fatigue. Multi-shift operations become more feasible, and this can be an important element in the cost justification.

Another often-mentioned justification is freedom from industrial relations problems. The lower skill levels required for conventional warehousing contribute to high personnel turnover or militant unions with restrictive practices. With fewer hourly workers, and with the increased use of engineering and process control skills, higher wages can be paid and recruitment policy can be more selective. Selection and training costs may be higher per person, but the number of people is reduced.

The use of human operators becomes subject to the law of diminishing returns with increasing warehouse size. Put quite simply, workers get in each others' way; yet restricting workers zones produces the problem of work balance and load scheduling. Many warehouses see dramatic savings in the number of operators and lift trucks as a consequence of introducing automation. Compare these savings with a higher hourly wage and higher maintenance cost for automation equipment. It may also be necessary to pay separation costs for those who lose their jobs as a result of automation.

People cause errors. One benefit of automation is improved data capture resulting in greater customer satisfaction and reduced inventories. However, the same savings can be obtained at lower capital cost by the use of radio frequency terminals in conjunction with bar code readers.

People are often the cause of fires. The fewer people working in an area, the less risk of fire. However, fire insurance underwriters are concerned about the *chimney* effect of high stacks and narrow aisles. Storage racks often require a higher level of fire protection. Energy costs are increased to power additional equipment; but to offset this, heating and lighting costs can be minimal.

Some argue that the use of advanced technology improves a company's image. The creation of a *high-tech* image may be attractive to investors or to the manager who wants to work in a progressive company.

The risks of automation

Getting it completely wrong: The biggest risk is that the system will not do what you want it to do. Why should this be? It is extremely unlikely to be bad technology because, for the most part, equipment is reliable and well proven. It is most likely to be because you have failed to predict what you require the system to do.

Warehousing is subject to many variables. Throughput can fluctuate seasonally, daily, or hourly. Order size can vary, as can the number of lines per order. The number of SKUs and size of packages can change. In selecting equipment, omission of a factor from a performance specification is likely to cause failure. High technology systems are inflexible and you can't adjust for your errors or omissions by increasing personnel or adding a few more lengths of conveyor.

It is important to get the specifications right. You can get help from outside — consultants and the equipment suppliers will be only too pleased to advise. However, it is important that your operations managers should be responsible for planning. After all, no one understands your business better, and they have the best possible incentive to ensure that the systems work.

There can be no hiding behind the excuse, 'Don't blame us because it doesn't work; we had nothing to do with it.' If they are to be given the responsibility, operations managers should learn from the experience of others who have undertaken the same task by visiting similar warehouses.

They also need time. Experience shows that nearly everyone regrets that they did not allocate more time to the planning stage. System suppliers complain that they are pushed into contracts with earlier implementation dates than they consider desirable, only to find that the schedule cannot be met because the customer changes the specification. This is a clear case of *haste makes waste*.

Be sure that a task force structure considers the operational requirements and views of all the departments. Line managers seldom have the ability to carry out this work, even if they have the time. Inevitably it will be carried out by a group working in a staff relationship. A task force with representatives from each department and reporting to a committee chaired by the chief executive can ensure that the essential integration of views takes place. It also demonstrates the on-going commitment of the chief executive and heads of departments to the project.

Failing to contract successfully: Once you know what you want, you are ready to choose your contractor. During the earlier stages of the investigation, you will evaluate various equipment suppliers, making visits to installations and discussing their performance. A number of specialist subcontractors provide the building, the racking, lift trucks or stacker cranes, conveyors, computers, and controls. Resist the temptation to coordinate these yourself. Instead, choose a prime contractor with a clear legal responsibility to fulfill all your specifications.

Check all references and investigate the prospective contractor's financial status to be sure the company can complete the project. Contractors have been known to go bankrupt as the project sinks into difficulties.

Be sure the contract stipulates the maximum down-time that you are prepared to accept over a period of time. System reliability must be a matter of legal definition, including a rated throughput per hour, per shift, and per week.

Because the project must be completed and handed over on time, a time schedule should be written into the contract, including penalty payments in the event of failure.

It is at this stage that the additional time spent on the specification and pre-planning stage pays dividends. Pre-planning avoids last minute alterations that can lead to contractual amendments and disputes. There is considerable opportunity for misunderstanding in the complicated exchange of information in major automation projects and some projects do end with litigation. To prevent misunderstanding, all communication links should be made formal and detailed records carefully maintained.

Over-estimating your organization's ability to cope with change: This applies not only to the acquisition of new skills, but also to enabling managers to understand the issues involved and to make decisions.

Skills that may not exist in the organization are certain to be required. These include architectural specifications, mechanical system design, project management, computer systems, and process control. In addition, experience will be necessary in dealing with human relations problems resulting from change. These skills can be obtained by training or recruitment. Consultants may provide specialist advice and knowledge based on their wider experience, but they should never be used to impose a solution on the organization. These consultants should be members of the project team, and in no way should their presence usurp the ultimate authority of the operational managers.

Many operators are apprehensive of changes and some will be unable to make the transition to meet the challenge of using new techniques. This at least necessitates a planned communication and training program, and it might even suggest including a human relations specialist on the project team. Some organizations have completely rotated their personnel or organized retirement programs for older workers. A system can only be as effective as the skills of people allow it to be.

In conclusion

There is a large range of available technology for warehouse automation. The availability of technology is not an issue nor, for the most part, is the ability to design reliable systems. The problem is that business requirements and people are not completely predictable. Move with caution if you want to reduce the risk of failure.

Questions that solve problems

Because of the many risks involved in automating warehouse operations, managers cannot ask too many questions before making a decision. Furthermore, questions should be asked at all levels of the organization, from hourly worker to chief executive. It is important to control an unjustified urge to install warehouse automation. Here are some things that you should ask about automation:

Q How certain are we that the sizes and shapes of products stored in this warehouse will be the same ten years from now?

C In some automation situations, a major change in product specifications could cause the system to be unusable. If you anticipate such changes, then you must measure the flexibility of the system.

Q How certain are we that the planned volume will either stay the same or be greater in future years?

C If there is a risk that volume will drop or the location will be obsolete, then you must consider the payback time for the automation and the possibility that these changes will take place before the system has paid for itself.

Q Have we simulated precisely the way the warehouse will work with the proposed equipment?

C A simulation is designed to demonstrate any problems that might take place once the new system has been installed.

Q What risks do you see in making this investment?

C Beware of the advocate who sees no risk at all.

Q What steps will our company need to take to deal with the changes that will accompany warehouse automation?

C The answers will tell you how much detailed forward planning has gone into the proposal for automation. ❖

PART 7

Starting a New
Warehouse Operation

Chapter 30

Locating the warehouse

As you consider where to situate a warehouse, you should also ask why you are considering a new warehouse site. There are four common reasons:
- It is necessary to relocate an existing warehouse operation.
- The business is expanding and must move inventory into a new market.
- More warehouse space is needed to accommodate a growing inventory.
- Contingency planning requires some decentralization of existing warehousing — in other words, there are too many eggs in one basket.

Depending on which of these reasons is the motivator for seeking a new warehouse, the site search can take different forms.

Site selection is an art as well as a science. Decisions usually involve weighing priorities, determining which features are most critical, and then using a process of elimination. Since every location has both advantages and disadvantages, the final selection of a site invariably involves compromises.

Defining your requirements

The guideline for your location search will be a list of your company's specific requirements in their order of importance. Defining and listing them is the first step.

It is not possible to consider warehousing without also examining its relationship to transportation. In most industries, transportation is a larger part of the cost and a greater percent of sales than warehousing. Therefore, uneconomical transportation could easily destroy the value of an otherwise desirable warehouse location.

The four primary modes of transportation are: rail, highway, water, and air. The location of the distribution center, both its general geographical location as well as its specific position within a community, will be decided in part by the transport modes selected. This also will affect operating methods, labor, equipment, and plant layout. The warehouse layout must allow for efficient materials handling by the primary transport mode, and it must be flexible enough to adjust to transportation changes. Special conditions may influence transportation selection, including variable costs, local service conditions, and transit time. Traffic management includes the selection of transport modes to be used, and choosing specific carriers within the mode.

Transportation has the greatest influence on the location of a distribution center. In some cases, computer modeling techniques may be used to determine the optimum location (or locations) to serve a given market. The availability, speed, and reliability of transportation must be considered in determining how many distribution centers are needed. The type and quality of transportation must be considered in choosing cities to serve as distribution points.

Once planners select a city, the next step is a detailed study to locate a piece of land or an existing building. Again, transportation will be the primary factor in selecting the site. For example, if air freight has first priority, the site selector will give priority to airport accessibility. Waterfront sites will be sought if the user has determined that water transport is necessary. A limited selection of industrial property is available if rail is needed, and in some cases there will be economic or service advantages in seeking service from one particular railroad company.

The ultimate in rail flexibility gives a shipper access to two or more carriers. This may be achieved through reciprocal switching, a privilege that allows free switching to any carrier in the community. With deregulation, this privilege is negotiated less easily than in the past, so another alternative is service by a short-line railroad. Some communities have terminal railroads that exist to connect and switch for several carriers serving the city.

Proximity to a switching yard and availability of frequent switching service is important if rail volume is high. The widest selection of sites is available to a truck-oriented center, since virtually all industrial property has road access.

Ease of access is sometimes overlooked. The fact that the distribution center is located along the border of an expressway means little if trucks must make a long detour to the nearest interchange ramp. Be sure the access roads have the load-bearing capacity to accommodate trucks serving your warehouse. Any distribution center can be reached some way, but the question of how easily it can be reached is a most important issue.

To the extent that a warehouse is a marketing tool, it is important to consider the relationship of the proposed site to the locations of the customers. Consider transportation costs and order cycle times, and remember that your customer should not really care *where* the inventory is held, as long as product can be delivered in a timely fashion and at a reasonable price.

The labor market is probably less important for most warehouse operators than for the typical manufacturing plant. If the proposed operation has a high degree of automation and relatively little touch-labor, labor availability may be of minor importance. On the other hand, workforce quality and availability can be critical in a labor-intensive warehouse, such as packaging or assembly.

There can be wide variations in taxes, particularly inventory taxes, within a single metropolitan area. These taxes can be a critical competitive factor when the warehouse inventory has high value.

Community attitudes toward the new warehouse should be evaluated by every site seeker. Most development authorities consider a clean and quiet warehouse development to be preferable to manufacturing operations that cause pollution and congestion. Yet some communities are opposed to *any* new industrial development. If such opposition exists, it's best to recognize it and look elsewhere.

A requirement study should certainly determine whether a new building is necessary, or if an older one could be adapted. Rehabilitating older buildings is described in the next chapter.

Financial questions are an important part of defining requirements. How important is the availability of mortgage financing at favorable rates? This leads to the question of whether to own or lease the warehouse facility, which is also is covered in the next chapter.

If space needs are not fixed, the availability of overflow space, either in public warehouses or short-term lease space, is an important consideration. Because it is seldom possible to construct or purchase a building that is always the right size, the warehouse user should acquire minimal permanent space and use overflow space within the community for seasonal requirements.

The selection process

Once requirements are defined, the user should develop a selection process by proceeding from *macro* to a *micro* decision.

We might first determine that the new warehouse must be somewhere within the continental United States, then narrow the selection to the southwestern region of the country, the state of Texas, the Dallas-Ft. Worth metropolitan area, and finally to the southwest area of the city of Dallas — a specific site on Duncanville Road.

Be skeptical as you check sources of information in the transition from macro (region) to micro (location). If you're told that a specific site has never had a flood history, get a second opinion from another party who cannot possibly be influenced by the earlier informant. If multi-source checking produces the same answers to critical questions, one can then have some confidence in the information.

As you move through the selection process, and particularly as you zero in on a specific site, it is essential to have a contingency plan. Once you select the best site, make sure that you have an alternate location that is almost as good and equally available. Let the seller discover that you have a secondary site in the event that bargaining for the primary site should break down.

Location theory is a useful exercise in picking the site for a new warehouse. Whether you accept or reject the theory that follows, at least consider it as a potential guideline.

Over a century has passed since J. H. Von Thunen wrote about the advantages of growing the bulkiest and cheapest crops on the land closest to the city needing that commodity. The same principle can be applied to manufactured products: Location of inventory is most critical for those products that have the least value added. An inventory of gold or diamonds can be economically kept in one spot and moved by air freight all over the world, but the producer of bagged salt may find it necessary to keep inventories close to the market.

Sources of outside advice

As you work to pick a spot for a new warehouse, you may turn to people outside your organization for advice. For this reason, we should consider some commonly used advisory sources.

Real estate brokers are often involved in any search for new property. Remember that the broker's compensation for this activity is based on a successful transaction, so the broker is motivated to complete a commissionable sale. When the value of the broker's invested time begins to approach the value of the commission, the broker is likely to abandon the search.

Not all brokers have multiple-listing services. Furthermore, commission arrangements that may not be known to the prospective buyer could make it difficult for the broker to maintain objectivity as a source of outside advice. Not all real estate brokers are biased, of course, but the user must recognize that the commission system for brokerage tends to create pressures that influence the results.

If you are seeking public warehouse space, a sales representative could be useful. The public warehouse industry has several national marketing chains, with representation in major cities. Most chain sales representatives are not paid a sales commission, though a few may work on a commission as well as a salary basis. Since the chain sales agent normally cannot represent competing warehouses, each chain has its own representative in each major city.

The development departments of electric and gas utilities are excellent sources of outside advice, once you have established the general area for the facility. Most areas and their suburbs are served by just one electric utility and one gas utility, so the representatives of that utility should be unbiased in recommending sites throughout the entire metro area. These utility departments often work with all local real estate brokers to become a clearinghouse of information on available buildings and land within their service area.

Government development agencies, and chambers of commerce are reliable information sources, once the choice of community has been made. Some large metro areas have several chamber or government development officers. Since these people are motivated to attract new industry into their own area, make sure you have selected the area before relying on this source of advice.

Finally, a management consultant may be an unbiased source of advice. In selecting a consultant, be certain that the individual really is independent and objective in approaching the site search. Some individuals who use the term *consultant* also are involved in other activities, such as real estate brokerage, which may affect their objectivity in handling the site search.

There are three reasons to bring in an outside consultant. The most important of these is objectivity. Secondly, the consultant who has extensive experience in site seeking will save time. Finally, the consultant is a source of executive expertise with no long-term commitments. A detailed site search takes many hours, but hiring new executives to handle it would be foolish if their job will end once the site has been selected.

Check and double check

Because the consequences of a site selection error can be extremely costly, checking the accuracy of information received cannot be overemphasized. A site analysis checklist is shown on the following pages. This checklist deals with the search for existing buildings as well as construction sites. Whether or not outside information sources are used, confirm any information given to you. When a contradiction arises, be sure you know why and investigate further to determine which source is correct.

Site selection is a critical decision in warehousing.

A checklist to locate your next warehouse

Editor's note: most of this checklist is designed to use whether you plan to build a new facility or acquire an existing structure. However, a final section contains items used only for new construction.

Governmental restrictions

1. Is the property zoned for warehousing and related uses?
2. Will the zoning description impede conversion to other uses?
3. Are there any variances or special exceptions in the zoning?
4. What are the limits or restrictions on employee parking?
5. What is the maximum expansion capability of the facility?
6. Are there any easements or protective covenants on the property?
7. Are there any restrictive load limits on roads leading to this facility?

Geographic restrictions

1. Are there grade problems on the land?
2. Are there any problems with drainage?
3. Are there streams, lakes, or wetlands near this site?
4. If so, what is the 100 year flood plan?
5. What is the level of the ground water table?
6. Is there any history of earthquake in the area?
7. If so, have we received the US Geodetic Survey of fault lines?
8. Does the site have any fill?
9. If so, what material was used?
10. What is the load bearing capacity of nearby soil?
11. Is any part of the site wooded?
12. Are there any restrictions on tree removal?

Transportation

1. What is best access to nearest freeway interchange?
2. What is distance from primary motor freight terminals?
3. Have you interviewed motor freight managers?
4. Is the facility inside the commercial delivery zone of the city?
5. If not, what is the extra delivery cost compared to deliveries within the commercial zone?
6. Is rail access available?
7. If there is no rail siding now, what is the cost of adding one?

8. What is cartage cost to a TOFC (piggyback) terminal?
9. What is cartage cost to nearest marine terminal?
10. What is cartage cost to nearest air freight terminal?
11. Will those customers who pick up at your warehouse have any transportation problem with this facility?

Utilities

1. What is the size of the water main serving the site?
2. What is the water pressure and when was it last tested?
3. Are there water meters on hydrants and sprinkler systems?
4. What is the source of the water supply?
5. What is the electric power capacity?
6. Is submetering of electricity permitted?
7. Have we received copies of recent utility bills?
8. Are incentives available for reducing peak electric demand or installing HID lighting?
9. Is submetering of gas permitted?
10. Are there limitations on capacity or demand?
11. If fuel oil is used for heat, what is the source of supply?

Security considerations

1. Does the sprinkler system meet preferred risk standards?
2. If not, what is the cost of upgrading the system?
3. Is the sprinkler capable of conversion to ESFR?
4. If so, what is conversion cost?
5. Is there a secondary water source for the sprinkler system?
6. Have we seen insurance inspection reports?
7. Have we interviewed law enforcement officials?
8. Have we interviewed neighboring managers?

Labor market

1. Are neighboring businesses unionized?
2. Have we measured community attitudes toward unions?
3. Is there a labor shortage or high unemployment?
4. How are nearby schools rated in comparison to other sites?

Community attitudes
1. Do community leaders welcome industrial expansion?
2. Is there any discernable opposition to warehouse operations?
3. Is there any history of difficulty in rezoning?

Taxation:
1. What is the date of the most recent property appraisal?
2. What is real estate tax history over the last ten years?
3. Have there been any recent tax assessments?
4. Are there any tax abatement programs in effect or available?
5. Is the facility in a duty free or enterprise zone?
6. Are there planned public improvements?
7. How do inventory tax levels compare with other sites?
8. Is this a free port state?
9. What are tax rates for?:
   - Corporate income tax
   - Payroll tax
   - Unemployment compensation
   - Sales tax
   - Workers compensation
   - Franchise tax
   - Other taxes
10. What are recent trends in taxation?
11. Are industrial revenue bonds available, and can we qualify?

New construction considerations
1. Have test borings been made at all key points on the site?
2. Are there landscaping or buffer zone requirements?
3. How will roof drainage be discharged?
4. What are estimated costs and time requirements for all construction and occupancy permits?

Questions that solve problems

Because the requirements definition is so important in a location process, your first questions should test the validity of the definition that has been prepared.

Q Who was involved in the preparation of this requirement list?

C The answer should reveal that everyone who could possibly be influenced by the location of the new warehouse has had some input into the requirements definition. At the very least, be sure that all executives involved in logistics, marketing, and finance were consulted. Opinions from manufacturing will be important in some organizations. You can't get too much input at this stage.

Q Have we considered all the contingencies in picking a location?

C Try to think of everything that could go wrong. For example, if only one rail carrier serves the site, that carrier could be disabled by a strike. This questioning tests the ability of your people to be creative in considering every possible contingency.

Q Do we have an alternate in case the preferred site does not work out?

C Lack of available alternates suggests that your people have not been open-minded in looking at all the possibilities.

Q Do we have a site selection checklist, and has it been reviewed by everyone involved in the process?

C Failure to have any checklist suggests that the location decision has not been developed as an orderly management process. ❖

Chapter 31

Real estate – lease, buy, or rebuild?

Real estate decisions are frequently driven by corporate policy. While you may or may not be able to influence your company's policy, you at least should understand it. Furthermore, if you are handling warehouse real estate in a certain way because *we've always done it that way*, you should recognize that you may be a victim of management inertia.

Handling real estate calls for strategic decisions, and the strategy for warehousing real estate might differ from that used for real estate assets devoted to production or administration.*

Though about one quarter of the corporate assets in the United States consist of real estate, the great majority of corporations in this country do not put a realistic value on their real estate assets. Following accounting custom, most companies value real estate at a declining book value: The original cost of the facility, less all depreciation taken since the real estate was first acquired. Using this system, some companies own thirty-year-old warehouses that are well located, in good condition, functionally efficient, and significantly under-valued. The book value is often a tiny fraction of the property's replacement cost or resale value.

When such distortions in valuation exist, they can cause corporate managers to make foolish decisions.

In considering strategy, you should seek a harmonious relationship between real estate strategy and three other strategies that are important to every corporation. The first of these is overall corporate strategy, the deter-

---

*   Adapted from an article by Bruce Abels and Duane Ottenstroer. The article appeared in *Warehousing Forum*, Volume 2, Number 7, ©Ackerman Company.

mination of what businesses the company will be in and why. Of equal importance is the investment strategy — what rate of return does the company seek, and where do you want to make investments? Third, consider your overall strategy for logistics. Have you made long-term decisions about where you want warehouses? How certain are you that those locations will still be valid in the light of anticipated changes in your business over the next five, ten, or twenty years?

As you review corporate strategy, you must also recognize the distinct differences in warehousing. In some situations, the best operations decision is not the best real estate decision. Warehouse strategy must be flexible and respond to change, meaning a long-term lease may not be the best lease. Your warehouse strategy should be influenced by opportunity costs. These costs are determined by the fair market value of the warehouse and the reasonable chance of renting or selling that warehouse to a third party.

Three options in managing real estate

As you develop a real estate strategy, consider that there are three primary options in property management:

- ◆ Control costs — be sure they are minimized and stabilized.
- ◆ Generate maximum cash return.
- ◆ Generate maximum corporate profit.

From an operational standpoint, controlling costs always has first priority. In most corporations, surprises are troublesome, so most managers seek stable real estate costs, preferably with only moderate cost fluctuations anticipated for many years ahead. But when the market or other conditions change rapidly, the manager may elect to sacrifice stability for flexibility. If you have reason to believe that you will not want to be in the same warehouse three or five years from now, a short-term lease is preferred even though rent escalations might be anticipated when the lease expires.

The second option is to generate maximum cash return from real estate, usually by looking for chances to purchase properties at a below-market price and to sell surplus properties at an attractive gain. Generating cash returns usually requires the constant buying and selling of properties.

The third option is to operate warehouses as a profitable real estate business. This could include a decision to enter into public warehousing as a profit center.

In examining the options, the warehouse user frequently finds conflict between two central questions as shown below:

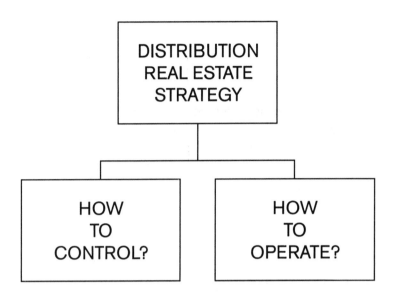

Many warehouse users assume that they can best control warehouse facility costs by owning or long-term leasing. They further assume that it is then necessary to operate the warehouse with their own people.

The development of contract warehousing as an alternative to traditional public warehousing has provided another option, that of controlling the real estate without operating the warehouse. While the commitment to the real estate may be long-term, the commitment to the contract *operator* can be of relatively short term. Because contract operators do not have a big investment in the operation, they should not require long-term guarantees.

The ultimate facility cost control comes from owning the warehouse building. Second is a long-term lease of five years or more with no (or tightly limited) escalation clauses.

A more flexible option is a rolling lease or *evergreen* contract, an agreement that is subject to cancellation or modification by either party with twelve months notice. This lease provides assurance that either party will have twelve months to make other arrangements, but it also allows either party to modify the agreement after this waiting period.

The most flexible option is public warehousing, which typically involves a commitment of only thirty days. However, that commitment is subject to modification with thirty day notice by either party.

When you measure the issues of flexibility and control, consider ten principal factors for change in your business that influence your use of warehousing:

- Volumes increases or decreases.
- Customers change.
- Transportation rates or services change.
- Transportation modes change.
- Service policies change.
- Products change.
- Order profiles change.
- Businesses acquired/divested.
- Property values change.
- Space is needed for other purposes.

In any dynamic business, these factors change frequently, and more than one can change simultaneously. When such changes take place, you may find that your warehouse is too large, too small, or in the wrong location.

Understanding real estate costs

The ownership of property has both visible costs and hidden costs. The five visible costs are:

- Rent.
- Taxes.
- Insurance.
- Utilities.
- Maintenance.

Even if you own the property, you must calculate the equivalent of rent. Because these costs are likely to change, it is important to revise your calculations often.

In addition to the five visible costs, there is a group of hidden costs:

- Cost of vacancy.
- Professional expenses (legal, engineering, project management and property management).
- Corporate staff support.

♦ Losses of insurance deductibles.
♦ Relocation.
♦ Travel.
♦ Opportunity costs.

No warehouse is full all of the time, yet few corporate budgets calculate the cost of vacancy. Opportunity cost is listed to be sure that you consider the difference between the book value of the real estate and the market value for that property.

The influence of ROA accounting

A growing number of corporations emphasize *return on assets* rather than return on sales. The emphasis on ROA shifts attention from the exclusive focus on cost to the trade-offs between costs, assets, and risks. The ROA-oriented manager will improve return on assets either by increasing the amount of return or by reducing the dollar value of assets in the company.

To improve ROA in warehousing:

♦ Dispose of property so that it is no longer owned or leased.
♦ Acquire use of warehouses through public warehousing, a
   very short-term lease, or an operating agreement instead of
   a formal lease.

As you consider these techniques, you must balance the improved ROA with changes in your ability to control real estate costs.

As you seek the best strategy for warehouse property management, you walk the fine line of maximizing real estate return without damaging your warehouse operation.

The buy/lease decision

In deciding whether to buy or lease a warehouse, consider both financial and non-financial issues. The financial issues typically involve a worksheet to compare the positive and negative cash flows of purchasing or leasing. Figure 1 shows a worksheet that your financial people may wish to use to guide the decision.*

Figure 1	Buy/Lease Decision
Buy?	
Positive cash flows:	
Present value of the interest deducted after tax.	$
Present value of the depreciation deduction after tax.	
Present value of the land at end of lease.	
Present value of the building at end of lease.	
Negative cash flows:	
Cash down payment.	
Present value of the future mortgage payments.	
Total	$
Lease?	
Positive cash flows:	
Present value of the lease payment deduction after tax.	$
Present value of the down payment.	
Negative cash flows:	
Present value of the future lease payments.	
Total	$

The results will differ depending on whether the purchase is made with cash, through mortgage financing, or a combination of the two. The addition of mortgage debt to purchase a warehouse usually reduces the company's borrowing ability or other future opportunities.

---

*   Adapted from material written by David P. Lauer, partner in charge, Deloitte and Touche, Columbus, Ohio.

Under the simplest form of lease, the company could direct the construction of the building and either sell it after it is completed or enter into an agreement with a property owner as the project begins. The present value approach is used in completing the worksheet, enabling the user to assign a value in today's dollars to cash flows at a given date.

Once the financial impact is measured, be sure to consider the non-financial factors, which include the following:

- Existing location compared to possible future location.
- Changes in the business or product that may require a different type of warehouse.
- Construction innovations that cannot be retro-fitted in an older building.
- Influence of the warehouse on the asset values of the business.

When should you build?

The decision to build will be influenced by location, supply and demand of existing buildings, construction costs and capabilities, and financing considerations.

If you have determined that there is only one appropriate location for your new warehouse, and if there are no suitable buildings at that location, the logical conclusion is that you must construct the new building. For example, a manufacturer determines that a finished product warehouse is needed at a location within conveyor distance of the production plant. The project is justified by a reduction of trucking to remote warehouses. Since no existing warehouses are available within conveyor travel of the plant, a new warehouse must be constructed.

Supply and demand will influence the decision. You may find that existing buildings are available near the desired location, but scarcity of warehousing has driven the prices so high that they exceed the occupancy cost of a new building. In that situation, you may decide building a new facility is more economical than leasing or buying.

Financing may influence the decision to build or buy because obtaining financing for a new building is often easier than financing the purchase of an old one. At other times, an older building can be purchased by assuming a mortgage that has an interest rate below the current prevailing rate. Attractive financing is often a prime reason for buying an existing property.

You must also consider obsolescence. One characteristic all used buildings have in common is that their original owners no longer want them. The buyer should carefully examine an existing property to determine whether its location, design, or construction is likely to become obsolete in the foreseeable future.

The rehabilitation alternative

The preservation, conservation, and adaptive re-use of older buildings has gained increasing attention in recent years. Some of this interest has been spurred by legislation that provided significant tax credits for rehabilitating both historic structures and other buildings over 50 years old.

Rehabilitation may have economic incentives regardless of taxation. Sometimes the best location for growth is an available building in the center of the city, and it may be more economical to rehabilitate that structure than to build a new one. The community in which an older building is located may offer tax abatement, favorable financing, or other incentives to induce the investor to purchase an older building. These incentives must be balanced against the cost of rejuvenating the building. Then compare operating costs in that building versus costs in a new structure.

Rejuvenating warehouse roofs

The two most critical construction components in a warehouse building are the floors and the roof. By comparison, walls are relatively easy to change or fix. A roof or a floor with a serious problem can be most expensive to correct.*

The great majority of roofs in industrial and warehouse buildings in the United States are called *built-up roofs* because they consist of a series of layers of felt material, bonded and saturated with hot asphalt coating. Sometimes a coating of tar and gravel is applied, with the gravel providing

---

*   This subchapter is based on material provided by the Ruscilli Construction Company, Columbus, Ohio. Most of this originally appeared in *Warehousing and Physical Distribution Productivity Report*, Volume 19, Number 7, ©Alexander Communications, Inc., New York, NY.

protection and insulation. Heat, moisture, and ultra-violet rays cause the surface to deteriorate, and this process can be aggravated by windstorms and occasional roof traffic. Ponding water and thermal shock can also cause built-up roofs to deteriorate.

Built-up roofs can be repaired in a variety of ways. A coating of either hot or cold asphalt material will seal spot leaks. New plies of roofing material can be installed over the older roof, unless the surface is in poor condition. In that case, old plies are removed before new material is applied.

A newer alternative is the single-ply roof, similar to a giant rubber sheet. Sometimes the best way to stop persistent leaks, the single-ply system is lighter and simpler than installing additional plies of built-up roof. Single ply can be installed with or without ballast, but you should check with a professional engineer to see if the structure can support the additional weight of a ballasted system. Figure 2 shows maintenance features of single-ply and built-up roofs as well as metal roofs.

Some roofing problems are corrected by installing a foam roof, a plastic compound that foams as it is applied to create a surface that provides insulation as well as protection from leaks. Questions remain regarding the long-term life of a foam installation.

Figure 2   **Checklist of Roof Maintenance**

Metal roof

☐ Check all flashings and fasteners at least twice a year. Look for areas that are no longer watertight and may be rusting.

☐ Check the deck itself, looking for any rusting. Color changes are a key indicator of rust.

☐ If rusting is found, the area can be coated with an appropriate sealer or protective agent.

Built-up roof

☐ Check flashings. Check for areas that are no longer watertight, and look for areas where the flashings have split open.

☐ Re-coat damaged areas with a polymer-modified asphalt designed for such purposes. This is especially good for vertical surfaces because it will not slide off.

☐ Check the surface of the roof itself. Look for puncture damage. The roof may need a top-coating from time to time to cover up punctures, particularly if the felt on the roof is visible.

☐ Check areas where drains are located to make sure they are air-tight and are not leaking. If you find leaks, an emulsion may solve the problem.

Single-ply roof

☐ Very little maintenance is needed for these roofs; they either work or not. But if coating is desired, do it when the roof is new.

☐ As with other roofs, always check the flashings to make sure they are not pulling or punctured.

Rejuvenating warehouse floors

In some ways, a warehouse floor is like a highway, but forklift trucks have small, solid tires and the front tires of a counterbalanced forklift truck carry the weight of the load as well as a portion of the truck's weight.* They thus load the floor more heavily than any highway and are heavier than most storage loads. The loaded legs that support storage rack also concentrate a heavy weight on a small area of the floor. For these reasons, floor composition of a warehouse is most important.

---

*   John Dixon of Ohio Ready Mixed Concrete Association provided substantial assistance in preparing this subchapter, most of which originally appeared in *Warehousing and Physical Distribution Productivity Report*, Volume 19, Number 18 ©Marketing Publications, Inc., Silver Spring, Maryland.

Many subsoils offer particular challenges. Some regions have expansive soil (clays and certain slags) that swells when it gets wet and shrinks when it dries. The result is a shifting that will severely damage floors. Uncontrolled expansive soil has virtually ruined warehouse floors, but such soil can be stabilized by being treated with lime, which soaks up any water in the soil and creates a hard, sealed surface.

One way to correct floor problems is to install a new floor over the old floor. Options include using a bonded overlay, a partially bonded overlay, or an unbonded overlay.

A **bonded overlay** is best used on a floor that has excellent subsoil but is badly worn, for example in the aisle areas of a busy grocery warehouse where thousands of poundings by lift trucks have simply weathered and worn the floor. The floor is first cleaned and sandblasted to ensure that there is a perfect surface to allow bonding of the two layers of concrete, then covered with approximately two inches of concrete.

The **partially bonded floor** is probably the least expensive means of getting a new surface. No effort is made to clean the old floor; a new surface is just put over it. Cracks in the old surface are likely to migrate up to the new one. However, if there are no cracks and cost is the primary consideration, this is a good option.

Probably the best method of treating a floor in very poor condition is the **unbonded overlay**. An unbonded overlay consists of an application of either asphalt slurry or two sheets of polyethylene as a buffer between the old concrete and the new. After the buffer is applied, the new floor is poured: three-and-one-half to five inches of concrete. The buffer keeps cracks from appearing in the new surface.

In cases of extreme deterioration, some preparation must be done before the unbonded overlay is applied. This may involve finding and filling voids in the floor. In a poorly prepared subsoil, sections of concrete slab may have no soil directly beneath them. These voids can be discovered by tapping the floor with a metal rod or a small hammer and listening for hollow sounds. A mud pump should be used to fill any such voids.

The unbonded overlay can be successfully used for all but the most severe expansive soil deterioration. Before the overlay is applied, the subsoil condition should be corrected. In the case of expansive soil, no repair attempt should be made until the soil has been stabilized by lime, a process that takes about two years.

Less serious floor problems can be dealt with more simply. Concrete floors commonly develop joints or cracks that tend to widen or spall as they are repeatedly hit by lift truck wheels. Such conditions can be stabilized and corrected by filling these joints and cracks with a flexible sealant, a flexible epoxy, or an elastomeric compound. Use a filler that is flexible rather than rigid, otherwise the movement between the two slabs on either side of the crack will quickly destroy the filler.

Spalling is the dislodging of pieces of floor at the edges of the joint, and it happens through the normal wear and tear of warehouse work. Where much material has been removed from the floor by spalling, the entire cavity needs to be patched. After the patching is complete, a saw cut is made to restore the joint. The joint in the patch must be at least as wide as the old opening and at least as deep, otherwise spalling will occur again.

Sometimes a carelessly poured floor contains sections thicker than necessary or thinner than needed to support traffic and loading. In extreme conditions, the unbonded overlay may be the only way to save such a floor. In other cases, the floor can be fixed by tearing out abnormally thin portions, removing enough subsoil to allow a slab of normal thickness, and then pouring new concrete.

Questions that solve problems

When your people announce their preferred program for developing real estate, your questions should be designed to insure they have considered all the options.

Q Why are we better off to build than to repair or enlarge an existing building?

C The answers will show whether or not your people have really thought through a real estate strategy.

Q Should we own the facility or lease it?

C The answers should be readily available from your financial people, and they should be able to defend the decision in terms of corporate policy as well as the best answer from a current cash flow standpoint.

Q Why don't we rehabilitate the warehouse we already have?

C As you look at the options, be sure to compare the total costs of rehabilitation with the cost of moving or constructing new space. There could be taxation consequences, and these should be reviewed by your financial people. ❖

Chapter 32

Elements of warehouse construction

Constructing a new warehouse is an opportunity to correct the deficiencies of an existing facility and to create a more productive workplace. This job is far too important to be left to the specialists; it deserves your people's input — particularly those who will operate the building.*

The stories of warehouse design errors are countless, and can be both amusing and tragic.

◆ One developer started a warehouse in southern Indiana, a region famous for stone, but neglected to perform soil tests. When the graders hit rock, they were forced to do blasting despite the fact that steel had been erected.

◆ In north Texas, a warehouse was constructed on soil known to be unstable. While soil can be stabilized, the developer poured a floor without taking any corrective action. When the building was finished, the floor heaved and soon had a rough surface. Ultimately the building was torn down because the floor could not be used.

◆ In Ohio, a new warehouse was constructed using high-intensity lighting, but there was an additional $25,000 expense before the building could be opened because the contractor had to relocate the lights so they would be over the aisles. Furthermore, any future aisle changes will cause similar expenses.

---

* This chapter was written with substantial assistance from John Ensign and Tim Kelton of Ruscilli Construction Company, Columbus, Ohio.

No matter how large or small the construction project, you must be involved. Everyone who will have anything to do with the new warehouse should also be consulted on those decisions that cannot be changed once construction is started.

Understanding total development costs

Economy is of great concern to any warehouse developer, and before construction begins you should question the total development cost of the selected site. That cost can vary significantly depending on the condition of the land, costs of providing access, and zoning restrictions.

For example, most communities restrict the amount of land that can be occupied by buildings. One common limitation is 45 percent building coverage, but some areas set the limit at 30 percent. A cheaper site that permits only 30 percent coverage may prove to be more expensive than an alternate site allowing 45 percent coverage.

If the soil is unstable or rocky, the cost of site preparation can exceed the cost of the land itself. Therefore, when you compare sites, be sure that the total cost and development time for the site selected will not destroy either your budget or your time schedule. An apparently inexpensive site may be far more costly in the long run.

Test borings

The floor and the foundation are the most critical elements of any warehouse construction. The quality of foundations and floors depends upon the land under them, and that can be measured only with soil tests.

Soil tests to determine the load-bearing capacity of the site are essential. The tests may pinpoint the best location for the building on the piece of land because load-bearing capacities vary from 1,000 pounds per square foot up to well over 10,000 pounds per square foot. Remember: No warehouse floor is any stronger than the land beneath it. Independent soil testing laboratories are found in all major cities, and use of one is an essential early step in any construction project.

Test borings limit the risk of underground problems. These include aquifers, peat bogs, old foundations, and other hidden underground structures. You may find rock that requires extensive blasting before construction. All of these are unwelcome and costly surprises, but they can be mitigated with a comprehensive test boring pattern.

Governmental considerations

Municipal zoning and permits should be considered very early in the site
selection process. Environmental impact studies are needed in some states.
In one community, for example, local government agencies require three to
six months to approve a site development plan and will not permit the developer to apply for a building permit until after the site development plan
has been approved. The building permit process requires additional
months. As a result, the process of obtaining the necessary permits can con-
sume an entire year. One of your first questions should be: *How much lead
time is required to obtain necessary permits?*

Storm water management

One site planning aspect for which local governments have been increasingly alert is how to deal with flash floods during sudden heavy rains. Many
municipalities require that developers show the ability to handle storm
water. There are four generally accepted ways of doing this:

- ◆ Excavate a detention pond.
- ◆ Install a detention tank.
- ◆ Build a recessed parking lot that can be flooded to a depth
  of six inches. In a flash flood, this may inconvenience people who parked there, but flood water will not be deep
  enough to damage the cars.
- ◆ Install oversized pipe or culverts to handle maximum storm
  water capacity.

A typical storm water policy is that the site shall not drain more water
onto neighboring land than was deposited before the new structure was
built.

Some state authorities have added environmental constraints on storm
water management. Such regulation substantially complicates the process
of putting up a new building. Some require sedimentation control during
construction. This constraint is designed to protect against potential migra-
tion of earth and other sediment during the process of grading and construction. Others require pre-treatment of storm water discharge if there is
any chance that the discharge could contain pollutants. Any building that

includes a chemical treatment process could have such exposure, and the storm water management system will be far more complex.

A careful study of state and local storm water management ordinances is critical before construction commences. In extreme cases, such ordinances could make construction of the building uneconomical.

Utilities

Planning for all utilities must take place before construction starts, and you should determine the minimum requirements for electricity, natural gas, and telephones. Check the capacity and capability of existing utility systems, and the cost of expanding them if they are inadequate.

Of particular importance is water pressure, which is essential for fire protection. Adequate water pressure and flow can eliminate the need for costly fire pumps. The best and newest sprinkler systems require substantially more water than the older systems, and your ability to use the latest sprinkler technology is likely to be limited by the characteristics of your water supply. Fire protection underwriters are likely to be more adamant about the availability of water than local fire protection codes and ordinances.

Before construction starts, be sure that all utilities are adequate to support your warehouse operation.

Risk management

Ask your insurance underwriter about features that will reduce your insurance cost. Building insurance rates and contents rates are always related. Since most warehouses today contain an inventory worth many times the cost of the building, the contents rating is more important than building coverage.

Construction codes vary throughout the country, but all are concerned with structural design adequate to withstand a given number of pounds per square foot of wind load or pounds per square foot of uplift. However, insurance underwriters often have requirements that exceed the local codes.

Wind loads are higher in areas where hurricanes are common. By allowing your underwriter to review construction plans before the project is underway, you will avoid errors that might be costly or difficult to correct.

Fire protection systems

The insurance underwriter should always be involved in fire protection system design. Most protection standards specify fire lanes around a building to allow access by fire-fighting equipment. Lanes and roads must be designed with the proper width and turning radius to accommodate fire engines.

Nearly all warehouses in the United States use sprinkler systems to fight fires, and many systems have booster pumps to provide additional water pressure. If your facility has such a pump, consider the benefits of installing a larger unit than the minimum required size. The larger pump may increase the cost by 10 to 15 percent while providing 55 percent more water capacity. This allows higher stacking and greater cube utilization in the warehouse.

The underwriter is likely to ask for hose stations, hose racks, and intermediate sprinklers in storage racks. Don't be afraid to negotiate these items, testing to see if they could be eliminated by providing greater water capacity or other safeguards at lower cost. Be sure you consider the use of Early Suppression Fast Response (ESFR) sprinklers or similar new designs which often eliminate the need for sprinklers in storage racks. Underwriters are familiar with trade-offs, and they will help you find alternative ways to provide adequate protection.

Layout design

Many warehousing professionals question the advice of architects and engineers. Clearly, no building can be built without them, but the best source of layout advice comes from your own warehousing people. The best warehouses are designed from the inside out.

Before starting the project, design your own layout based on necessary stack heights, aisle widths, staging areas, bulk storage, order-picking lines, and so forth. Then have an architect or engineer fit the building to your layout. Be sure you consider the construction cost options, such as possible savings from using standard bay sizes, or varying the layout to permit more economical building practices.

By starting with your own preferred layout and receiving feedback from the contractor, you will find the trade-offs between the most economical building from a construction standpoint and the most efficient building from a warehousing standpoint.

Since you are the one who must make the operation run efficiently after the building is built, remember that construction cost is a one-time expense, but the cost of operating the building is likely to increase each year.

As you develop storage plans, make sure you understand the relationship of building costs to layout. From a construction standpoint, the lowest-cost warehouse is square. This provides the maximum number of square feet per linear foot of wall, yet a square building might be inefficient to operate by creating long travel runs between rail dock and truck dock or dock and storage areas.

Bay size (the space between upright columns) is a factor in layout and construction costs. For many structures, the most economical bay size is 25 by 50 feet, or 30 by 30 feet. A 40 by 40-foot bay will require a relatively small premium. A 40 by 50-foot bay may prove more economical than a 40 by 40-foot bay, but construction costs will escalate rapidly when bay sizes exceed 50 by 50 feet, particularly if the roof must bear heavy snow loads.

The building contract

Some construction firms offer a contract by which they become responsible for the design and construction of the facility. Using a *design-and-build* contractor expedites the overall construction process. When the contractor is also responsible for the design, the possibility of an adversary relationship between the builder and the owner's architect is eliminated, and the project is usually completed more rapidly. The greatest disadvantage to the buyer is the difficulty in comparing bids, since each bidder may propose, design, and build different details in construction.

A *construction management* approach addresses the competitive issues by creating a team that includes the owner, the architect, the construction manager, and the warehouse manager. Early in the planning process, the team addresses the issues of schedule, budgets, materials, and constructability. The team must insure the existence of checks and balances as the needs of each party are recognized.

The team monitors progress and establishes competitive bidding for each major component. The team qualifies all potential bidders to be sure that each is a reputable trade contractor. The construction manager monitors all construction activities.

In drawing up construction contracts there are several bases for an agreement. These include lump-sum contracts, cost-plus-fixed-dollar contracts, guaranteed maximum costs with cost-plus-fixed dollar fees, and guaranteed maximums with sharing of savings.

Cost-plus percentage fees provide no incentive for the contractor. The builder should receive a bonus for early completion or completion under budget, but should be penalized for late completion. The maximum markup for changes should be specified.

Changes are always expensive, particularly after construction is underway. A change order costs everyone additional time and money. For this reason, it is important to have all drawings and specifications checked while the project is still in the planning stage.

Building a firm foundation

The two most important parts of any warehouse are the roof and the floor. Floors, like roadways, are merely a wearing surface with minimal tensile strength. They are no stronger than the material beneath them.

Close inspection and adherence to specified compaction standards should be made right up to the actual pouring of the concrete on the base. If inspection is not made constantly throughout the compaction process, early precautions can be wasted. Concrete cylinder tests should be made throughout the pouring of the concrete floor and core samples should be taken if any such tests provide a warning signal.

Meticulous inspection by an independent source, such as a testing laboratory, is critically important in every phase of floor construction. A badly constructed floor may never be correctable at an economical cost.

Roof design and construction

The type of roof you select will influence both construction and operating costs. A conventional built-up roof, made from layers of felt roofing and asphalt, weighs eight to ten pounds per square foot, while an insulated metal roof weighs one pound or less per square foot.

Both metal and built-up roofs are available in materials adequate for a 20-year bond. Roof bonds should be examined with care, since they usually have many escape clauses. Some contractors offer a 20-year weather tightness guarantee. The best metal roof has an aluminum-and-zinc-coated surface, and it is built with a standing-seam process. The standing-seam provides superior protection against leakage and allows construction of a roof with a less pronounced pitch than older metal roofs. Earlier metal roofs required a pitch of one inch in 12 inches, but standing-seam roof allows a pitch as gentle as one in 36.

An excellent alternative to the built-up roof is the single-ply rubber roof, now frequently used to replace worn out built-up roofs.

Inspect the roof during construction to be sure that the materials are being applied correctly. Because roofing is dirty, hard work, some laborers will take short-cuts.

Roads

Roadway design and construction are critical parts of any warehouse development. The drainage is critical because the asphalt or concrete is merely a wearing surface, while the strength is in the base below. A base that is not properly drained will lose its bearing strength and fail. Inspection and testing of the base of roadways is as important as it is for warehouse floors.

Even if your company does not operate any trucks, the design of truck maneuvering areas to save labor costs should be important to you. Reducing costs for your transportation suppliers will ultimately reduce your own costs. Many warehouses have truck areas apparently designed by people who knew nothing about driving a truck. While architectural standards state that 85 feet from the edge of the truck dock to the outside edge of the maneuvering area is adequate, a maneuvering area of at least 110 feet — and preferably 120 to 124 feet — will greatly improve truck movement. The truck berth should be a minimum of 12 feet wide.

The truck apron, like the roadway or the warehouse floor, is no stronger than the base material beneath it. With the extreme wear on the truck parking pad, it is best to install a concrete apron seven to eight inches thick, reinforced with wire mesh.

Some truck docks are constructed of asphalt, but these must have a concrete dolly strip to provide support in the event trailers are left at the loading dock. If you need a dolly strip, be sure the architect knows that location of trailer dollies varies. Therefore, the dolly strip must be wide enough to allow for maximum variance.

Docks

An item once referred to simply as a 'truck door' is an important tool for the operation of the warehouse. Today it is likely to include a mechanical dock leveler and pit, a thermally efficient overhead door, a dock shelter to provide a weather seal between the truck body and the warehouse, and a concrete pad for the trailer.

A few years ago, trucking industry standards called for a dock height of 50 to 51 inches above the pad. If you will be using refrigerated trucking equipment, remember that the presence of insulation will raise the height of the trailer bed at least two inches and sometimes more. Truck tires are smaller, and current industry recommendations call for a dock height of 48 inches.

The door itself should be larger. In 1984, the federal government encouraged adoption by all the states of a trailer width of 102 inches, or 8.5 feet.

At the time, most warehouse doors were eight feet wide and nine feet high. Today's preferred door is nine feet wide by ten feet high. The nine-foot width brings the entire truck body within the door area, even if the driver misses the mark by a few inches. A narrower door creates loading problems if the truck is just slightly off center. The ten-foot height provides total clearance of 14 feet from door jamb to the truck pad. This ensures that any truck that is within the 13-foot, 6-inch highway clearance limitation will not damage the top of the door jamb or the building.

Because of heat loss, uninsulated metals should never be used in door construction. Wood construction provides better thermal efficiency than plain metal.

Wear and tear

Protection of the building from battering by highway trucks and fork-lift trucks is frequently overlooked. A few dollars spent on placing six-inch diameter pipes where they will protect overhead door tracks, door jambs, electrical apparatus, building corners, or other vulnerable items is well worth the investment. These protector pipes should be filled with sand, capped with concrete, and painted yellow for visibility.

Such pipes also may be placed on critical points in the radius of a curve in a roadway or at sensitive points in the truck maneuvering area. Inspect the condition of roadways and maneuvering areas after the facility has been in operation for a month or so. You are likely to find other places where guard posts should be installed to further protect the pavement or the facility.

Railroads and rail docks

Drainage is as important for railroad tracks as it is for roadways, whether the rail lead is inside or outside the warehouse. Poor drainage is often indicated by a rail lead *pumping* when the locomotive rolls over it. Such action eventually makes it necessary to realign the rails, and will be a continuing problem until proper drainage is established.

The usual railroad side clearance is 8.5 feet from center line of the rail lead to the building wall. However, it is possible to establish closer clearance for an inside rail dock, down to 5 feet 9 inches. The approval process usually involves the state public utilities commission and sometimes the railway union.

Securing close clearance is well worth the trouble because it enables the warehouse operator to use a much shorter dock plate, which improves materials handling speed and safety. Since approval of a close clearance may take up to four months, it is important to start early.

Walls

While most warehouse users and nearly all lenders place great emphasis on the warehouse walls, this is the least critical component of warehouse construction. You have a choice of many construction materials.

Most lenders and users like masonry because it gives a feeling of permanence and strength. The masonry may be either concrete block or block with a brick veneer. Poured concrete panels have grown in popularity because they are less expensive to construct than masonry. Concrete is a poor insulator, though new designs include an insulation sandwich within the panels. These are called *tilt-up* panels because they are poured at the site and then tilted into place.

Insulated metal wall panels are less costly than either masonry or tilt-up and provide maximum energy conservation. One compromise is masonry or tilt-up concrete to a height of 10 feet above the floor, with insulated metal panels above for maximum economy and energy conservation. The concrete wall provides a substantial barrier to bumps from trucks and fork-lifts, as well as adding to the esthetics of the building exterior.

Heating

Since products will be damaged by freezing, nearly all facilities in temperate climates have some heating equipment. Additional insulation is a sound investment, particularly in a time of accelerating energy costs.

In many cities, energy codes now force the developer to prevent heat loss. Insulation value is indicated with R-rating, referring to resistance to heat loss. Warehouses may be required to reach R-19, which is considered to be the point of diminishing returns for an industrial building. Depending on the type of insulation used, a blanket of four to ten inches may be needed to provide the required R factor.

In examining heating paybacks, consider using the lowest heat level possible. Warehousing is a strenuous job and workers do not need warm surroundings. By using low-range temperature thermostats and reducing heat to 45 degrees Fahrenheit, it is possible to cut energy consumption by nearly 40 percent.

Supplemental heating at the point of loss is often installed at dock areas or other doors in order to prevent cold air from moving into the building.

Air rotation furnaces are a newer alternative to overhead gas-fired heaters. These furnaces are floor-mounted and move large amounts of air to equalize temperatures at the floor and ceiling. The heaters are designed to handle nearly 100,000 square feet of space, and some users report that such systems are far more economical than conventional overhead unit heaters.

Illumination

Like other aspects of warehousing, lighting has changed greatly in recent years. Many warehouses rely heavily on skylights and translucent wall panels to provide the cheapest and best form of light available — sunlight. Skylights may be installed easily in a steel roof, and newer construction techniques eliminate the leak problems that were common with older skylights. However, skylights do nothing for the work environment of the night shift, and in a cold climate the heat lost through skylights costs more than the illumination saving.

The biggest payback of good illumination is a reduction of errors and an increase in morale. Many users have reported better shipping accuracy after improving warehouse lighting. Everyone reacts unfavorably to darkness, and bright light makes people feel better about the job they are doing.

Beyond accuracy and morale, there are other reasons for installing modern light fixtures. Utility rebates and credits offered by many electric companies can make the modernization less costly. A guide to utility rebates published by *Electrical Contractor Magazine* listed 41 electric utilities that offered a rebate for replacing fluorescent lights with high intensity discharge (HID) fixtures. The rebates offered are sometimes based on wattage and the number of lamps. These rebates can be significant. One company received a rebate equal to three quarters of the cost of the new light fixtures.

Further savings are offered in maintenance — lamp replacement and fixture cleaning. HID lamps have a far longer life than other light sources. While fluorescent tubes are commonly rated at 12,000 hours of life, HID lamps last up to 24,000 hours. This means that relamping is needed half as often as with older lighting sources.

Most warehouses constructed just a few years ago used eight-foot fluorescent fixtures. One problem with fluorescent lamps, however, is that the light output deteriorates substantially at temperatures below 60 degrees, a common occurrence in many warehouses. Furthermore, they lose their lighting power as they age, but energy consumption remains the same.

If you are considering high-intensity electric lamps, you have a choice of three types: mercury vapor, metal halide, and high-pressure sodium. Metal halide and sodium lamps are far more efficient than the earlier lamps in the amount of light they produce for each watt of electricity.

High-intensity lighting is superior to fluorescent lights in many ways, but early installations were not sufficiently flexible to accommodate new aisle layouts. The warehouse operator who anticipated an aisle change stayed with fluorescents and long cords so that each fixture could be moved. Today's high intensity fixtures are available with the same long cords found in fluorescent fixtures.

Mercury vapor lamps cause some change in color and are therefore risky whenever color coding is used for product identification. Coupled with their relatively low efficiency and lamp life, they are now considered obsolete for warehouse use.

High-pressure sodium lights make minor changes in color values, but not enough to affect product identification. These lamps do distort color sufficiently to increase the error rate on some bar code scanning equipment. The metal halide lamp, while less efficient and with a shorter bulb life than sodium, provides the best color values and least potential for distortion.

Landscape

When the structure is completed, don't forget landscaping. There is no building that cannot be enhanced with greenery, and there is no better value in improving the appearance of your warehouse.

Some landscaping plans require extensive maintenance. Others provide greenery with minimal care. It is often better to pay a little more in initial cost to achieve a landscaping system that minimizes maintenance.

Questions that solve problems

When a construction project is planned for your company, your questions should be designed to verify that operations people have designed the building from the inside out and have not left key questions to be resolved by outsiders. Here are a few questions designed to check key points:

Q Who has checked all of the specifications for this building, and when were these checks made?

C If all of the checks were made by architects and engineers with minimal input from your employees, you have a dangerously incomplete project.

Q Have the fire underwriters approved every aspect of the design?

C If anyone in your company tries to cut corners in this area, you will face serious consequences later.

Q Are we sure that roadways and truck maneuvering areas are designed for tomorrow's equipment rather than today's?

C Be sure your planners anticipate the largest equipment that might be allowed on the highways in the future.

Q Have the designers anticipated normal wear and tear?

C Consider the battering that every warehouse takes from highway trucks, lift trucks, and extreme weather.

Q Are we sure that heating and illumination systems are current state-of-the-art?

C Not every supplier knows about the latest developments in both heating and lighting. Be sure you get more than one opinion. ❖

Chapter 33

Planning and procedures

A key to warehousing success is a detailed plan supplemented by carefully described procedures. In contrast, many failures in warehousing reflect a failure to plan and a lack of specific procedures. Most decisions on warehouse layout are influenced by the two major activities: storage and handling.

Storage requirements

Because housekeeping is the most important barometer of warehouse management, an excellent layout either improves or maintains good housekeeping.

As you look at housekeeping considerations in planning a layout, ask these questions:

1. Will the new layout facilitate removal and reconditioning of damaged stock?
2. Will the layout allow easy cleaning of aisles and staging areas?
3. Does the layout allow ample transmission of daylight or artificial light so that carton markings are easy to read?

The environmental requirements for different products vary, and this must be considered in space planning. For example, some merchandise may require temperature or humidity control, other products may be hazardous, and still others represent abnormal security risks. Some products must be stored in racks because packaging limits the ability to stack them. Some pallets must be stored in racks because of volume considerations, while others have both the quantity and packaging to allow a tall free-standing stack.

How much can your warehouse hold?

In essence, the warehouse protects stored goods in a minimal amount of space. Minimizing space usage while protecting the inventory requires careful planning.

Assume that a warehouse operator needs to develop a total space plan for toilet paper. A carton measures 20 inches by 24 inches by 10 inches and arrives in boxcars containing 1,500 cases, with just one line-item per car. The product can be stacked 15 feet high. The operator determines that the product can be stacked in tiers measuring two units by two, five tiers high on a 48 by 40 inch pallet. With a stacking limitation of 15 units, this converts to a height limitation of three pallets. A pallet load, allowing for normal overhang, will occupy 15 square feet.

Layout plans show that 40 percent of the building will be used for aisles, docks, and staging areas, leaving 60 percent available for storage. From this 60 percent net storage, an additional 20 percent is lost to *honeycombing*. (The space lost in front of partial stacks.)

After making the space calculation shown in Exhibit 1, we find that 31.25 square feet are needed for each stack, or .52 square feet per case of product. This information is adequate to plan the total space requirement. Similar calculations should be made for each item planned in the inventory.

Exhibit 1   **Storage Space Calculation**

Assumptions

1. A portion of gross space must be dedicated to aisled and staging, leaving 60% net space.

2. Honeycombing losses further reduce net space, leaving only 80% typically in use.

Calculations

A. Each pallet of a product contains 5 tiers with 4 cases per tier, or 20 cases total.

B. Each stack of 3 pallets contains 60 cases.

C. Each stack is the size of one pallet plus 1" overhang on each side (42"x50"), or 2,100 square inches. This is 14.6 feet, which we round to 15.

D. Gross square feet needed per stack is 15 / 60% = 25.

E. Square feet per stack after honeycombing is 25 / 80% = 31.25

F. Square feet per case is 31.25 / 60 cases = .52083.

Interaction of storage and handling systems

The storage layout and handling system in a warehouse are inseparable. The handling system must fit the building and the storage job and the storage plan must fit the handling system and aisle width requirements. It is impossible to plan one without considering the other.

While the storage method aims at maximum cube use, the warehouse operator must recognize the ever-increasing cost of labor. Balance is essential between an effective storage system and an effective handling system. This balance changes if labor costs increase faster than storage costs. The goal is to plan a distribution center that operates at maximum cost efficiency today, but can be modified to keep in step with changes in the cost relationship between storage and handling.

Simulating warehouse handling

One way to understand how a new warehouse layout will function is to create visual aids that help you to visualize what the warehouse will look like.

There are several ways to accomplish these simulations. One of the oldest and most dependable is the process of making flow charts. Flow charting helps the planner learn more about the job by describing it step by step. Flow charting identifies questions that may have been overlooked. It also imposes a discipline, makes you plan ahead, and provides a clue as to what layout options might be available that you may have failed to anticipate.

A more modern visual aid to simulate the layout is computer aided design (CAD). CAD uses a plotting machine to develop a detailed picture of the warehouse layout. This technique enables the planner to get a better visual preview of how the warehouse will look when layout recommendations are implemented.

As you review either flow charts or CAD layouts, answer these questions to be sure that logic prevails in planning the warehouse operation:

Purpose
- What is done?
- Why is it done?

Place
- Where is it done?
- Why is it done there?
- Where else might it be done?
- Where should it be done?

Sequence
- When is it done?
- Why is it done then?
- When might it be done?
- When should it be done?

Person
- Who does it?
- Why does that person do it?
- Who else might do it?
- Who should do it?

Means
- How is it done?
- Why is it done that way?
- How else might it be done?
- How should it be done?

Planning for change

The layout must be adaptable to change as well as the functions of storage and handling. What changes will be made if inventory grows to twice the size it is today? What changes will be made if inventory is cut in half? If the handling operation includes use of highly specialized equipment such as a turret truck, what will you do when that truck breaks down? What provisions have been made for casualty losses or disaster such as fire, windstorm damage, earthquake, or more common breakdowns: Power failure, equipment failure, and computer breakdown? Both future planning and contingency planning must be considered as the warehouse layout is designed.

The prime objective of a warehouse layout is to use available space effectively so that materials can be moved at minimum cost. The layout planner must allow maximum flexibility to deal with changes, some of which cannot be anticipated.

The right layout for you cannot be discovered without measuring and considering all of these variables. Therefore, developing an effective warehouse layout is really a *process* rather than a *formula*. Once you understand the process, you can develop a formula that will work well in your own operation.

Why and how to write an operating manual

An operating manual is important regardless of the size of your warehouse. The smallest operation needs the best manual because the absence of one key person can be critical. The operating manual documents the way the work is done.

The writing must involve people who are intimately familiar with the work to be done. While they may not be good at writing, this skill can be monitored by others who are. If the manual is to be useful to those who work in the warehouse, it must be prepared by many of these same people.

Contents of an operating manual

A good operating manual might have six major sections:
- Introduction and objectives.
- Storage layout and product location.
- Job descriptions.
- Staffing and work flow.
- Quality assurance.
- Glossary of terms and definitions.

The goal of an operating manual is to describe how the warehouse works, and this must be made clear in the first section. Since a warehouse is partially a storage location, the logic of that storage is described in one section.

The job of the warehouse is the sum total of the jobs of all employees, and therefore job descriptions become a critical part of the operating manual.

Work flow is even more important than storage in many modern distribution centers, so a description of that flow is essential.

Definition and the importance of quality should be part of any operating manual.

A glossary is readily overlooked, but you must consider the fact that many people entering warehousing have never even seen a warehouse before. The terms you take for granted are new to these workers, and definitions can be a valuable part of any training document.

Key issues for the operating manual

The manual provides a guideline for effective use of space, labor, and equipment. It must also consider seasonal factors. If you have dramatic swings in volume between peak shipping periods and slack periods, a prime function of your operating manual is to show how you can meet the seasonal peaks and avoid undue waste of space and labor during the slow season. Your operating procedures must provide for a high level of effectiveness during the rush season.

The manual must also recognize probable changes. If your products are like most, product families will change as new items are added and others deleted. As these products change, will the systems controlling them need to be changed? How will these changes affect the storage layout or the way in which the orders are selected? Which has greatest priority, integrity of operations or labor efficiency? Your procedures will depend on the answer.

Think of all the questions that are or might be asked about your warehouse, and then try to provide answers in the operating manual. Here are a few starter questions, and no doubt you can add to the list:

- ◆ How should we handle damaged merchandise discovered at the receiving dock?
- ◆ How should we handle damage discovered in the warehouse?
- ◆ How should we handle overages or shortages discovered in the warehouse?
- ◆ What procedure is followed if we cannot find an item which is shown on the book inventory?

◆ What do we do when we cannot find sufficient space to put away an inbound shipment?

◆ What are the ground rules for hiring new warehouse employees, and who is responsible?

◆ How will new employees be trained?

◆ If there is a date coding system, how does the code function?

◆ If stock rotation is necessary, what should be done when an error causes newer stock to be shipped?

Planning for equipment use

In most warehouse tasks, as well as many office tasks, the number of hours needed to finish a job will depend on the equipment or tools available to the worker. The planner begins by considering the kinds of equipment available.

For example, lift trucks are available with a wide array of attachments besides the conventional forks. A warehouse operation designed for carton-clamp handling will require significantly different planning for space and people than one designed to receive loose-piled cases that will be palletized at the receiving dock. Use of slip-sheet handling devices requires still different planning. The best time to do this planning is before the warehouse is opened.

At the planning stage, the warehouse manager should select the kinds of equipment that can best be used in the operation, taking into account lifting capacities and storage heights, and any environmental considerations that would restrict the design of the lift trucks. For example, internal combustion engine trucks may not be acceptable in freezers or other confined areas.

Six basic items of information should be gathered during the process of worker and equipment planning:

◆ The average order-size provides a good indication of the amount of time needed to ship each order.

◆ Physical characteristics of the merchandise also may define the amount of effort needed to handle it.

◆ The ratio of receiving units to shipping units, and the question of whether goods are received in bulk or as individual units will greatly affect the effort involved.

◆ Seasonal variations and the intensity of these seasonal swings must be measured.
◆ Shipping and receiving requirements should be defined, including the times of day when goods will be received and shipped.
◆ Picking requirements must be defined. A strict first-in first-out system is more costly both in labor and space.

Once the planner has collected this data, a useful definition of manpower and equipment needs can be reliably projected.

Contingency planning

Contingency planning is preparing in advance for emergencies not considered in the regular planning process.*

The best approach is to ask the question, *What if?* For example, what if our major suppliers are on strike? What if we are unable to obtain sufficient fuel to run our truck fleets? What if an earthquake or a tornado destroys our biggest distribution center? What if we cannot find enough secretaries, order pickers, or industrial engineers to staff our distribution facilities? What if we have to recall a major product?

A contingency plan should have certain characteristics. First of all, the probability of an adverse occurrence should be lower than for events covered by the regular planning process. Second, if a critical event occurs that could cause serious damage, the contingency plan must provide the means for a prompt response.

Contingency plans should be specific. For instance, an organization may develop a contingency plan to be implemented in the event of a drop in sales below a certain level. *If sales drop by 10 percent below plan, our net income will decline by 5 million dollars. In order to reduce this loss it will be necessary to defer the expansion of our distribution center, reduce the number of employees by 50 and to cut variable production costs.*

Wherever possible, the expected results of the actions taken should be calculated in financial terms, or in other meaningful measures, such as mar-

---

*   Based on an article by Bernard J. Hale, *Warehousing & Physical Distribution Productivity Report*, Volume 14, Number 3, ©Alexander Communication, Inc., New York, NY.

ket share, capacity, and available labor.

Trigger points

Contingency plans must specify trigger points, or warning signals, of the imminence of the event for which the plan was developed. In some cases, such as fire, the trigger point is obviously the event itself. In others, however, the point is not so clear. But a trigger point should be specified and the contingency plan should indicate the action to be taken at the trigger point.

Distribution managers should consider developing contingency plans for such potentially serious disruptions as strikes, energy shortages, labor shortages, natural disasters, and product recalls.

Planning steps

There are four steps in preparing a contingency plan:

- ◆ Identify the contingency and describe your objectives. For example, if the computer goes down, will your major objective be to get the equipment back in operation, or will you switch from computer to manual systems?
- ◆ Identify departments that will be affected by the contingency. For example, will the computer breakdown affect both office operations and warehouse operations? How will each of these departments cope with the situation?
- ◆ Determine what action should be taken to lessen the impact of the event. For instance, would the maintenance and testing of standby manual systems ease the transition in the event of a computer breakdown?
- ◆ Determine what connection one event will have with another. For example, how will the computer breakdown affect shipping and receiving operations?

The increased attention to contingency planning is the result of a comparable increase in business uncertainty in recent years. Supply situations taken for granted in earlier years must be the subject of contingency planning today. In a time of increased government involvement in quality control, the contingency of product recall is more common.

If the contingency event occurs — however unlikely it may be — the prudent manager will have an available plan of action.

Questions that solve problems

The best questions to ask about planning and procedures are those that require your people to demonstrate and illustrate the plans and procedures that they should already have prepared. Here are a few questions to stimulate the process:

Q What do we project as storage requirements, and how were those requirements developed?

C Be sure the answer demonstrates ample detail as well as a good process.

Q Do we know how much material our warehouse can hold? How did we arrive at this calculation?

C Again, the process is as important as the answer.

Q Have we simulated a warehouse layout, and if so what does it look like?

C Be sure to inspect the simulation and probe into methods used.

Q Have we developed an operating manual, and is it being used?

C Take a critical look at a random sample of procedures.

Q Do we have a contingency plan, and how recently has it been reviewed?

C The plan should be carefully reviewed and criticized. ❖

Chapter 34

Starting or moving a warehouse

Long before the warehouse accepts its first shipment, you should develop a general job outline. This job outline should include a review of anticipated customer service needs and of how these customer service levels are to be achieved.

Careful analysis of expected operating costs is important whether the proposed center is private or third party. Never overlook the fact that a private warehouse has internal costs that are expressed as imputed rates.

Third party warehouse operators calculate costs and then add profit to quote a rate. If you have a private distribution center, imputed rates allow you to evaluate the alternative of using an outside contractor. Therefore, a basic understanding of the costs of operating a warehouse helps control the new operation.

You should also develop a detailed plan for the opening to allow proper lead times and to minimize confusion during the start-up phase. The checklist at the end of this chapter can serve as a guide.

Initial planning

Early in the planning stages for the distribution center, consider communications, packaging, transportation, security and perishability of stored products. Communications includes the method of data transmission and its frequency. Examine package sizes, their handling characteristics, opportunities for unitization, and bulk storage versus warehousing of packaged goods. Consider the best mode for both inbound and outbound transportation. Problems of security include both fire and theft protection. Nearly everything is perishable to some degree, and a means of protecting product is a key consideration.

Costs

Warehousing costs divide into two categories — external and internal. External costs are those that originate outside the warehouse but would not occur if it were not there. Internal costs are those generated within the facility and are directly controlled by warehouse management.

External costs are the following:

♦ Transportation to and from the warehouse.

♦ Inventory taxes on goods stored at the warehouse.

♦ Insurance on warehoused inventories.

♦ Costs of controlling the warehouse.

Internal costs include:

♦ Storage.

♦ Handling.

♦ Clerical services.

♦ Administration.

While some cost accountants would assign other headings or cost categories, the eight cost centers listed above are typically found in warehouse operations.

Transportation

The largest external cost in most warehouses is transportation. After deregulation, some warehouse locations became uneconomical because they were based on artificially regulated transportation rates. Freight rates for goods moving to and from a distribution center may now be affected more by negotiation than the exact location of the distribution facility. On the other hand, selecting a location to maximize backhaul opportunities is a proven way to reduce transportation costs.

Design of the facility also influences transportation costs. If dock doors are inadequate, or if dock ramps are congested, the building may be costly for either the private or common carrier to serve. Design of the building and the ability to turn around vehicles quickly can directly influence overall distribution costs. Locating close to a freeway system will reduce driving time for private trucks. When air or marine freight is used, proximity to airport or wharf is a cost consideration.

Taxation

Second in importance as an external cost is the local tax on inventories, which can vary significantly from one location to another. A few states or other taxing authorities have used inventory as the basis for levying franchise, income or other taxes on the owner of property in storage. A user may shift inventories from a state that has created a significant tax burden by radical changes in tax policy. As transportation has improved, manufacturers can provide reasonable delivery service to their customers and still avoid those states and municipalities that have created what amounts to tax harassment.

Individual states differ widely in their approach to inventory taxes. At the same time, rates of taxation within states or even within counties or towns also can show significant differences.

Taxation rates and attitudes toward taxation are in a constant state of change. The trend seems to be toward eliminating inventory taxes, as state governments have recognized they must take this step to remain competitive with their neighbors. Because state tax situations change frequently, expert advice should be sought when making comparisons about tax policies of individual states or communities.

Insurance on goods in storage

In both private and public warehouses, casualty insurance for goods in storage is the responsibility of the owner of the inventory.

A building considered to be a firetrap will have high insurance rates for both the building and its contents. Types of goods stored in the warehouse affect the insurance rates. The quality of the fire department serving the area, the underwriter's assessment of housekeeping, and management interest in property conservation also will influence rates.

While insurance costs are normally a minor part of total physical distribution cost, insurance rates are an excellent yardstick for measuring the quality of a warehouse operation. Because the underwriters have a good reason for giving a warehouse a high risk rating, a public warehouse with unusually high rates is likely to be either badly managed or in a poor building, or both.

Control costs

Every warehouse must be controlled by someone who is responsible for its quality, and these control costs should be recognized as a separate item. If the warehouse is operated by a third party, control costs would include re-negotiation of the contract as well as periodic quality checks.

Storage

The first of the four internal cost categories is storage. Storage costs are best defined as those which are associated with goods at rest. They are those costs which would be incurred every month whether any of the freight was moved or not. Some warehouse operators assign to storage all costs which cannot be readily reduced, including lease payments or depreciation on materials handling equipment. They do this with the argument that the equipment could not sensibly be disposed of at a time of temporary down turn, and therefore a portion of the equipment cost is fixed and should be charged to storage. Storage costs would of course include all costs related to the buildings and property.

Handling costs

Those costs associated with goods in motion are typically charged to han-dling. They are all of those costs incurred when freight is moved. There are cases where certain cost areas must be divided between storage and han-dling. For example, an operator of electric trucks would pro-rate the monthly electric bill to reflect that electricity charge associated with the building (fixed costs) and that portion of electricity which is used to re-charge lift truck batteries. Cost of goods in motion are totally variable, and they are presumably reduced or increased as the velocity of freight move-ment goes up or down.

Clerical service costs

This group of costs are those associated with the office functions related to warehousing. Some operators will include these costs with materials han-dling, since they are closely related to goods in motion. If nothing were received or shipped, presumably clerical costs would virtually disappear. By isolating the clerical costs, the warehouse operator may better justify investments in office technology designed to reduce these costs.

Administrative costs

This cost center describes the internal administrative burden of operating the warehouse. It is the rough internal equivalent of the control costs described earlier, except that this cost center is internal rather than external. It represents those managerial and supervisory costs which are relatively fixed and would not be reduced in proportion to rising or falling volume.

Moving a warehouse

When planning a warehouse location change, you must estimate the cost of the move and include that cost in the primary decision of whether or not to move.

To calculate this cost, start with a target date for the move. This may change several times, but a target date is essential for planning purposes. Weather and seasonal inventory level variations need to be taken into consideration, and basing the cost estimate on a specific date allows this. Be extremely wary of establishing a target date based on a construction contractor's promise — contractors are eternally optimistic. Managers have had to move an operation into an incomplete warehouse because relocation plans were based on a contractor's completion date estimate and it later became impossible to postpone the move. To avoid this, add a comfortable cushion to the contractor's promise date.

Estimating the cost of moving

After setting the target date, estimate the inventory to be on hand on that date. The simplest approach forecasts the future date's inventory levels as a percentage of today's inventory levels.

Remember that it's possible to plan the moving date to coincide with a lower inventory level period or a period of reduced shipping activity — as long as the new building is ready.

After estimating the level of on-hand inventory, determine the number of transfer loads currently. You can do this by counting the full and partial pallet loads and pallet equivalents, and then dividing the number of pallets per load into the total.

For example, assume the current inventory level consists of 3,500 full and partially loaded pallets and pallet equivalents. (Pallet equivalents are items, not palletized, that equal a pallet in cube requirements.) Anticipate 26 pallets per transfer load. The number of loads of inventory to be transferred may be calculated as:

3,500 pallets/26 pallets per load = 134.6 loads

134.6 current inventory loads adjusted by a 92 percent factor to compensate for reduced inventory levels on the move date yields 123.8 loads of inventory (rounds to 124) to be transferred on the targeted move date.

Experience has shown that, for a short-distance move, floor loads (goods stacked just one pallet high) allow for quicker turnaround of transfer vehicles and are more efficient. For longer moves, fully loaded vehicles are more economical. When the trucks used to move the inventory can be turned around quickly by using a floor load, you'll be able to reduce driver waiting time.

The cost of each load to be transferred can be calculated by summing the following costs:

- ◆ Transfer vehicle operating cost, or vehicle rental cost, plus driver labor, and fuel, per round-trip.
- ◆ Outloading manpower and machine cost per load.
- ◆ Unloading and put-away cost per load.
- ◆ An allowance for damage, clerical labor, and contingencies.

The sum of these costs is the cost per load which is multiplied by the number of loads to be transferred to yield the total cost of transferring the inventory.

An example

Truck cost: 20 miles/round-trip @ $1.80/mile 36.00

Outloading cost: 0.3 hours/load @ $22.00/hr 6.60

Unloading/putaway cost: 0.25 hours @ $22.00/hr 5.50

Overtime allowance @ 25% x labor cost 3.03

Damage/clerical/contingency allowance @ . . . . __1.44__

Total cost per transfer load $52.57

In addition to relocating the inventory, the warehouse support functions must also be moved. So the following costs should be added:

- ◆ Cost of relocating the office operation.
- ◆ Cost of relocating the warehouse maintenance shop.
- ◆ Cost of transferring the materials handling equipment.
- ◆ Cost of moving value-added services (packaging, recooper-ing, assembly, and so forth).
- ◆ Cost of disassembling, transferring, reassembling, and lag-ging down storage racks.

These can be costed in the same way, then adding additional labor costs for rack reassembly and lag-down labor.

How long will it take?

The following is an example of how to calculate the number of days that will be required to make the move:

Volume Assumptions:

Inventory loads to be transferred . . . . 124 loads

Additional loads to move the support services . . . . 5 loads

Total loads to be transferred . . . . 129 loads

Time Assumptions:

Truck travel time, one way loaded . . . . 25 minutes

Return trip time, one way not loaded . . . . 25 minutes

Outloading time, one lift operator . . . . 18 minutes

Unloading and putaway time, one lift operator . . . . . . 15 minutes

Total round-trip cycle time . . . . 83 minutes

Time available, one shift operation

Available truck time, 7.5 hours . . . . 450 minutes

Minus allowance for delays/ interruptions, 10% . . . . . 45 minutes

Minutes available per truck per shift . . . . 405 minutes

Calculations

◆ 405 minutes per truck per shift divided by 83 minutes per round trip cycle = 4.9 loads/truck/shift.

◆ With moderate overtime or extra efficiency, five loads may be achieved per shift per truckload with one lift operator loading and another unloading.

The 129 total loads to be moved will require:

◆ 129 loads / 5 per day = 25.8 days with one truck, two lift operators on one shift

◆ 129 / 10 = 12.9 days with two trucks

◆ 129 / 15 = 8.6 days with three trucks.

Continue services or suspend operations?

A vital question is deciding whether to continue services or suspend operations during the move. *Customer service considerations* should take priority.

The warehouse operating manager's preference will probably be to shut down because moving costs can be minimized and coordination of the move is much simpler. When operations are suspended, all that is required is thorough planning, having everything ready in advance, and a few hectic days of concentrated activity. Overtime costs may be significant but the period of disruption can be kept to a minimum. Overtime days and weekends may be best for this type of move.

The customers should be the deciding factor in whether or not to close during the move. Moving a warehouse without a break in normal customer service requires special coordination. First, and of critical importance, is communication. Each customer must be contacted during the early planning stages to discuss the move and to outline the tentative plan and timetable.

As the move date approaches, there must be frequent contacts on the administrative and clerical levels between the warehouse and its users to assure that loads dispatched to the warehouse are routed to the new location on the proper dates, and that carriers are sent to the proper location for pick-up of outbound shipments. There may be a short-term requirement for carriers to pick up outbound shipments from both the old and new locations.

Communications

Customers need to be sold — tactfully — on the benefits of the proposed move. All customers must be informed well in advance of the move, and then provided with frequent progress reports. An over-informed customer seldom complains.

Points that must be covered in communications with customers include:

♦ Out-of-service dates, if the warehouse is to suspend operations during the move. Also provide for the emergency service requirements, that surely will arise.

♦ Date and time of transfer of each class of inventory. This is needed to coordinate delivery and pick-up carriers. It requires daily, even hourly, contact.

♦ Phone number and address changes and their effective dates.

♦ Dates and times when data communications may be out of service.

♦ Directions to the new location.

♦ New hours of service, if these are to change.

♦ Changes in service charges or standards of service.

Common carriers, employees, suppliers, the phone company, and the postal service need to have timely notice of the move.

Employees should hear about the relocation well in advance; if you don't inform them, the grapevine will. Explain what is happening, why, and what to expect at the new site. Employees should be given regular information updates, and it is important that they tour the future facility. A complete walk-around, explanation of the location system, and any needed training in the use of new or different equipment will pay off in higher morale and a faster learning curve at the new site. Union organizers may take advantage of any uncertainty to play on employee concerns, and good communications will help you avoid this.

Carriers also need to be informed. This is a good time to look at any special arrangements with carriers. For example, for nighttime rail switching, the rail crew needs a key to the rail door and the security system.

Opening the relocated warehouse

Relocating a warehouse inventory or opening a new warehouse is a major undertaking. Moving or opening a new center involves planning, communications, more planning, and more communications. You cannot have too much of either.

Checklists are always an important part of planning, the checklist which follows covers warehouse administration, receiving, shipping, operations, space use, and safety.

A warehouse start-up checklist

Using the checklist: This checklist is divided into six sections. It is designed to provide reminders to help insure that nothing is overlooked during the busy time before you open a new facility. Never assume that this is a complete checklist. Each user should consider it as a starter and will add additional checkpoints to cover specific features of your own warehouse operation.

Personnel administration

1. Is the application form used for hiring thorough and in compliance with Federal and local law?
2. Are adequate personnel available to carefully and thoroughly interview each job applicant?
3. Has a company doctor been selected to perform physical examinations for each new person hired?
4. Has a personnel manual been prepared to explain responsibilities, benefits, and personnel procedures?
5. Has a detailed training program been prepared for both warehousing and clerical personnel?
6. Who will supervise the training? Is an adequate cadre of experienced people available to train the new people in the new operation?
7. Are all supervisory personnel hired and already in place before hiring hourly people?
8. What checking procedures are available to detect problems with substance abuse, dishonesty, or credit problems of job applicants?

Receiving

1. Has a detailed procedure been prepared for receiving of freight?
2. Is a manifest or other form designed to cover receiving?
3. Will bar coding be used to identify received materials correctly?
4. What procedure will be used for shipments which arrive without manifests or without any advance notification of what is in the load?
5. What procedure is established to handle overages, shortage, and damage (OS&D)? Who will be responsible for checking OS&D re-

ports? Who will be responsible for checking the accuracy of each receipt?

6. What procedure will be followed to document the time which each vehicle is held at the dock in order to approve or dispute carrier detention charges?

7. What procedure variations will be established for receipt of merchandise returned by customers?

8. How will receiving reports and other reports for the receiving dock be routed through the warehouse office?

9. If lot numbers are used, how will they be assigned at the receiving dock?

10. When product is palletized at the receiving dock, what pallet pattern will be used? What control will be exercised to be sure that all product is palletized according to the prescribed pattern?

11. How will storage location be determined when goods are received at the dock?

12. As merchandise is staged to be moved to storage, how will stacking limitations, stock rotation and other storage specifications be communicated?

13. If a locator system is used, what checks will be made to be sure that the product is actually stored where ordered?

14. Has an appointment procedure for inbound carriers been established? How will it be enforced?

15. Do all inventory procedures go as far as they could to prevent fraud or dishonesty in receiving?

Shipping

1. Has a detailed shipping procedure been prepared?

2. Will there be a priority system for handling of outbound orders?

3. What checking procedure will be established to insure accuracy in shipping?

4. Has an appointment procedure for outbound carriers been established? How will it be enforced?

5. Will we include a manifest or load plan with the outbound shipment?

6. Will special procedures be developed for shipping of hazardous products, freezable merchandise, or other goods requiring special treatment in transit?

7. Do all inventory procedures discourage fraud or dishonesty in shipping?

Materials Handling Operations

1. Will lift trucks or other mobile equipment be owned or leased?
2. Are the specifications for this equipment appropriate for the new warehouse operation?
3. Will aisle turning radius be adequate? Are lift heights adequate?
4. Is each piece of mobile equipment properly identified and equipped with an hour meter?
5. If used equipment will be acquired, is it in perfect operating condition?
6. Is there a training procedure to orient equipment operators?
7. Is storage equipment adequate to maximize cube utilization?
8. What mix of pallet rack, drive-in rack, drive-through rack, flow rack, self-supporting pallet rack, or other storage equipment will be used?
9. Has all rack been lag bolted to the warehouse floor?
10. Is there a training procedure to discourage abuse of storage rack?
11. In materials handling equipment, what will be used?
12. Have the safety hazards for each piece of mobile and storage equipment been determined and communicated?
13. Will records display the age and maintenance cost per year for each piece of equipment used in the warehouse?

Use of Space

1. Will one person be designated as a space planner?
2. What space planning procedures will be followed?
3. Which merchandise, is on a first-in/first-out basis?
4. Has a detailed layout for the warehouse been prepared?
5. Has the layout been reconciled with the types of storage and handling equipment which will be used?
6. Has the layout been checked against fire regulations and safety procedures?
7. What procedures will enforce proper storage procedures, including maintenance of aisles, housekeeping, and stacking limitations?
8. What procedures will minimize honeycombing space losses?

9. Is the location, width, and number of aisles adequate to allow effective movement of all materials?
10. Is there adequate space to stage inbound and outbound cargo?
11. Are storage pallets of uniform specification, in good repair, and in sufficient quantity to hold the planned inventory?
12. Is storage of surplus pallets in compliance with fire regulation?
13. Will storage locations be random, fixed, or a combination of the two?
14. Will a pick line be used for all or a portion of the inventory?
15. How many units of product can be stored in your new warehouse?
16. What percent of capacity is occupied at any given time?

Sanitation, Security, and Safety

1. Has a detailed housekeeping procedure been prepared?
2. Do you know which stockkeeping units, if any, are subject to inspection by the Food and Drug Administration (FDA)?
3. If a portion of the product is FDA controlled, do you know FDA's requirements for safe storage of this product?
4. Is a member of the warehouse staff specifically assigned to sanitation maintenance? Is that individual also responsible for safety and security?
5. Has a professional sanitation service been retained?
6. Have training procedures for sanitation been established?
7. Is there a procedure for checking the percentage of lost time accidents to total hours worked and comparing the safety record with other operations?
8. Have the safety hazards of all equipment been identified and made part of the training program?
9. Have any safety guards or other safety devices been deactivated for any reason?
10. Have you anticipated all the ways in which equipment or tools might be used in an unsafe manner?
11. Have refueling procedures been reviewed?
12. Have all warehouse operations procedures been reviewed by insurance underwriting inspectors to check on fire safety?
13. Is a no smoking policy strictly enforced?
14. Are hazardous materials segregated from other materials?

15. Will random unloading and reloading of outbound shipments be performed? If so, how frequently will random checks be made?
16. Will check weighing procedures prevent deliberate overloading of outbound vehicles or under-receiving of inbounds?
17. How will physical counting procedures be used to improve security?
18. What procedures are used to control pilferage?
19. Do procedures warn employees of the consequences of pilferage or theft?
20. Will undercover procedures be used to detect dishonesty?
21. What procedures will be used to prevent unauthorized people from entering into parking lots, grounds, or other outdoor property adjacent to the warehouse facility?
22. How will lighting be used to discourage unauthorized entry?
23. What kinds of alarms, watch services, or other procedures will be used to detect unauthorized entry?

Questions that solve problems

As you review the steps your people have taken to prepare for a start-up, use the checklist included in this chapter as a means of reviewing your readiness.

To be sure that budget surprises don't come later, the review should start with exposure of all planned costs. These would include the external and internal costs described earlier in this chapter.

If your people disagree among themselves about the expected cost in any area, it is essential to find out who is right and why the other people are wrong in their perception.

Once costs are identified, move through the start-up checklist on the preceding pages to be sure that your people have considered everything that is likely to happen as the warehouse is opened.

Q Which points in the start-up checklist are not included in our current plans?

C Why?

Q How much will it cost us to open the next warehouse?

C Is the number well defended?

Q Who checked our numbers and how did we reconcile differing opinions?

C Be sure there was ample constructive dialog.

Q Are we sure that one capable manager has taken responsibility for planning the move?

C In a distressing number of cases, each manager thinks someone else has the situation under control. Moving need not be traumatic, but it certainly could be unless a good manager anticipates and plans for all of the normal occurrences. ❖

The Future

Chapter 35

Warehousing in a world economy

The rate of growth of international business transactions in recent years has been far higher than the growth of transactions in most domestic economies. Global commerce is not a dream, it is now a reality.*

International logistics is characterized by four D's: distance, demand, diversity, and documentation.

Transportation expenditures as a percent of total logistics cost in the United States have been gradually increasing in recent years. In most situations, an international shipment travels further than a domestic transaction. Distance equates to transportation dependency and because greater distances are involved, a reliable transportation system is more critical. Many warehousing organizations do not have direct control over the transportation link, particularly transport across borders. Ability to obtain control of transportation could have a key role in the success of international warehousing operations.

Customer demand for many products and services is country specific. Some prestigious products, such as quality jewelry or tableware, can meet the same design standards all over the world. However, automobiles must be customized to suit the pollution or safety regulations requirements of individual countries. Nearly every product must conform to local or national regulations relating to labeling.

An ideal answer for dealing with customized demand is a postponement strategy, and this will be described later.

---

* Adapted from *Framing Global Logistics Requirements,* an address given at the 1992 Council of Logistics Management Conference by Professor Donald J. Bowersox of Michigan State University.

International trade requires accommodation to diversity. Customer tastes differ, and each country has unique requirements for safety, performance, styling, and power supply. Dealing with this diversity may also require use of the postponement strategy.

Though free trade agreements in North America, Europe, and elsewhere promise to simplify import and exports, documentation for international shipments will always be more complex than domestic shipments. The warehouse operator has a responsibility to control this documentation, and doing it correctly involves training and constant quality checks. Customs brokers, freight forwarders, and third-party distribution services may all be involved in cross-border commerce.

In Central America, for example, many third-party warehouses specialize in facilitating customs clearance. Sometimes the customs officer is stationed at the public warehouse and is motivated to facilitate the trade which moves through the operation.

Postponement

Postponement in distribution is the art of putting off to the last possible moment the final labeling, assembly, or formulation of a product. The theory of postponement is nothing new. It has been discussed in marketing and logistics textbooks for decades.

Although the theory is not new, the concept's full potential for saving money in the warehouse has not been reached. For example, an inventory of 20,000 units could replace an inventory of 100,000 simply by converting branded merchandise into products with no brand name. It's being done today in some industries.

Postponement was practiced long before marketing theorists started writing about it. Coca Cola used the process early in the 20th century. Postponement was described by a marketing theorist as the opposite of speculation.

Postponement can take any of several forms:
- ◆ Postponement of commitment.
- ◆ Postponement of passage of title.
- ◆ Postponement of branding.
- ◆ Postponement of consumer packaging.
- ◆ Postponement of final assembly.
- ◆ Postponement of mixture or blending.

What does postponement do for warehousing efficiency? Basically, it enables one inventory to do the work of many. Where blending is postponed, the warehouse can have a single stockkeeping unit that is convertible to many different products as the final brand is applied. To illustrate, consider one line of automotive batteries: The only difference between brands is a decal applied to the top of the battery. By delaying the application of the decal and the final consumer package until the last moment, the number of line items in the warehouse is dramatically reduced.

Figure 1

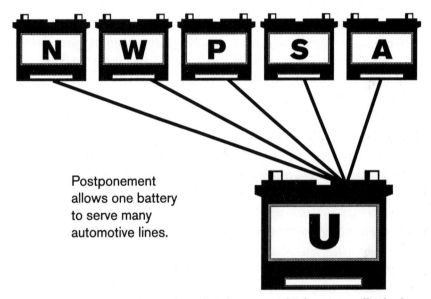

Postponement allows one battery to serve many automotive lines.

Postponement can also reduce freight costs, which are usually the largest component of physical distribution costs. One example of postponement involves an Italian toy manufacturer producing a light-density item. The item is shipped in bulk boxes to a warehouse at the port of entry. Consumer packages purchased in the United States are shipped to the same warehouse where workers package the bulk items for consumer sale. Not only are freight costs reduced, but the consumer package is more attractive because it has not been subjected to the wear and tear of trans-Atlantic transportation.

Delaying final branding or packaging also reduces the risk of obsolescence. Certain brands may decline in popularity, reducing warehouse turnover and increasing the risk that the product will become stale.

Postponement problems

While productivity advantages in the use of postponement are substantial, the challenges are equally so.

Postponement at a warehouse requires the warehouse operator to enter a whole new business — that of assembly and packaging. This creates additional risks in quality control. In the course of packaging, the product may be damaged or contaminated. It could even be mislabeled or put in the wrong package. Quality control in final assembly may be compromised.

Ultimately, the widespread use of postponement could turn today's distribution centers into tomorrow's packaging and light-assembly centers. However, the management and labor skills involved at the warehouse level will need to be higher than those needed for receiving, storing, and reshipping.

Dealing with developing regions

A majority of our planet consists of countries that are relatively undeveloped. In some nations, logistical competency and infrastructure are not well developed. The concept of warehousing as practiced in the United States is virtually unknown. This represents both challenge and opportunity for today's warehouse operator.

A study done by Michigan State University shows that total estimated logistics costs in the United States are more than twice the size of the next largest reporting country, Japan. Yet American logistics costs are a lower *percent* of gross domestic product than in other countries. This research suggests that American logistics companies could have a significant adjustment as they adapt to local conditions overseas.

Worldwide warehousing will also be influenced by time-based competition. Toyota has been a leader in time-based production systems, emphasizing just-in-time production, total quality controls, close supplier relations, and employee decision making on the factory floor.

The time-based competition strategy depends on a cycle of flexible manufacturing, quick response, and expanding variety.* The time-based competitor places factories close to the customers to be served or uses premium transportation to reduce order cycle time. Some American companies using time-based competition are The Limited, Federal Express, Dominos Pizza, and McDonalds.

Warehousing can be a critical factor in time-based competition. It is not always practical to rely on the transportation pipeline for precisely timed JIT deliveries. Warehousing is frequently the best and most economical way to achieve this.

While time-based competition might have existed without a global market, its importance has been emphasized by today's international trade.

International third-party providers

Public warehousing has evolved from a business that consisted primarily of single-city or regional companies to national warehouse networks. The trend has continued on a global basis:

- ◆ The public warehousing subsidiary of an American machine manufacturer offers third-party warehousing on every continent except Antarctica.
- ◆ The Japanese have developed third-party warehouse systems to support their automotive manufacturing in branch plants far from Japan.
- ◆ A British trucking company has acquired third-party warehousing units in several parts of the world.
- ◆ An Australian firm has developed trucking and warehousing outlets in the Americas and Europe.

While a truly global network of third-party warehousing services does not exist today, it is reasonable to presume that such a network will exist in the foreseeable future.

---

*   From *Time — The Next Source of Competitive Advantage*, by George Stalk, Jr., Harvard Business Review, July/August 1988.

The future of world logistics technology

Mankind's progress in producing goods can be divided into three waves, or significant changes.*

The first wave was *agrarian*, marked by the abandonment of hunting and gathering and the development of agriculture. This period lasted for 4,000 years. Warehousing was critical to distribution of agricultural products since granaries and other storehouses enabled people to protect themselves from famine. They accomplished this by keeping a bank of surplus food to be used at times of food shortages.

The second wave is commonly called the *industrial revolution* and it lasted less than 400 years. People moved from the farms into the cities to work in factories. Logistics systems were developed to handle the movement of raw materials from source to factory and the outbound movement of manufactured products from factory to customer.

The third wave is the *information age*, and we are just entering it now. This wave is based on the computer and on communication among computers. The third wave will be characterized by eight major changes:

1. A shorter product life.
2. Increased product variety.
3. Increased competition.
4. Increased cost of labor, space, and capital.
5. Increased concern for health and safety.
6. Increased use of computers.
7. Faster transport systems.
8. Lower inventories.

Warehousing practices will adjust to meet the third wave. Third- wave thinking is characterized by interdependence of suppliers and customers. The warehouse is frequently the buffer between them, which means that the warehouse must adapt to these changes.

Because the third wave is still new, it is difficult to describe how it will influence warehousing in the future. It is increasingly obvious, however, that the traditional role of warehousing in the information age is changing

---

*   Adapted from a presentation by J. M. Williams at the Eighth International Logistics
      Congress, 1989, Beijing, China.

rapidly.

A logistical renaissance

The practice of logistics changed more during the 1980s then it had in all of the decades since the industrial revolution began hundreds of years ago. Warehousing was a key factor in this change.*

Part of the change was a great increase in the awareness of logistics as a critical business activity. Managers who did not even know what logistics meant in 1980 were vitally concerned with it by the end of the decade.

An important challenge was to reach a new degree of excellence in logistics performance. Transportation companies such as Federal Express showed a degree of reliability and information support which were undreamed of in earlier years. The perfection of bar coding systems to support warehouse order picking allowed shippers to achieve a previously unattainable level of accuracy. Finally, faster and cheaper computing allowed logistics managers to achieve a degree of control never before possible.

Change remains as a driving force of the developing information age.

---

*   Bowersox, Op. Cit.

Questions that solve problems

Q Is our warehouse now involved in international shipping and receiving transactions? If not, are we prepared to handle such transactions in the future?

C As you consider this, measure the training needed to deal with customs documentation and other procedures found only in international transactions.

Q Have we explored every opportunity to use postponement as a means of meeting world markets or saving money in inventory management?

C When you explore this, be sure that imaginations can flow to consider the wildest ideas in postponement. The most aggressive kinds of postponement require a major restructuring in the traditional ways of building and distributing products.

Q Can we expand our warehousing operation to other parts of the world?

C Discussion will depend on whether you are in manufacturing, wholesale or retail distribution, or third-party warehousing. If a global vision seems too broad, perhaps you should start with a regional approach, such as all of North America rather than just the U.S.A. ❖

Chapter 36

Staying current in the future

Once you have mastered the business of warehousing, what will you do to stay current? As in every other field, the state-of-the-art changes constantly. To keep up, you need to use the sources of new information and training that are available.

Information sources

In the United States, many trade and professional associations deal totally or partially with warehousing.

The outstanding professional society specializing in warehousing is called **Warehousing Education and Research Council** (WERC) . Headquartered in Illinois, its international membership includes people from many occupations who share an interest in the field of warehousing.

The Council publishes a steady stream of technical articles dealing with every aspect of warehousing. An annual conference provides the chance to hear presentations and exchange ideas with professionals from all over the world. WERC has also established a university research center to allow in-depth studies of several projects each year. As a professional society, WERC grants membership to individuals rather than to corporations.

Older and larger than WERC is Council of Logistics Management (CLM). The prime difference between the two societies is the size of membership and the breadth of focus.

CLM's agenda includes every aspect of logistics. Because its agenda is broader, it is not unusual for the senior logistics officer of a company to belong to CLM, while the warehousing executive belongs to WERC.

The fact that the activities of the two groups are similar is no accident — WERC modeled much of its structure on the larger organization. Both groups are strictly non-commercial, and the use of membership for sales purposes is discouraged. Both are liberal in their membership policy, willing to admit members from any occupation, including those who are temporarily unemployed.

The American Warehouse Association (AWA) is a trade association, so its members are companies rather than individuals. One of the oldest trade associations in the United States, AWA was formed at the end of 19th century for the purpose of lobbying to prevent railway domination of commercial warehousing. AWA's membership is limited to third-party warehousing companies. To an increasing extent, AWA offers seminars, publications, and other services to non-members.

Other United States organizations devoting part of their agenda to warehousing are the following:

- ◆ American Production and Inventory Control Society (APICS).
- ◆ American Society of Transportation and Logistics (ASTL).
- ◆ Delta Nu Alpha.
- ◆ Institute of Industrial Engineers.
- ◆ International Association of Refrigerated Warehouses.
- ◆ Material Handling Institute.
- ◆ National Industrial Transportation League (NITL).

Outside the United States, many similar counterpart organizations exist. Any warehousing professional who wishes to stay current on the newest developments would be well advised to belong to at least one of the above organizations, and to be an active member.

Publications

Many trade magazines that deal partially with warehousing are available at no charge to qualified subscribers. To qualify, you must demonstrate that your company is involved in warehousing and at least open to buy the products advertised in the magazine. These controlled subscription trade publications include warehouse directories, journals about materials handling, magazines dealing with transportation, and publications that emphasize warehousing and logistics management.

Trade magazines with substantial coverage of warehousing include the following:

- *Distribution.*
- *Transportation & Distribution.*
- *Traffic Management.*
- *Grocery Distribution.*
- *Materials Handling Engineering.*
- *Modern Materials Handling.*

While these publications are available primarily inside the United States, similar trade magazines exist elsewhere throughout the world.

There are two directories of third-party warehouses: American Public Warehouse Register, and Distribution Magazine's Logistics Annual Report.

At least two subscription newsletters deal with warehousing: The Ackerman Company publishes *Warehousing Forum*, a monthly newsletter. Another publication called *Distribution Center Management* is published by Alexander Communications.

Seminars

Programs ranging from one day to a full week are offered by both trade associations and professional societies, including those listed above. Management consultants have also packaged their own seminars. Some of these are offered at universities, but the potential buyer should note the difference between a seminar actually sponsored by a university and one that is simply held on a campus. Several seminar packagers have purchased the use of a university campus and the university seal. Other programs are actually sponsored and controlled by a university. The buyer should at least recognize the difference.

Seminars can be valuable for two reasons: The attendee should learn some new information about warehousing, of course. But additionally the attendee may make useful contacts with peers in other industries who have similar challenges. The professional network developed by seminar attendance could be as valuable as the seminar material itself.

Train and develop people

No warehouse is any better than the people who work in it. While some people in your company may still think that the warehouse is a dumping ground for the marginal employee, your warehousing operation can gain the respect of other corporate departments. This respect occurs only when you have demonstrated an excellence in performance through the employment of talented and motivated people. Part of the process is to hire the best people and to remove those *box kickers* who show no potential for growth. The professionalism of warehousing people is enhanced by the use of the information sources described earlier. Training is a process with no beginning and no end.

Upgrading the tools

The most important component of warehousing is people, but even the best people need good tools. These tools are the plant, the equipment, and the information system.

Is your warehousing plant in the right location and does its design meet today's state-of-the-art? If the answers are no, fixing it may be beyond your control. However, eventually a new plant will be needed, and you should look for the opportunity to replace your warehouse with a new one.

The best thing about warehouse equipment is that it is portable and depreciable on a much shorter life than the building. Obsolete equipment should be replaced with new and better machinery.

The information system is the most important tool of all, and the one which will become obsolete most rapidly. The search for a better information system should, therefore, be one that never ends. Improving your information system may not require replacing it, and you should look for ways to modify the system to meet tomorrow's needs.

Putting it all together

This book was designed to help you understand why warehousing is important and what it can do to improve the profitability of your organization. Perhaps the most important message is that no warehouse is ever perfect.

Warehousing is always more complex than those outside the field think it is. A troubled warehouse can take months to fix, and one that seems to be running well can disintegrate quickly. Warehousing is a profession, not just an art or craft. As such, it requires professionals who are constantly absorbing the newest information about the business.

Every living thing either grows or dies. Be sure that you and your people are always growing.

Questions that solve problems

Q Does anyone in our group belong to a professional society, and which ones?

C If you draw a blank on this, find out why.

Q Which trade magazines come to our warehouse?

C Get feedback on quality as well as quantity.

Q Who has been to a warehousing seminar and what was the "take-home" value?

C If feedback is negative, find out why. ❖

Index

A

B

C

D

E

F

G

H

I

J

K

kan ban 19–20
Kelton, Tim 333
Kota, J. Michael 39
Kroger 8

L

La Londe, Bernard J. 11, 57
labor
    cost 71, 96
labor bottlenecks 61, 91
labor requirements plan 133–134
Lauer, David P. 324
layout 50, 52, 58–59, 91, 98, 101–102, 109, 111, 181, 208, 219, 222–223, 225, 274, 310, 337, 344, 347, 349, 351, 369
liability 107
LIFO 31, 297
lift truck
    fleet 112
    rebuilding 115
    training 160
lighting 120, 122
location theory 312
locator systems 59, 92, 120, 219–220, 222, 226, 282, 368

M

management by walking around (MBWA) 152
Material Handling Institute 382
Materials Handling Engineering 383
McDade, Bill 281
McDonalds 377
McMillan, D. F. 54
mentoring 159
Menzies, John T. 127
Michigan State University 376
miscommitment 20
Modern Materials Handling 383
MS-DOS 282
Mulder, Dallas 133

N

O

P

present value 324
Prior, R. L. 143
probation 143, 145
Procter and Gamble 244
Professional Air Traffic Controllers Association (PATCO) 7
proficiency tests 143
Progress 282

Q

quality circles 153
quality management 56
quick response 32, 377

R

R-rating 343
radio frequency (RF) terminals 27, 228, 287, 302, 305
Ransom, William J. 215, 233
re-use 13–14, 48
real estate brokers 313
recalls 47–49, 52, 354–355
reciprocal switching 310
recycle 11, 13–14, 48–49
reduce 13–14
rehabilitation 326
repackaging 23, 51
replevin, action for 37
request for proposal (RFP) 75, 77–80, 83
restricted access 190
return on assets (ROA) 323
return-on-assets 13, 71
reverse logistics 51, 262
reverse order picking 230, 237
Richards, Mark 75
roadway design 340, 346
Rogala, Richard E. 148
roofs 189, 205, 209, 253, 326–327, 338–340
RSX 282
Ryan, Tom 252

U

U.S. Army 7
U.S. Department of Transportation (D.O.T.) 255–256
U.S. Postal Service 7, 245
undercover investigation 189, 200–202
Uniform Commercial Code (UCC) 107, 185
uniforms 38, 54, 195–196
Uniforum 286
unions 15, 35–45, 72, 78–79, 129, 304, 342
UNIX 282
UPS 232
US Geodetic Survey 315
USDA 275
utilities 313, 316

V

vandalism 108, 205, 210
very narrow aisle (VNA) 302
very-narrow-aisle trucks 277

W

Walther, Robert T. 256
warehouse audit form 130
Warehousing Education and Research Council (WERC) 76, 381
Warehousing Forum 383
Weber, Joel 252
Westburgh, Jesse 230, 252
wet-pipe systems 207
Williams, J. M. 378
Williams, John 301
windstorm 205, 208, 213
WINS (Warehouse Information Network Standards) 78
work teams 15

X

Xenix 283

Y

Yeomans, Morton T. 298

Z